Higher Results in
Textual
Analysis

Christine Findlay

the buzz saw snarled

He had thought himself

The leaves were in full voice

lush velvet couches

OXFORD
UNIVERSITY PRESS

OXFORD
UNIVERSITY PRESS

Great Clarendon Street, Oxford OX2 6DP

Oxford University Press is a department of the University of Oxford.
It furthers the University's objective of excellence in research, scholarship,
and education by publishing worldwide in

Oxford New York

Auckland Bangkok Buenos Aires Cape Town Chennai
Dar es Salaam Delhi Hong Kong Istanbul Karachi Kolkata
Kuala Lumpur Madrid Melbourne Mexico City Mumbai Nairobi
São Paulo Shanghai Singapore Taipei Tokyo Toronto

with an associated company in Berlin

Oxford is a registered trade mark of Oxford University Press
in the UK and in certain other countries

British Library Cataloguing in Publication Data

Data available

ISBN 0 19 8314833

1 3 5 7 9 10 8 6 4 2

Typeset in Great Britain by AFS Image Setters Ltd, Glasgow

Printed in Great Britain by Alden Press Ltd, Oxford

CONTENTS

ACKNOWLEDGEMENTS

The author would like to offer grateful thanks to former teaching colleagues for their continuing interest and support. To Angela McEwan at Media Matters, a very special thank you for her professional input and her tireless encouragement. To husband and family, sincere thanks for sustaining motivation and for showing patient tolerance throughout the project. Since its completion, they have stoically avoided the phrase 'textual analysis'!

Permission to include the following is gratefully acknowledged:

Beryl Bainbridge: extract from *Master Georgie* (Abacus, 1999), reprinted by permission of Little Brown and Company (UK).

Robert Bolt: extract from *A Man for All Seasons* (Heinemann Educational, 1960) reprinted by permission of the publishers.

George McKay Brown: extract from 'Andrina' in *Andrina and Other Stories* (Chatto & Windus, 1983) and extract from Scene 4 of *A Spell for Green Corn* (The Hogarth Press, 1970), reprinted by permission of John Murray (Publishers) Ltd.

John Burnside: 'The Blind' from *A Normal Skin* (Jonathan Cape, 1997), reprinted by permission of The Random House Group Ltd.

J. M. Coetzee: extract from *Disgrace* (Secker & Warburg, 1999), reprinted by permission of David Higham Associates.

Anne Donovan: extract from 'The Ice Horse' and extract from 'Zimmerobics' from *Hyroglyphics and Other Stories* (Canongate, 2001), reprinted by permission of the publishers, Canongate Books, Edinburgh.

Douglas Dunn: 'A Silver Air Force' from *Elegies* (1985) and 'Landscape with One Figure' from *Terry Street* (1969), reprinted by permission of the publishers, Faber & Faber Ltd.

Sebastian Faulks: extract from *Birdsong* (Hutchinson, 1993), copyright © 1993 Sebastian Faulks, reprinted by permission of The Random House Group Ltd and Gillon Aitken Associates.

Robert Frost: 'Out, Out' from *The Poetry of Robert Frost* edited by Edward Connery Lathem (Jonathan Cape, 1972), copyright 1916, © 1969 by Henry Holt & Co, copyright 1944 by Robert Frost, reprinted by permission of The Random House Group Ltd on behalf of the Estate of Robert Frost, and Henry Holt & Company, LLC.

Athol Fugard: extract from 'Valley Song' in *Plays* (1998), reprinted by permission of the publishers, Faber & Faber Ltd.

John Glenday: 'The Apple Ghost' from *The Apple Ghost* (Peterloo Poets, 1989), reprinted by permission of the publishers.

Lewis Grassic Gibbon: extract from *Smeddum* edited by Dr Valentina Bold (Canongate Classics), reprinted by permission of the publishers, Canongate Books, Edinburgh.

Chris Hannan: extract from Scene 7 of 'Elizabeth Gordon Quinn' in *Scot-Free: New Scottish Plays* edited by Alasdair Cameron (1990), reprinted by permission of Nick Hern Books, The Glasshouse, 49a Goldhawk Road, W12 8QP; www.nickhernbooks.co.uk.

Seamus Heaney: 'Twice Shy' from *Death of a Naturalist* (1966) and 'Follower' from *New Selected Poems 1966–1987* (1990), reprinted by permission of the publishers, Faber & Faber Ltd.

Nick Hornby: extract from *High Fidelity* (Gollancz, 1995), copyright © Nick Hornby 1995, reprinted by permission of Penguin Books Ltd.

Ted Hughes: lines from 'Wind' from *The Hawk in the Rain* (1957), and lines from 'Rain' and 'Tractor' from *Moortown Diary* (1989), reprinted by permission of the publishers, Faber & Faber Ltd.

Henrik Ibsen: extract from Act I of *A Doll's House* translated by James McFarlane (World's Classics, OUP, 1981), reprinted by permission of Oxford University Press.

Kazuo Ishiguro: extract from *The Remains of the Day* (1989), reprinted by permission of the publishers, Faber & Faber Ltd.

Liz Lochhead: extract from Scene 5 of *Mary Queen of Scots Got Her Head Chopped Off* (Penguin Plays, 1987), copyright © Liz Lochhead 1997, reprinted by permission of Penguin Books Ltd; and 'My Rival's House' from *Dreaming Frankenstein and Selected Poems* (1981), copyright © Liz Lochhead 1981, reprinted by permission of the publisher, Polygon Press.

Christine de Luca: 'Strength Made Perfect in Weakness' from *Wast Wi Da Walkyries* (The Shetland Library, 1997) reprinted by permission of the author and the publishers.

Bernard MacLaverty: extract from *Lamb* (Jonathan Cape, 1980), reprinted by permission of The Random House Group Ltd.

Arthur Miller: extracts from Act 2 of *Death of a Salesman* (1949), copyright © Arthur Miller 1949, and extract from Act 2 of *All My Sons* (1947) copyright © Arthur Miller 1947, both reprinted by permission of International Creative Management, Inc.

Edwin Morgan: 'Girl' from *The New Divan* (1977), reprinted by permission of the publisher, Carcanet Press Ltd.

Rona Munro: extracts Scene 3 and Scene 4 of *Bold Girls* (available in an edition published by Hodder & Stoughton), reprinted by permission of Nick Hern Books.

Sean O'Casey: extract from Act I of *Juno and the Paycock* (Macmillan, 1928), reprinted by permission of Macnaughton Lord 2000 Ltd.

Frank O'Connor: extract from 'Masculine Protest' from *Masculine Protest and Other Stories: Collection Three* (Macmillan, 1969); extract from 'The Mad Lomasneys' from *The Mad Lomasneys and Other Stories: Collection Two* (Macmillan, 1964), reprinted by permission of PFD on behalf of Frank O'Connor.

Donny O'Rourke: 'Clockwork', 'Angus in his 80s', and 'All Leave Cancelled' from *The Waistband and Other Poems* (1997), reprinted by permission of the publisher, Polygon Press.

Tony Parsons: extract from *Man and Boy* (HarperCollins, 1999), reprinted by permission of HarperCollins Publishers Ltd.

Alastair Reid: 'Scotland' from *Weathering* (Canongate Press, 1978), reprinted by permission of the author.

Arundhati Roy: extract from *The God of Small Things* (Flamingo, 1997), reprinted by permission of HarperCollins Publishers Ltd.

Willy Russell: extracts from *Educating Rita* (1981), reprinted by permission of Methuen Publishing Ltd.

Bernhard Schlink: extract from *The Reader* (Phoenix, 1998), translated by Carol Brown Janeway, translation copyright © 1997 by Carol Brown Janeway, reprinted by permission of The Orion Publishing Group Ltd and Pantheon Books, a division of Random House, Inc.

Bernard Shaw: extract from Act 3 of *The Devil's Disciple*, reprinted by permission of The Society of Authors on behalf of the Bernard Shaw Estate.

R. C. Sherriff: extract from Act 2, Scene 2 of *Journey's End* (Heinemann), copyright © R. C. Sherriff 1929, reprinted by permission of Curtis Brown Group Ltd, London, on behalf of the Estate of R. C. Sherriff.

Ena Lamont Stewart: extract from Act I Scene 2 of *Men Should Weep*, copyright © Ena Lamont Stewart, reprinted by permission of the copyright agent, Alan Brodie Representation Ltd, 211 Piccadilly, London W1J 9HF.

and the **Scottish Qualifications Authority** for permission to reproduce sample questions from SQA Analysis and Appreciation papers Intermediate and Higher, 2000/2001.

INTRODUCTION

What is **textual analysis**? Let's start with a dictionary definition of 'analysis':

'The division of a physical or abstract whole into its component parts to examine or determine their relationship or value.' (*The Oxford English Dictionary*)

Well, yes, that's one way of putting it! But it does make the process of exploring a text sound a bit like taking a car engine to bits to learn how the thing works and to see if it runs better with or without some of the parts.

So what does the term **textual analysis** mean in practice?

Let's begin by looking at a short extract from the very familiar fairy tale, *Cinderella*.

EXTRACT Ⓐ

In the royal palace, and in the royal gardens, over which shone the same stars which had looked down upon Cinderella's pumpkins, the ball was at its height: with scores and scores of couples dancing on the waxed floor to the music of the violins; and under the trees, where the music throbbed in faint echoes, other scores of couples moving, passing and repassing, listening to the plash of the fountains and inhaling the sweet scent of the flowers. [Paragraph 1]

Now, as the King's son walked among his guests, word was brought to him by his Chamberlain that a grand Princess, whom nobody knew, had just arrived and desired admission. [Paragraph 2]

'She will not tell her name,' said the Chamberlain, 'but that she is a Princess of a very high dignity cannot be doubted. Apart from the beauty and the perfection of her address (of which your Royal Highness, perhaps, will allow me to be no mean judge), I may mention that the very jewels in her hair are worth a whole province.' [Paragraph 3]

The King's son hastened to the gate to receive the fair stranger, handed her down from the coach, and led her through the ballroom, where at once a great silence fell, the dancing was broken off, the violins ceased to play, so taken, so ravished was everybody by the vision of this unknown one. Everywhere ran the murmur, 'Ah, how beautiful she is!' The King himself, old as he was, could not take his eyes off her, and confided to the Queen in a low voice that it was long since he had seen so adorable a creature. [Paragraph 4]

All the ladies were busily studying her headdress and her ball-gown, that they might order the like the next day for themselves, if only (vain hope!) they could find materials so exquisite and dressmakers clever enough. [Paragraph 5]

The King's son took her to the place of honour, and afterwards led her out to dance. She danced so gracefully that all admired her yet the more. A splendid supper was served, but the young Prince ate nothing of it, so intent was he on gazing upon her. [Paragraph 6]

She went and sat by her sisters, who bridled with pleasure at the honour. She did them a thousand civilities, sharing with them the nectarines and citrons which the prince brought her; and still not recognising her, they marvelled at this, being quite unused (as they never deserved) to be selected for attentions so flattering. [Paragraph 7]

Comments

Over the page is a random selection of comments on this extract from a group of students:

Paragraph 1

'I like the way the scene is set — the polished dance floor is crowded and the music is lively.'

'Yes, and it's good the way there's a contrast between the crushed, noisy scene inside and the quieter scene out in the gardens.'

Paragraph 3

'What about the Chamberlain's words to the Prince? He's a real snob — impressed by her speech and her expensive jewellery!'

Paragraph 4

'There's a real build up of tension when Cinderella is escorted to the ballroom — silence falls, the music and the dancing stop. The guests seem to be in a kind of trance, stunned by her beauty.'

'The old King's a bit of a character! He can't take his eyes off Cinderella. I bet the Queen noticed that!'

Paragraph 5

'You get a real sense of the society of the time — with the ladies making fashion notes about Cinderella's headdress and gown and planning on trying to order something similar for themselves. No different, I suppose, from today really — wanting to imitate the dress styles of models and film stars.'

These comments are examples of **textual analysis** in action in a number of key areas:

- they are exploring meaning(s), using some evidence to demonstrate their **understanding (U)**
- they are beginning to **analyse** aspects of style **(A)**
- they are making critical statements to **evaluate** the effectiveness of certain aspects of the text **(E)**

Next step

The next step for these students is to develop and polish the skills of **understanding, analysis** and **evaluation** to better equip them to respond with maximum appreciation to a wide range of literature, in both private and class reading. Refining these skills will also better prepare these students to respond with confidence to questions on an unseen literary text under assessment conditions.

SQA assessment criteria for Textual Analysis at Intermediate 2
Grade C Performance Criteria

a) **Understanding**
   Responses demonstrate understanding of key elements, central concerns and significant details of the text.

b) **Analysis**
   Responses explain in some detail ways in which aspects of structure/style/language contribute to meaning/effect/impact.

c) **Evaluation**
   Responses reveal engagement with the text or aspects of the text and stated or implied evaluation of effectiveness, using some appropriate critical terminology and substantiated with some relevant evidence from the text.

SQA assessment criteria for Textual Analysis at Higher
Grade C Performance Criteria

a) **Understanding**
Responses demonstrate secure understanding of key elements, central concerns and significant details of the text.

b) **Analysis**
Responses explain accurately and in detail ways in which aspects of structure/style/language contribute to meaning/effect/impact.

c) **Evaluation**
Responses reveal clear engagement with the text or aspects of the text and stated or implied evaluation of the effectiveness, using appropriate critical terminology and substantiated with detailed and relevant evidence from the text.

ACTIVITY

Initial reactions

You've read what this group of students had to say about the *Cinderella* piece. Now let's hear your initial reactions to the following poem and drama extract. After reading them, discuss your reactions with a group, and then make some brief notes. Your discussion should concentrate on the following areas:

- content and meaning
- the more obvious aspects of style used to put across meaning

Poetry

TEXT B

Scotland

It was a day peculiar to this piece of the planet,
when larks rose on long thin strings of singing
and the air shifted with the shimmer of actual angels.
Greenness entered the body. The grasses
shivered with presences, and sunlight
stayed like a halo on hair and heather and hills.
Walking into town, I saw, in a radiant raincoat,
the woman from the fish-shop. 'What a day it is!'
cried I, like a sunstruck madman.
And what did she have to say for it?
Her brow grew bleak, her ancestors raged in their graves
as she spoke with their ancient misery:
'We'll pay for it, we'll pay for it, we'll pay for it!'

Alistair Reid

Feedback questions

What sort of areas did your group's reactions cover?
- particular content details?
- imagery?
- figurative language?
- mood?
- tone?
- others?

Can you identify any of the group's comments where evidence was being closely examined? (**analysis**)

Can you identify any of the group's comments which were saying something about the *effectiveness* of a particular aspect of the text? (**evaluation**)

Drama

(The play is set in the poverty-stricken East End of Glasgow during the 1930s Depression. In this scene, John Morrison waits up to confront his teenage daughter.)

EXTRACT C

Maggie: Come tae bed, John.

John: Jenny's doon there wi a fella.

Maggie: If she's safe hame, ye needna worry —

John: I'm gaun doon. *(He puts on his jacket)*

Maggie: Don't go doon, John — ye'll only vex her, I tell ye! Speak tae her in the mornin.

John: Whit's the matter wi ye, Maggie? Are ye no carin whit sort o life Jenny's leadin?

Maggie: I'm no wantin her tae leave hame! I'm no wantin ony trouble atween the three o us.

John: She's got to be spoke tae.

(He goes out)

(Maggie sits up straight, her eyes straining at the door through which presently come angry voices. John comes in holding Jenny by the arm. She is about eighteen, made up boldly — for the 1930s —: her lipstick is spread over her mouth, her coat and blouse undone, her hair tousled)

Jenny *(furious)*: Leave me go! *(She shakes herself free and she and John stand glaring at each other. Maggie is watching fearfully)* Makin a bloomin fool o me in front o ma friend!

John: Where hae you been til this time o night?

Jenny: That's nane o your business. I'm grown up noo.

John: Don't you speak tae me like that. I asked ye whaur ye'd been.

Jenny: And I tell't ye! Nane o your damned interferin business!

Maggie: Jenny! John!

(John takes Jenny by the shoulders and shakes her)

John: Where wis ye? Answer me!

Jenny: At the pickshers.

John: The pickshers comes oot at hauf ten. Where wis ye efter?

Jenny *(sullen)*: Wi Nessie Tait an a couple friends.

(He lets her go and she flops into a chair, glaring sullenly at him and rubbing her shoulder)

John: I don't approve o yon Nessie Tait.

Jenny:	That's a peety. I dae.
John:	Ye impident little bitch! What I ought is tak ma belt tae ye.
Jenny:	Jist you try it!
John:	The next time you come in here at this time o night wi yer paint smeared a ower yer face, I wull! Look at yersel! *(He drags her over to the mirror, then propels her, resisting, to the sink, where, holding her under his arm, he scrubs off her make-up)* There, and in future, you'll let yer hair grow the colour God meant it tae be an leave it that way.
Jenny:	Mebbe I wull – an mebbe I'll no. It jist depends.
John:	I'm wantin nae mair sauce frae you, Jenny. I'm speakin tae ye for yer ain good. Whit'll the neighbours think, you comin hame at this time o night an staundin in the door wi a man.
Jenny:	Whit dae I care whit the neighbours thinks? An I suppose you never stood in a close yersel?

From Men Should Weep *by Ena Lamont Stewart*

Feedback questions

What sort of areas did your group's reactions cover?
- situation?
- character?
- dialogue?
- stage directions?
- language?
- tone?
- others?

Can you identify any of the group's comments where evidence was being closely examined? **(analysis)**

Can you identify any of the group's comments which were saying something about the *effectiveness* of a particular aspect of the text? **(evaluation)**

Hopefully, your answers will show that you have been actively engaging in the process of textual analysis, even if you don't recognize it under that name! So, we've made a good start. We've shown that we're all capable of responding to a piece of literature in a variety of different ways: some simple and direct, others more sophisticated and complex.

That's because we've discovered that we have, in fact, been building the necessary skills to do this over previous years.

We are now ready to take the next steps:
- ensuring a clear grasp of the **building blocks** for **textual analysis**
- practising exploring both short and longer literary texts or extracts from texts
- learning how to decode questions on **textual analysis** in preparation for assessment.

INTERMEDIATE 2

CHAPTER 1 *Prose*

BUILDING BLOCKS TO UNDERSTANDING

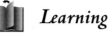 *Learning*

What? Why? How?

In the Introduction, we quoted a dictionary definition of the term 'analysis' but found it wasn't very helpful in explaining exactly what we mean by the phrase **textual analysis**. So the question remains: **What** is it?

Textual analysis is the close study of a text, or extract from a text, using the skills of analysis (**A**) and evaluation (**E**), to show meaning(s), to explore effects and to assess effectiveness of the writer's stylistic techniques.

Now that there is a clearer notion of what we mean by textual analysis, the next obvious question from an English student's perspective is to ask **why** he or she should study it. There are many possible explanations, but here are three key reasons:
  ◆ Its study needs mental discipline, so it trains the mind to look under the surface – a vital skill which can be applied to all subjects.
  ◆ It helps the student to appreciate the craft of the writer, using the tools of his or her trade with skill and imagination.
  ◆ Above all, it can bring real pleasure by encouraging a genuine love for literature and a willingness to explore new texts from all genres.

So, by the time you've worked your way through these chapters, the hope is that you will have found riches!

How do I find these riches? Firstly, by learning to recognize and interpret the **building blocks** which form the crucial foundation on which our understanding of the process of textual analysis is built.

Understanding is the most important **building block**. Picture an arched, stone-built bridge. The keystone (or keystane in Scots) is the central stone which connects and supports the whole structure. Similarly, **understanding** is the keystone in building a bridge to a full appreciation of a piece of literature.

Building blocks to understanding prose

BLOCK A	BLOCK B
Understanding of main ideas through: *structure; key words and phrases*	Understanding of significant detail through: *punctuation and tone*

Block A shows us that one of the most important building blocks of understanding that we need to learn to recognize and interpret is **structure**;

in other words, the way a piece of writing is arranged and organized on the page. Any piece of literature will have:

- an outer shape or structure (for example, a novel may be arranged in chapters which may have linked titles)
- an inner structure made up of connected paragraphs and sentences.

The recognition and accurate interpretation of these structures is vital to our understanding of meaning. Let's look at a specific example to see structure in action.

EXTRACT **A**

'Don't forget his leash,' Carrie called from the kitchen.

'I won't, darling.'

key words — *'Be careful,' she said. 'Don't step on any snakes.'*

'Valletta will protect me,' I said, and off we went.

note description of setting — *The leaves were in full voice, brassy overhead, rasping underfoot. Valletta kept backing off on the*   5
***red** leather leash, stubbornly planting himself every ten feet or so into the woods, trying to turn back to the house where his beloved mistress awaited his return. I kept assuring him that we were safe under the trees, leaves dropping gently everywhere around us. 'Come, little babypup,' I*
double underline indicates sounds — *cooed, 'come little woofikins, there's nothing can hurt you here in the woods.'*

The air was crisp as a cleric's collar.   10

key word — *When we had come a far-enough distance from the house, I reached into my pocket and took out the gun. 'See this, Valletta?' I said. 'I am going to shoot you with this. You are never going to bark again, Valletta. You are going to be the most silent dog on earth. Do you understand,*
single underline indicates absence of sound — *Valletta?'*

He began barking.   15

'Quiet,' I said. He would not stop barking.

'Damn you!' I shouted. 'Shut up!'

note description of setting — *And suddenly he yanked the leash from my hands and darted away like the sneaky little sissydog he was, all **white** and furry against the **orange** and **yellow** and **brown** of the forest floor,*
bold type indicates colour — *racing like a ragged whisper through the carpet of leaves, trailing the **red** leash behind him like a*   20
*narrow trickle of **blood**. I came thrashing after him. I was no more than six feet behind him*
example of complex sentence — *when he ran into a clearing saturated with **golden light**. I followed him with the gun hand, aiming at him. Just as my finger tightened on the trigger, Carrie burst into the clearing from the opposite end.*

'No!' she shouted, and dropped to her knees to scoop him protectively into her arms, the explosion   25
shattering the incessant whisper of the leaves, the dog leaping into her embrace, blood flowering on
key word — *her chest, oh dear God, no, I thought, oh dear sweet Jesus no, and dropped the gun and ran to her and pressed her bleeding and still against me while the damn dumb dog barked and barked.*

example of simple sentence — *He has not barked since.*

From Barking at Butterflies *by Evan Hunter*

Look closely at the annotations to the extract to help you with the following activities.

BLOCK A

Understanding the main ideas through: *structure; key words and phrases*

■ **ACTIVITY 1**

Recognizing and interpreting structure of narrative

a) The extract divides itself into a number of stages, each stage moving the narrative forward. Can you identify where each of the following stages begins and ends?
- ◆ leaving the house
- ◆ walking into the woods
- ◆ preparing to shoot the dog
- ◆ Valletta's escape
- ◆ accidental shooting of Carrie
- ◆ Valletta's death

b) How are these stages linked? It may help to consider some, or all, of the following possible linking devices:
- ◆ words
- ◆ ideas
- ◆ sound
- ◆ colour
- ◆ setting
- ◆ time

■ **ACTIVITY 2**

Recognizing and interpreting sentence structure

Below are the three most commonly used types of sentence structure, and a reminder of how to recognize each type.
- ◆ **Simple:** contains a single main point
- ◆ **Compound:** contains two or more linked main points
- ◆ **Complex:** contains a main point, plus one or more subordinate points

a) Simple sentences are often used to create particular effects: for example, to emphasize an important point; to shock or surprise the reader; to create tension.

Look carefully at this list of simple sentences.

'The air was crisp as a cleric's collar.' (line 10)
'I am going to shoot you with this.' (line 12)
'You are never going to bark again, Valletta.' (lines 12–13)
'You are going to be the most silent dog on earth.' (line 13)
'He would not stop barking.' (line 16)
'I came thrashing after him.' (line 21)
'He has not barked since.' (line 29)

Now look at the list of comments over the page, describing possible ways in which these sentences contribute to our understanding of aspects of the extract. See if you can match individual comments to particular sentences.

Comments:
- ◆ contributes to our understanding of atmosphere
- ◆ contributes to our understanding of character's thoughts
- ◆ contributes to our understanding of character's feelings
- ◆ contributes to our understanding of character's reactions

b) *And suddenly he <u>yanked</u> the leash from my hands and <u>darted</u> away like the sneaky little sissydog he was, all white and furry against the orange and yellow and brown of the forest floor, <u>racing</u> like a ragged whisper through the carpet of leaves, <u>trailing</u> the red leash behind him like a narrow trickle of blood.* (lines 18 to 21)

This is a much longer, looser sentence type than the simple sentence. How is our understanding of the dog's situation helped by the way in which the sentence has been put together? Pay particular attention to the part played by punctuation and the underlined verbs in developing the sentence.

c) *'No!' she <u>shouted</u>, and <u>dropped</u> to her knees to scoop him protectively into her arms, the explosion <u>shattering</u> the incessant whisper of the leaves, the dog <u>leaping</u> into her embrace, blood <u>flowering</u> on her chest, oh dear God, no, I thought, oh dear sweet Jesus no, and <u>dropped</u> the gun and <u>ran</u> to her and <u>pressed</u> her bleeding and still against me while the damn dumb dog <u>barked</u> and <u>barked</u>.* (lines 25 to 28)

Strictly speaking, this is not one sentence but several. The writer has chosen to use this unusual structure for a particular reason.

What do you learn about a) the shooting and b) the man's reaction to it from the way in which the sentence has been put together? Pay particular attention to the part played by punctuation and the underlined verbs in developing the sentence.

ACTIVITY 3

Recognizing and interpreting key words and phrases

Specific words and phrases within an extract, sometimes repeated and/or contrasted, can help the reader to grasp main ideas.

For example, look at the repetition of the word '*barking*' in this extract. Every time it is repeated, we sense the man's mounting anger, which helps us to understand why he feels compelled to kill the dog.

The words and phrases in the boxes on the next page share some areas of meaning. (**R** = repeated)

For each group, write a sentence which sums up what contribution it makes to your understanding of any area of the extract such as: narrative; character; atmosphere; setting and theme.

	1	**2**	**3**		**4**
R	barking	silent	beloved		hurt
	brassy	quiet	assuring	**R**	gun
	rasping	shut up	safe	**R**	blood
	explosion	still	gently		bleeding
	shattering		cooed		
	shouted		protectively		
			embrace		

	5	**6**	**7**	**8**
R	leaves	red	babypup	sissydog
	woods	white	woofikins	damn dumb dog
	forest	orange		
	clearing	yellow		
		brown		
		golden		

ACTIVITY 4

Recognizing and interpreting features of punctuation

Accurate reading for understanding depends on our ability to interpret the various functions of punctuation marks. Commas, inverted commas, colons, semi-colons, question marks, exclamation marks, brackets and dashes can all impact on meaning. By this stage in your school career, you should be familiar with the different functions of all key forms of punctuation. If you're still uncertain about any of these, now is the time to check them out.

In the section on sentence structure, you looked at two examples of long, loose structures. The comma is used regularly in these examples to separate the stages of the structure. Sometimes the result is a list of actions:

' ... he yanked the leash ... and darted away ... , racing like a ragged whisper ... , trailing the red leash behind him ... '

' ... she shouted, and dropped to her knees ... , the explosion shattering the incessant whisper ... , the dog leaping into her embrace ... , blood flowering on her chest ... '

Here, the punctuation helps us to break down the stages of the narrative, giving us a clearer picture of the events themselves as well as reactions to them.

Look at the use of the question mark in paragraph seven, beginning 'When we had come a far-enough distance.'

What does it tell you about the man's mood at this point in the narrative?

Look at the use of the exclamation mark in 'Damn you!', 'Shut up!' (line 17) and 'No!' (line 25). Do these examples give the reader any clues about what is going to happen?

■ **ACTIVITY 5**

Recognizing and interpreting features of tone

The **tone** which a writer adopts is another important tool which helps to shape meaning. By tone, we mean the 'speaking' voice of the writer or character. In the same way as our conversational tones will change and range widely, depending on the situation and the individuals to whom we are speaking, written tones will also vary across a wide range, from sympathetic to aggressive, from mocking to amused, and so on.

If you feel uncertain about recognizing a particular tone, speak the written words aloud and listen carefully to catch the rhythm and emphasis of the words, both of which help to determine tone.

Here are three examples to give you some practice.

Example 1   *'You don't say! I would have thought you could have worked that one out all by yourself.'*

Example 2   *Kathleen's voice cracked as she broke the news to her sister: she reached out and grasped her hand, praying that the gesture of friendship would be accepted.*

Example 3   *She was not going to be dragged down by events: she would show the world that this woman had what it took to pull herself out of the mess.*

Below is a list of adjectives which could apply to a range of tones used in the *Barking at Butterflies* extract. See if you can match each of the adjectives to particular examples, using quotation to support your findings.

- ◆ angry
- ◆ horrified
- ◆ chilling
- ◆ sinister
- ◆ tense
- ◆ threatening
- ◆ anguished
- ◆ desperate
- ◆ excited

CHAPTER 2 *Prose*

BUILDING BLOCKS TO UNDERSTANDING

 Developing

BLOCK A

Understanding of main ideas, central concerns through: *structure; key words and phrases*

BLOCK B

Understanding of significant detail through: *punctuation and tone*

Practice in developing understanding

Chapter 1 showed you how the keystone of understanding of meaning connects and supports all the elements which combine to create a text. Already you may be feeling you've uncovered glimpses of the riches we spoke of in that chapter because you can see how the building blocks work.

Going for Gold!

With further practice, you will be better equipped to complete the treasure hunt and reward yourself with some surprises. See what riches you can find underneath the surface of the following three extracts.

EXTRACT A (An elderly woman has been forced to move to sheltered accommodation. In this opening sequence to the short story, her niece, Catherine, visits her, encouraging her to take more of an interest in things, but she prefers to sit and daydream.)

A self-contained flat: one bedroom, security entrance and a view of the communal garden. A lovely house, with its fresh white walls and a green swirly patterned carpet that doesn't show the dirt. Catherine, my niece, went to a lot of trouble to do it up.

'Better than where you were. You had no view there. You're so lucky.'

I know I'm lucky and I didn't mean to be ungrateful. It's just that a sheltered house meant the end of everything. This was it, this view, for the rest of my life.

It's not really a life anyone would choose, getting old. Things don't work properly any more, not so badly that I'm helpless, just enough to be annoying. I can walk with a Zimmer but it's so much trouble to shove the thing in front of me that most of the time I can't be bothered. Stupid name, Zimmer. Why is it called that? Zimmer is German for room but it can't be that. Maybe it's the noise it makes as you shuffle along with it — zim, zim, zim.

And there's this constant feeling of awareness in every part of my body: jaggy pains in my elbows and knees, vertebrae grinding against one another, bits that used to fit together smoothly now clicking and crunking like the central heating boiler starting up. I did once try to explain it to Catherine.

'It's like the shows, those games where you get a circle on a stick and you have to feed it along a piece of twisted wire, very carefully without touching it and, if you touch the wire a bell rings.'

'Uh-uh.' She is busy rearranging ornaments on the mantelpiece.

'It's like that. I have to do everything really slowly and carefully, otherwise it hurts.'

Catherine gave me one of her looks and said I should take more interest in things. She knows I can't knit any more and reading tires me but she's always trying to get me to put photographs in albums or watch the TV.

'Top Hat's on TV this afternoon,' she said as she was getting ready to leave. 'Fred Astaire and Ginger Rogers.'

'Oh, is it?'

'It starts at two-thirty and it's all set for you. I'm away for the two o'clock bus. See you on Friday.'

I didn't watch the film. I'd rather sit and daydream out of the window, lost inside my own head. Catherine can't understand as it's not her nature to daydream or dawdle or drift. She's like an office stapler, precisely snapping shut, securing papers in the correct order forever. She never lets anything go.

From Zimmerobics by Anne Donovan

ACTIVITY 1

Structure of extract

BLOCK A

Understanding of main ideas, central concerns through:

structure; key words and phrases

a) The extract opens with an outline of the setting. How does the structure develop thereafter?

As part of your discussion, you may find it helpful to consider the following questions:
   ◆ Does it move outwards to consider aspects outside the immediate setting?
   ◆ Does it move inwards to focus on a narrower subject, concentrating our attention on a specific area?
   ◆ Does the last paragraph have any structural link to the opening one?

b) What role does the first person narrator play in the structure? How much control does she have over the direction of the narrative?

ACTIVITY 2

Structure of dialogue

a) There are two characters speaking here: the elderly woman and her niece, Catherine. What does the structure of their dialogue tell you about their relationship?

Look at what each character says and its context.

Catherine: *'Better than where you were. You had no view there. You're so lucky.'*

'Uh-uh.'

'Top Hat's on TV this afternoon … Fred Astaire and Ginger Rogers … It starts at two-thirty and it's all set for you. I'm away for the two o'clock bus. See you on Friday.'

Woman: *'It's like the shows, those games where you get a circle on a stick and you have to feed it along a piece of twisted wire, very carefully without touching it and, if you touch the wire a bell rings.'*

'It's like that. I have to do everything really slowly and carefully, otherwise it hurts.'

b) Much of the extract is taken up with another type of 'speaking', what we call **interior monologue** (monologue, rather than dialogue, because there is only one person speaking). The purpose of interior monologue is to show the inner thoughts and feelings of a character.

Look at paragraphs **3, 4, 5** and **11**. For each of these paragraphs write a sentence which sums up what you learn from it about the character's thoughts and feelings.

ACTIVITY 3

Structure of sentences

Sentence structure reflects the mood and personality of the characters. Which of the following words would you use to describe

- ◆ the structure of Catherine's sentences
- ◆ the structure of the elderly woman's sentences
- ◆ the structure of the narrator's sentences?

---

complex   loosely-linked   flowing   simple   short   conversational   abrupt
disjointed

ACTIVITY 4

Key words and phrases

Many of the words and phrases used in the extract give us an insight into

- ◆ the thoughts and feelings of the elderly woman
- ◆ the character of Catherine as her aunt sees her.

What do you learn about either of these two characters from these groups of key words and phrases?

1	2	3	4
the end of everything	self-contained	lost inside my own head	getting old
the rest of my life	security	daydream	don't work properly
not really a life	sheltered	dawdle	annoying
forever		drift	Zimmer
			so much trouble
			can't be bothered

5	6	7
jaggy pains	lucky	rearranging
grinding	explain	one of her looks
clicking	ungrateful	can't understand
crunking		precisely snapping shut
slowly		securing
carefully		correct order
hurts		never lets anything go

ACTIVITY 5

Punctuation

The colon is always a useful signpost to meaning: what comes after the colon relates directly to what has come before, in the form of an explanation, or an example or list of examples, or a contrast. The first part of the sentence is usually a general, abstract statement, while the second part is usually a particular, concrete explanation or illustration.

Example 1 '*A self-contained flat: one bedroom, security entrance and a view of the communal garden.*'

Example 2 '*And there's this constant feeling of awareness in every part of my body: jaggy pains in my elbows and knees, vertebrae grinding against one another ... starting up.*'

◆ Can you identify any other places in the extract where the author could have used a colon, rather than a full stop?
◆ Would it have altered meaning in any way if she had chosen to do this?

ACTIVITY 6

Tone

The use of first-person narrative dictates the tone, giving us a lot of information about character.

Look at the following examples:

'*Catherine, my niece, went to a lot of trouble to do it up.*'

'*Better than where you were. You had no view there. You're so lucky.*'

'*This was it, this view, for the rest of my life.*'

'*I can walk with a Zimmer but it's so much trouble to shove the thing in front of me that most of the time I can't be bothered.*'

'*I did once try to explain it to Catherine.*'

'*I'd rather sit and daydream out of the window, lost inside my own head.*'

'*She's like an office stapler, precisely snapping shut, securing papers in the correct order forever.*'

Which of the following adjectives could you use to describe the tone of each of these examples?

(Any one of the listed adjectives may apply to more than one example, or there may be examples to which you feel you could apply more than one of the listed words.)

irritable	depressed	regretful
nostalgic	resentful	accusatory/scolding
dreamy	sad	frustrated
self-pitying	dismissive	cynical
despairing	uninterested	

EXTRACT **B** (As he approaches his thirtieth birthday, Harry feel he needs a new image.)

The car smelled like somebody else's life. Like freedom.

It was parked right in the window of the showroom, a wedge-shaped sports car which, even with its top off, looked as sleek and compact as muscle.

Naturally it was red — a flaming, testosterone-stuffed red. When I was a little bit younger, such blatant macho corn would have made me sneer, or snigger, or puke, or all of the above.

Now I found it didn't bother me at all. In fact, it seemed to be just what I was looking for at this stage of my life.

I'm not really the kind of man who knows what cars are called, but I made it my business — furtively lingering over the ads in glossy magazines — to find out the handle of this particular hot little number. Yes, it's true, our eyes had met before.

But its name didn't really matter. I just loved the way it looked. And that smell. Above all, that smell. That anything-can-happen smell. What was it about that smell?

Amidst the perfume of leather, rubber and all those yards of freshly sprayed steel, you could smell a heartbreaking newness, a newness so shocking that it almost overwhelmed me. This newness intimated another world that was limitless and free, an open road leading to all the unruined days of the future. Somehow they had never heard of traffic cones or physical decay or my thirtieth birthday.

I knew that smell from somewhere and I recognised the way it made me feel. Funnily enough, it reminded me of that feeling you get when you hold a new born baby.

The analogy was far from perfect — the car couldn't squint up at me with eyes that had just started to see, or grasp one of my fingers in a tiny, tiny fist, or give me a gummy little smile. But for a moment there it felt like it just might.

'You only live once,' the car salesman said, his heels clicking across the showroom floor.

From Man and Boy *by Tony Parsons*

ACTIVITY 1

Structure of extract

The extract is structured in the form of a personal experience which is like a dream: the wonderful, magical object of his dream is *'a wedge-shaped sports car which ... looked as sleek and compact as muscle.'*

Can you identify the stages of the 'dream', showing how it develops and where it is finally broken?

ACTIVITY 2

Paragraph structure

The average length of paragraphs in this extract is two sentences. What contribution does this feature make to your understanding of the mood of the character?

■ **ACTIVITY 3**

Sentence structure

Look at the following lines from paragraph 6. *'And that smell. Above all, that smell. That anything-can-happen smell.'*
   ◆ What is unusual about the structure of these sentences?
   ◆ How does this particular structure contribute to our understanding of the mood of the character?

■ **ACTIVITY 4**

Key words and phrases

1	2	3	4
sleek	that smell	somebody else's life	unruined days
compact as muscle	perfume	red	future
testosterone-stuffed	newness	flaming	
macho		another world	
glossy		limitless	
hot little number		open road	
		only live once	
	5		
	heartbreaking		
	shocking		
	overwhelmed		

What do these groups of key words and phrases add to your understanding of any of the following:
   ◆ character
   ◆ theme
   ◆ symbolism?

■ **ACTIVITY 5**

Punctuation

Specific punctuation features add to the feeling of boyish excitement which characterizes the extract.

Look closely at the punctuation in paragraphs **3, 5, 7,** and **9.** Pick out some examples from these paragraphs where you recognize particular punctuation features contributing to this mood of excitement.

■ **ACTIVITY 6**

Tone

Which word would you select to describe the predominant tone of the extract?

   mocking   humorous   overawed   excited   intoxicated   exhilarated

Use evidence to support your choice.

CHAPTER 3 *Prose*

BUILDING BLOCKS TO UNDERSTANDING

 Demonstrating

Collecting the prize

So far you've been concentrating on learning to identify and interpret the building blocks of meaning. Your treasure hunt is nearly finished! But, before you can collect the prize, you'll need to show that you are able to explore an unseen prose extract, using the tools of textual analysis to uncover what may be several layers of meaning.

Below is an extract from the novel *Master Georgie* by Beryl Bainbridge. Following this, you will find a full commentary, showing how the key elements of building blocks A and B have helped the reader to an understanding of this extract. Use this sample commentary to help you in your own independent exploration of the final extract in this chapter.

EXTRACT A (Myrtle, adoptive sister of Master Georgie, a surgeon, has followed him out to the Crimean War. Here she goes out riding with an acquaintance, Mrs Yardley. The period is the 1850s.)

Presently the path widened and we saw in the distance a little whitewashed house beside a square of vineyard. I was all for making a detour to avoid coming too close. 'There'll be dogs,' I warned. Mrs Yardley didn't appear to have heard me and trotted on regardless.

Sure enough, we had advanced but a little way when the air was shattered by a deep and awesome howl; Mrs Yardley's horse stopped dead in its tracks. An animal the size of a small calf and much emaciated appeared round the side of the house and tore towards us, followed by a smaller creature, black all over and running on three legs.

'Don't move,' I called out to Mrs Yardley, though indeed, the slither of claws on the stony path and the ferocious barking that rent the luminous day had turned her to stone in the saddle. Fortunately the horses stood firm, being no doubt used to such alarms. Some six yards away, the dogs halted, tongues lolling. I concentrated on the larger of the two, forcing myself to gaze into its hateful eyes; whining, it lay down, ears flattened to its mean and bony skull. Mrs Yardley was whimpering, but not loudly enough to provoke an assault.

After what seemed like hours a bow-legged man emerged from the vineyard and whistled off the brutes. Approaching, he beckoned us forward. We were led past the house to a courtyard beyond, where a woman squatted on the dust pummelling a lump of dough. Fawning, the man urged us to dismount and gestured towards a rickety table. Half a dozen children, some crawling, materialised as though by magic and began to pluck at our clothes.

Mrs Yardley was trembling; a pin-prick of blood stood on her cheek.

'Forgive me,' she said. 'I should have listened to you.'

'Think of what to give them,' I urged. 'Have you any money?'

'Money,' she said. 'Why do we need money?'

'In return for hospitality,' I said, vexed. 'Nothing is for free in this world.'

The man set before us two small bowls and a pitcher of milk. The children got under his feet and he kicked out, scattering them squawking and fluttering, chicken-like into the corners of the yard.

'Pig,' I exclaimed, though I was careful to smile. I thought it was no wonder the smaller dog had a leg missing.

Mrs Yardley was staring down at the jug, at the insects floating atop the milk. 'You must drink it,' I told her. 'If you don't they'll only bring us something worse.'

'At least they're past biting,' she said and gamely drank.

The woman slapped the circle of dough on to a flat stone; she pointed to the sun, then patted her stomach, indicating the bread would be good to eat when baked. As she lifted her arm her gown fell back and there was an infant stuck to her breast, scalp springing with hair the colour of tar.

'Think,' I urged Mrs Yardley. 'Think what we can give them.' I myself had nothing, save a handkerchief at my wrist, mislaid by Georgie; she, a silk scarf at her throat.

All at once a curious giggling sound came from somewhere close to the vineyard wall. The bow-legged man swaggered off, and shortly returned carrying a struggling goat which he dropped on to its feet on the table. The children surged forward.

'If he's going to cut its throat in front of us,' Mrs Yardley promised, 'I shall scream.'

From Master Georgie *by Beryl Bainbridge*

BLOCK A

Understanding of main ideas, central concerns through: *structure; key words and phrases*

BLOCK B

Understanding of significant detail through: *punctuation and tone*

Sample commentary on extract from *Master Georgie*

Structure of extract

The structure of the extract resembles that of an episode from a serialized drama: a recognizable opening: 'There'll be dogs,' I warned; the development of plot, setting and character; a definite turning point and climax (the struggling goat appears) and a 'cliff-hanger' closure: *'If he's going to cut its throat in front of us,' Mrs Yardley promised, 'I shall scream.'*

Structure of paragraphs

These are mainly quite short, helping the reader to follow the frequent shifts in the narrative. The third paragraph is slightly longer as it deals with a high point in the action. The short paragraphs help the reader to appreciate the tense atmosphere of the episode.

Structure of dialogue

Something of the personalities of the two individuals can be gathered from their dialogue. For example, the narrator (the 'I' character) tends to issue warnings or orders:

'There'll be dogs,' I warned.

'Don't move,' I called out to Mrs Yardley.

'Think of what to give them.'

'You must drink it.'

'Think,' I urged Mrs Yardley. 'Think what we can give them.'

From this we can deduce a number of things: she is an authoritative figure, someone who takes control of a situation, someone decisive; she is also quite calm, not prone to panic; she is a practical, realistic woman who foresees the problem with the dogs and realizes that the man and his wife are expecting some form of payment in exchange for their hospitality.

From the structure of her dialogue, Mrs Yardley appears as a foil to her companion: she seems a rather naive, timid woman who leaves it to other people to take the initiative.

'Forgive me,' she said. 'I should have listened to you.'

'Money,' she said. 'Why do we need money?'

'If he's going to cut its throat in front of us,' Mrs Yardley promised, 'I shall scream.'

Key words and phrases

1	2	3
warned	slither of claws	awesome howl
alarms	ferocious barking	hateful eyes
assault	brutes	mean and bony skull
urged	kicked out	
	cut its throat	
4	**5**	
whining	fawning	
whimpering	swaggered off	
trembling		
scattering		
squawking		
fluttering		
struggling		
scream		

When we group key words and phrases as above, we can see how they contribute to our understanding of a number of specific areas of the text.

Group 1 captures the main focus of the narrative, the danger of being attacked by the dogs and by the unknown, aggressive villager.

Group 2 focuses on the violent nature of both dogs and man.

Group 3 makes us aware, through its details, of the threatening atmosphere

Group 4 communicates the various reactions – sometimes vocal, sometimes physical – to the attacks.

Group 5 gives us clues to the man's character.

Punctuation

In this extract the semi-colon is used on a number of occasions, helping to maintain pace and heighten tension by close linking of narrative details. For example:

'Sure enough, we had advanced but a little way when the air was shattered by a deep and awesome howl; Mrs Yardley's horse stopped dead in its tracks.'

'I concentrated on the larger of the two, forcing myself to gaze into its hateful eyes; whining, it lay down, ears flattened to its mean and bony skull.'

'I myself had nothing, save a handkerchief at my wrist, mislaid by Georgie; she, a silk scarf at her throat.'

Tone

The use of first-person narrative directly affects the tone because the incident is recounted from a single viewpoint. Tone, therefore, contributes to our understanding of this character's personality. For example, when she says *'Mrs Yardley ... trotted on regardless'*, her tone could be irritated. When she comments: *'Mrs Yardley was whimpering, but not loudly enough to provoke an assault'*, we can hear a note of scorn in her voice at Mrs Yardley's behaviour. Her rather bossy tone can be heard when she orders Mrs Yardley: *'You must drink it'*.

Demonstrating understanding

In summary, using the building blocks approach, several readings of this extract have revealed a clearer understanding of the following aspects of meaning:

- situation
- plot
- mood/atmosphere
- character
- relationships

EXTRACT Ⓑ *She'd had nine of a family in her time, Mistress Menzies, and brought the nine of them up, forbye — some near by the scruff of the neck, you would say. They were sniftering and weakly, two-three of the bairns, sniftering in their cradles to get into their coffins; but she'd shake them to life, and dose them with salts and feed them up till they couldn't but live. And she'd plonk one down — finishing the wiping of the creature's neb* or the unco dosing of an ill bit stomach or the binding of a broken head — with a look on her face as much as to say **Die on me now and see what you'll get!***

*Big-boned she was by her fortieth year, like a big roan mare, and **If ever she was bonny 'twas in Noah's time**, Jock Menzies, her eldest son would say. She'd reddish hair and a high, skeugh* nose, and a hand that skelped her way through life; and if ever a soul had seen her at rest when the dark was done and the day was come he'd died of the shock and never let on.*

For from morn till night she was at it, work, work, on that ill bit croft that sloped to the sea. When there wasn't a mist on the cold, stone parks* there was more than likely the wheep of the rain, wheeling and dripping in from the sea that soughed* and plashed by the land's stiff edge. Kineff lay north, and at night in the south, if the sky was clear on the gloaming's edge, you'd see in that sky the Bervie lights come suddenly lit, far and away, with the quiet about you as you stood and looked, nothing to hear but a sea-bird's cry.

But feint the much time to look or to listen had Margaret Menzies of Tocherty toun. Day blinked and Meg did the same, and was out, up out of her bed, and about the house, making the porridge, and rousing the bairns, and out to the byre to milk the three kye*, the morning growing out in the east and a wind like a hail of knives from the hills. Syne back to the kitchen again she would be, and catch Jock, her eldest, a clout* in the lug that he hadn't roused up his sisters and brothers, and rouse them herself, and feed them and scold, pull up their breeks* and *straighten their frocks, and polish their shoes and set their caps straight.* **Off you get and see you're not late,** *she would cry,* **and see you behave yourselves at the school. And tell the Dominie, I'll be down the night to ask him what the mischief he meant leathering Jeannie and her not well.**

*neb = nose

*skeugh = squint

*parks = fields

*soughed = sighed in the wind

*kye = cattle

*clout = a hit/slap

*breeks = pants/trousers

From Smeddum *by Lewis Grassic Gibbon*

ACTIVITY

Now it's your turn to demonstrate what you've learnt about decoding meaning by exploring the prose extract above, from the short story *Smeddum* by Lewis Grassic Gibbon.

Use the following prompts to help direct your discussion of the extract.

Structure

Look closely at the content and structure of each of the four paragraphs which make up the extract.

- Which aspects of Meg's life and background does the writer introduce us to in these paragraphs?
- List them in sequence, using a word or phrase to sum up each aspect.
- How does he link each stage of his character sketch? Pay particular attention to the opening and closing sentences of each paragraph.
- The writer uses an unconventional style of sentence structure. What do you notice about the way he builds his sentences? Are there any particular features on which you could comment?
- Can you see any similarities between Meg's personality and the style of sentence structure?

Key words and phrases

1	2	3	4
work, work	big-boned	shake them to life	feed them up
day blinked	like a big roan mare	skelped her way	plonk one down
		catch a clout	pull up their breeks
		rouse	straighten their frocks
		scold	

5	6
ill bit croft	sniftering
cold, stone parks	weakly
wheeling	
dripping	
soughed	
plashed	
the land's stiff edge	

What contribution do these groups of keywords/phrases make to your understanding of setting, character and theme(s)?

Punctuation

What contribution do the following punctuation features make to your awareness of the atmosphere of the extract: comma; semi-colon; dash.

Tone

What impression of character do you gather from a) the narrator's tone and b) Meg's tone?

CHAPTER 4 *Prose*

BUILDING BLOCKS TO ANALYSIS AND EVALUATION

Learning

Armed with the building blocks to understanding dealt with in the first three chapters, you're now ready to extend your skills to enable you to respond more fully to prose texts. Knowing how to **analyse** and **evaluate** a text will help you to do this.

Look at the SQA criteria for Textual Analysis at Intermediate 2.

ANALYSIS	'Responses explain in some detail **ways in which** aspects of **structure/style/language** contribute to **meaning/effect/impact**.'
EVALUATION	'Responses reveal **engagement** with the text or aspects of the text and stated or implied evaluation of **effectiveness**, using some **appropriate critical terminology** and substantiated with some **relevant evidence** from the text.'

The words in **bold** highlight key ingredients in the process of analysing and evaluating. Some of these require further explanation.

Analysis

'ways in which' simply means *how* in a technical sense

'style' refers to the distinctive way in which an author uses the various tools of writing

'effect' relates to the particular response(s) produced in the reader as a result of the way in which an author has used a specific writing tool

NB Not to be confused with **effectiveness**. See below for note on 'effectiveness'.

Evaluation

'engagement' means obvious personal involvement with the text

'effectiveness' relates to the degree of success an author has had in using specific techniques to communicate effectively with the reader

'appropriate critical terminology' means the special vocabulary used when discussing specific literary features: for prose, some of these terms would be *genre, structure, pace, setting, characterization* ...

'relevant evidence' indicates that whatever statement is being made about a text or aspect of a text, this needs to be backed up by evidence which is directly related to that statement

The SQA criteria indicate the skills a candidate requires to demonstrate in order to achieve a pass at Intermediate 2 in Textual Analysis. Using these as our framework, let's see how they translate into useful building blocks.

BLOCK C *Analysis*
Examining aspects of structure, style, language to show HOW they contribute to meaning and effect.

BLOCK D *Evaluation*
Assessing the effectiveness of a text through personal response, supported by relevant evidence and appropriate critical vocabulary.

Analysis in action

Using the following extract from Evan Hunter's short story, *On the Sidewalk Bleeding*, let's explore further the **process** of analysis to see how it works in practice.

EXTRACT Ⓐ (Andy, a member of the Royals, has been stabbed by a rival gang member.)

He felt weak and very tired. He felt alone and wet and feverish and chilled, and he knew he was going to die now, and the knowledge made him suddenly sad. He was not frightened. For some reason, he was not frightened. He was only filled with an overwhelming sadness that his life would be over at sixteen. He felt all at once as if he had never done anything, never seen anything, never been anywhere. There were so many things to do, and he wondered why he'd never thought of them before, wondered why the rumbles and the jumps and the purple jacket had always seemed so important to him before, and now they seemed like such small things in a world he was missing, a world that was rushing past at the other end of the alley.

I don't want to die, he thought. I haven't lived yet.

It seemed very important to him to take off the purple jacket. He was very close to dying, and when they found him, he did not want them to say, 'Oh, it's a Royal.' With great effort, he rolled over onto his back. He felt the pain tearing at his stomach when he moved, a pain he did not think was possible. But he wanted to take the jacket off. If he never did another thing, he wanted to take the jacket off. The jacket had only one meaning now, and that was a very simple meaning.

If he had not been wearing the jacket, he would not have been stabbed. The knife had not been plunged in hatred of Andy. The knife hated only the purple jacket. The jacket was a stupid meaningless thing that was robbing him of his life. He wanted to take the jacket off his back. With an enormous loathing, he wanted to take the jacket off his back.

*He lay struggling with the shiny wet material. His arms were heavy, and pain ripped fire across his body whenever he moved. But he squirmed and fought and twisted until one arm was free and then the other, and then he rolled away from the jacket and lay quite still, breathing heavily, listening for the sound of his breathing and the sound of the rain and thinking **Rain is sweet, I'm Andy**.*

From On the Sidewalk Bleeding *by Evan Hunter*

The process of analysis could be said to involve three key stages: making a statement about an aspect of structure/style/language; providing relevant evidence to back up that statement, and then commenting on the effect of the selected aspect. For ease of memory, this process can be reduced to a neat acronym, **SEA**:

S	statement	
E	evidence	(SEA)
A	analysis	

Working with a few examples from *On the Sidewalk Bleeding*, let's look at this process in action.

Example 1　statement

Evan Hunter take us inside Andy's head, showing us his thoughts and feelings, helping us to identify with his situation.

evidence

'For some reason, he was not frightened. He was only filled with an overwhelming sadness that his life would be over at sixteen.'

analysis

Too late, Andy realizes what his life has been, up to now. The sadness this brings is *'overwhelming'* as if he cannot quite cope with the tragic realization that this is the end of his short life. The fact he is *'not frightened'* seems strange to us but, at the same time, it helps us to understand that his mind is so preoccupied with thinking about what he has missed in his life, that it has no room for fear.

Example 2　statement

The physical pain Andy experiences is shown in the use of detail.

evidence

He is *'weak and very tired'*, *'wet and feverish and chilled'*. When he tries to remove his jacket he feels *'the pain tearing at his stomach ... '* and *'His arms were heavy, and pain ripped across his body'*.

analysis

The phrase *'wet and feverish and chilled'* gives us a moving picture of Andy lying in the rain becoming colder and colder as his heart rate drops. At the same time, it also suggests the idea of the young boy confronting the 'chilling' realization that he is facing death. The onomatopoeic words *'tearing'* and *'ripping'* are particularly striking; metaphorically, they convey the sounds of a wild animal attacking human flesh.

Example 3　statement

The symbol of the jacket plays an important role in helping us to understand character.

evidence

> *'If he never did another thing, he wanted to take the jacket off. The jacket had only one meaning now, and that was a very simple meaning.'*
>
> *'The knife hated only the purple jacket.'*
>
> *'The jacket was a stupid meaningless thing that was robbing him of his life.'*

analysis

The boy realizes that he has become the jacket: he has lost his own identity as Andy. It is very important now, before he dies, that he throws away the jacket and becomes himself again. Tragically too late, he also realizes that the person who stabbed him was hitting out at a symbol, not at Andy, himself —

it was what the jacket had come to represent to the gang world that brought on the attack. The jacket, which Andy had once thought of as important, now seems 'stupid' and 'meaningless'.

Example 4   statement
The sentences are structured in a way that is very similar to the speech of a young boy.

evidence
They are a mix of short, simple statements and longer, looser structures, which repeat 'and' as a link word. For example, there are the short, direct statements such as:

'He felt weak and very tired.'

'He was not frightened.'

But these are mixed with longer structures such as:

'He felt alone and wet and feverish and chilled, and he knew he was going to die now, and the knowledge made him suddenly sad.'

'There were so many things to do, and he wondered why he'd never thought of them before, wondered why the rumbles and the jumps and the purple jacket had always seemed so important to him before, and now they seemed like such small things in a world he was missing, a world that was rushing past at the other end of the alley.'

analysis
The short, simple structures reflect the straightforward directness of the young boy's thoughts: until now he has not stopped to think in a more complex way. The longer, looser sentences sound like the rush of confused thoughts that are spinning through his head like a rushing stream. The 'and' links are typical of the way a young person might join a range of thoughts in an unsophisticated structure.

Example 5   statement
Repetition helps to reinforce important ideas in the extract.

evidence
The words 'die/dying' and 'life' are repeated, as is the word 'pain'. The fact that 'He wanted to take the jacket off' is repeated four times.

analysis
The stabbing of Andy is literally a life and death issue. The writer seems to be stressing the irony of the fact that it is only when facing his own death that Andy realizes what is truly important in life. The jacket stands as a terrible symbol of the life Andy has led, and now that he realizes its true value, he must remove it before he dies to reclaim his own identity.

ACTIVITY 1
Now try to provide **evidence** and **analysis** to support the following statements, using the above examples to help you.

statement A
Word choice helps the reader to feel sympathy for Andy.

evidence

analysis

statement B
The writer uses contrast to emphasise the difference between the confined world of the Royals and the wider outside world.

evidence

analysis

Evaluation in action

Although we've separated the two areas of analysis and evaluation for teaching purposes, they are, of course, very closely related. Often your evaluative comments will be based on specific aspects which you've already analysed. The emphasis, however, will be different. If you look at the **building block D** again, you'll see that the focus is on assessing the **effectiveness** of a text or aspects of a text through the following elements:

BLOCK D *Evaluation* Assessing the effectiveness of a text through personal response, supported by relevant evidence and appropriate critical vocabulary	personal response relevant evidence appropriate critical vocabulary

Let's go back to *On the Sidewalk Bleeding* to see some examples of the **evaluative process** in action.

Example 1   I think that Evan Hunter has been very successful in taking the reader inside the mind of young Andy **(PR)**. The interior monologue **(CV)** weaves very naturally into the narrative so that at times it is hard to distinguish who is talking, the narrator or Andy. For example, in paragraph three, we switch from Andy's inner voice saying, '*He did not want them to say, "Oh it's a Royal"*', to the narrator's voice recounting the action, '*With great effort, he rolled over onto his back*' **(E)**.

The frequent use of strong, forceful imagery **(CV)** seems to capture Andy's thoughts about his life as a member of the Royals: he feels strongly now that this life has led him down a futile road **(PR)**. He feels an '*overwhelming sadness*' **(E)** when he thinks of the world that is '*rushing past*' **(E)** him '*at the other end of the alley.*' He can feel the '*pain tearing at his stomach*' **(E)** as a result of the knife which '*had not been plunged in hatred*' **(E)**. The knife is personified **(CV)** as the killer who '*hated only the purple jacket*' **(E)**. You feel a great pity for Andy as he lies in terrible pain, knowing that there could have been another kind of life '*at the other end of the alley*', so near and yet so hopelessly far **(PR)**.

(PR = personal response; E = evidence; CV = critical vocabulary)

Example 2   What is most effective about this extract is the way in which the young boy's realization of what being a member of the Royals really means is so sympathetically handled (**PR**). The author describes the boy's physical condition, emphasizing his terrible pain but, more importantly, he focuses on his mental pain when he *'knew he was going to die now.'* This terrible knowledge makes him aware that: ' … *he had never done anything, never seen anything, never been anywhere'* (**E**). He is forced to accept that his life has been meaningless, a fact that is reinforced by the repeated use of *'never'*.

His sudden awakening to this fact is further underlined by the repetition (**CV**) of the words *'and he wondered why'* (**E**). He cannot believe that he is only now making this discovery about his life. The closing lines are particularly moving in the way in which they capture the boy's sudden awakening to the sweet taste of rain and to his own identity as Andy. *'Rain is sweet, I'm Andy'*, written as if the boy were speaking the words aloud, is a very poignant way of expressing this realization (**PR**).

ACTIVITY 2

The writer has succeeded in drawing a picture of a young boy who is more than just a stereotypical gang member (**PR**).

Try to develop this response, using 'relevant evidence' (**E**) and 'appropriate critical vocabulary' (**CV**) to back up what you say. Use the above examples to help you.

CHAPTER 5 *Prose*

BUILDING BLOCKS TO ANALYSIS AND EVALUATION

 *Developing*

Practice in developing the skills of analysis and evaluation

The next two extracts aim to provide you with opportunities to develop specific analytical and evaluative skills by focusing on key aspects of each text, exploring *how* individual writers have achieved particular effects and assessing their effectiveness.

EXTRACT A *All my life I've hated Sundays, for the obvious British reasons ('Songs of Praise', closed shops, congealing gravy that you don't want to go near but no one's going to let you escape from) and the obvious international reasons as well, but this Sunday is a corker. There are loads of things I could do; I've got tapes to make and videos to watch and phone calls to return. But I don't want to do any of them. I get back to the flat at one; by two, things have got so bad that I decide to go home — **home**, home, Mum and dad home, congealing gravy and 'Songs of Praise' home. It was waking up in the middle of the night and wondering where I belonged that did it: I don't belong at home, and I don't **want** to belong at home, but at least home is somewhere I know.*

Home, home is near Watford, a bus-ride away from the Metropolitan Line station. It was a terrible place to grow up, I suppose, but I didn't really mind. Until I was thirteen or so it was just a place where I could ride my bike; between thirteen and seventeen a place where I could meet girls. And I moved when I was eighteen, so I only spent a year seeing the place for what it was — a suburban shit-hole — and hating it. My mum and dad moved house about ten years ago, when my mum reluctantly accepted that I had gone and wasn't coming back but they only moved round the corner, to a two-bedroom semi, and they kept their phone number and their friends and their life.

In Bruce Springsteen songs, you can either stay and rot, or you can escape and burn. That's OK; he's a songwriter, after all, and he needs simple choices like that in his songs. But nobody ever writes about how it is possible to escape and rot — how escapes can go off at half-cock, how you can leave the suburbs for the city but end up living a limp suburban life anyway. That's what happened to me; that's what happens to most people.

From High Fidelity by Nick Hornby

ACTIVITY

a) Focus of interest for analysis: communicating thoughts and feelings.

How?
Areas for consideration:
- ◆ word choice
- ◆ tone
- ◆ imagery

Using the three listed elements as the basis for your discussion, explore *how* each of these elements helps to communicate the narrator's thoughts and feelings.

Remember to support your comments with evidence and analysis. Use the examples in Chapter 4 to remind you of the process of analysis.

Here is one example from each of the areas for consideration, to help start the discussion.

Example of word choice   Paragraph 3: '*rot*' — a short, strong word which is repeated to underline the strength of his negative feelings.

Example of tone   Paragraph 1: '*All my life ... , but this Sunday is a corker.*' Bitter, cynical tone which effectively conveys his feelings about a British Sunday.

Example of imagery   Paragraph 1: '*congealing gravy*'. 'Congealing' suggests that the gravy has been sitting around for a while and has gone cold: it is beginning to set into an unappetising, sticky state. It is a metaphor for the way he feels about Sundays, and about his own life, which he feels has 'set' into a solid, unappealing state.

b) Focus of interest for evaluation: theme of disillusionment

How successful is Nick Hornby in communicating the idea of life's dreams and ideals being shattered? Look, in particular, at the connection he makes between:

◆ Sundays
◆ home
◆ Bruce Springsteen songs

Remember to show a personal response to the extract, using appropriate critical vocabulary when making your evaluation. Use the examples in Chapter 4 to remind you of the process of evaluation.

EXTRACT B   (The incident described takes place in the rural heart of the North East of Scotland in the 1920s.)

She went through the Clatterin' Howe where she always had to walk up the steep brae, pushing her bicycle by the handlebars. Folk said it was called the Clatterin' Howe because at night-time you sometimes heard the clatter of horse hoofs, supposed to be pulling a hearse over the brae, where a tinker quine* was ravished and murdered long back, and you could just see the outline of the hearse in the dark from the lettered stone by the roadside that marked the evil spot. But Helen had gone through the Howe so many times in the dark, on her way to Bogmyrtle, and had never seen or heard anything unnatural, that she scarcely gave the story a thought, or if she did at all she mostly put it down to somebody's imagination; another ghost story, and that things like that were all in the mind.

But somehow tonight she remembered the story and a vague silence dogged her footsteps. The faint halo from her lamp gave shadows to the whins and brooms that grew by the roadside: weird, wind-blown shapes that might conceal a body with ill-intent, leaping out upon her from the dyke. But it was from behind that she was suspicious; something or somebody was following her, she felt sure of it; something sinister, but she was afraid to turn her head. There was no sound of footsteps in the whispering wind, only her own, and when she stopped there was silence. But she was aware of a presence; she was not alone, and in a moment of defiance she turned her bicycle and shone the feeble light down the brae. But there was nothing, nothing but the silent winking of the stars and the brooding darkness. She passed the lettered stone and bravely stared up the brae, where the rim of the road was outlined in the blackness but nothing else.

But the presence persisted, and she daren't look sideways, for she heard the rustle of clothes, like the swish of a heavy cloak, now caught up with her and bearing into the night; a priest-like figure robed to the ground and blacker than the night, without footsteps, without visual movement, silhouetted in the gas light against the sky, with sloping shoulders, its hands clasped in front like a minister in prayer, a rigid figure now ahead of her, aloof and silent, passing into the night. It might have been a woman, Helen wasn't sure, and as it poised on the rim of night a tremendous flash swallowed it from sight. Helen waited for the thunder, terrified, but it never came, only a dead silence that was even more terrifying; and with her aching eyes she stared into the night, half blinded by the flash. She stood on the brae and hung on her bicycle, praying to God there wouldn't be another flash, and that the thunder wouldn't come; that it was only fireflacht or winter lightning that folk said was harmless, though she had never seen it so close.

* *quine* = a North Eastern dialectal word for girl

From Blown Seed *by David Toulmin*

ACTIVITY

a) Focus of interest for analysis: establishing atmosphere.

How?

Areas for consideration:
- build up of tension
- imagery
- weather

Using the three listed elements as the basis for your discussion, explore *how* each of these elements helps to establish a convincing atmosphere.

Remember to support your comments with evidence and analysis. Use the examples in Chapter 4 to remind you of the process of analysis.

b) Focus of interest for evaluation: the supernatural.

How effective?

How convincing is the writer's handling of the supernatural?

You may find it helpful to consider the following aspects:
- details of night-time setting
- references to the alleged 'incident' on the Clatterin' Brae
- description of Helen's reaction to 'the presence'

Remember to show a personal response to the extract, using appropriate critical vocabulary when making your evaluation. Use the examples in Chapter 4 to remind you of the process of evaluation.

CHAPTER 6 *Prose*

BUILDING BLOCKS TO ANALYSIS AND EVALUATION

 Demonstrating

Demonstrating analysis and evaluation

In Chapter 3 we explored an extract from *Master Georgie* using the building blocks to understanding in order to provide a working model as preparation for your independent study of a text.

Now we're going to apply the **building blocks of analysis and evaluation** to this same extract in preparation for your own independent study of another, unseen extract.

BLOCK C *Analysis*	**BLOCK D** *Evaluation*
Examining aspects of structure, style, language to show HOW they contribute to meaning and effect.	Assessing the effectiveness of a text through personal response, supported by relevant evidence and appropriate critical vocabulary.

But first, as part of that preparation, a reminder about **denotation** and **connotation**.

Analysis of language

To ensure that writing is effective, a writer strives to use the tools of language with care and precision. Word choice not only communicates literal meaning (**denotation**) but, in many cases, sets up a range of additional associations in the reader's mind. These associations, or **connotations** as they are correctly known, are what gives a piece of writing its rich layers.

Imagine a group of words representing a line of doors, each of which has a key in its lock. Unlocking these 'doors' one by one will not produce the same views; some will be much more interesting than others. The more interesting views will lie behind those 'doors' or words which carry associations or **connotations**.

For example:

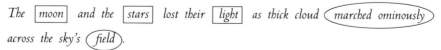
The moon *and the* stars *lost their* light *as thick cloud* marched ominously *across the sky's* field.

In this example, when we unlock the circled words we find they carry additional connotations: the clouds '*marching ominously*' suggest an army of soldiers striding out threateningly to do battle, while the word '*field*' picks up this association with war to suggest the sky is a battlefield waiting for an attack.

In this context the framed words *'moon'*, *'stars'* and *'light'* could also be said to carry certain connotations: the moon and the stars reflect light which, traditionally, has represented goodness. Here the light of goodness could be said to be at war with the dark clouds, forces of evil.

Your analysis of language features should always explore any relevant **connotations.**

Sample commentary on *Master Georgie* extract

Use the sample commentary which follows this extract to help you in your own independent exploration of the final unseen extract in this chapter.

EXTRACT Ⓐ (Myrtle, adoptive sister of Master Georgie, a surgeon, has followed him out to the Crimean War. Here she goes out riding with an acquaintance, Mrs Yardley. The period is the 1850s.)

Presently the path widened and we saw in the distance a little whitewashed house beside a square of vineyard. I was all for making a detour to avoid coming too close. 'There'll be dogs,' I warned. Mrs Yardley didn't appear to have heard me and trotted on regardless.

Sure enough, we had advanced but a little way when the air was shattered by a deep and awesome howl; Mrs Yardley's horse stopped dead in its tracks. An animal the size of a small calf and much emaciated appeared round the side of the house and tore towards us, followed by a smaller creature, black all over and running on three legs.

'Don't move,' I called out to Mrs Yardley, though indeed, the slither of claws on the stony path and the ferocious barking that rent the luminous day had turned her to stone in the saddle. Fortunately the horses stood firm, being no doubt used to such alarms. Some six yards away, the dogs halted, tongues lolling. I concentrated on the larger of the two, forcing myself to gaze into its hateful eyes; whining, it lay down, ears flattened to its mean and bony skull. Mrs Yardley was whimpering, but not loudly enough to provoke an assault.

After what seemed like hours a bow-legged man emerged from the vineyard and whistled off the brutes. Approaching, he beckoned us forward. We were led past the house to a courtyard beyond, where a woman squatted on the dust pummelling a lump of dough. Fawning, the man urged us to dismount and gestured towards a rickety table. Half a dozen children, some crawling, materialised as though by magic and began to pluck at our clothes.

Mrs Yardley was trembling; a pin-prick of blood stood on her cheek.

'Forgive me,' she said. 'I should have listened to you.'

'Think of what to give them,' I urged. 'Have you any money?'

'Money,' she said. 'Why do we need money?'

'In return for hospitality,' I said, vexed. 'Nothing is for free in this world.'

The man set before us two small bowls and a pitcher of milk. The children got under his feet and he kicked out, scattering them squawking and fluttering, chicken-like into the corners of the yard.

'Pig,' I exclaimed, though I was careful to smile. I thought it was no wonder the smaller dog had a leg missing.

Mrs Yardley was staring down at the jug, at the insects floating atop the milk. 'You must drink it,' I told her. 'If you don't they'll only bring us something worse.'

'At least they're past biting,' she said and gamely drank.

The woman slapped the circle of dough on to a flat stone; she pointed to the sun, then patted her stomach, indicating the bread would be good to eat when baked. As she lifted her arm her gown fell back and there was an infant stuck to her breast, scalp springing with hair the colour of tar.

'Think,' I urged Mrs Yardley. 'Think what we can give them.' I myself had nothing, save a handkerchief at my wrist, mislaid by Georgie; she, a silk scarf at her throat.

All at once a curious giggling sound came from somewhere close to the vineyard wall. The bow-legged man swaggered off, and shortly returned carrying a struggling goat which he dropped on to its feet on the table. The children surged forward.

'If he's going to cut its throat in front of us,' Mrs Yardley promised, 'I shall scream.'

From Master Georgie *by Beryl Bainbridge*

Analysis of structure of incident

The incident opens with an innocent approach to 'a little whitewashed house beside a square of vineyard'. But this peaceful setting is immediately interrupted by the warning of dogs which Mrs Yardley ignores, introducing tension to the scene. This tension is further heightened when the fearsome dogs actually do appear.

With the arrival of the 'bow-legged' man and his family, the scene begins to build a delicate balance between seemingly innocent actions and the possibility of more sinister events lying just beneath the surface. For example, a pitcher of milk is produced, but the suggestion is that if they don't drink it, they will be presented with 'something worse'.

The scene reaches a startling climax with the man producing the struggling goat, which Mrs Yardley suspects is about to have its throat cut.

The scene is carefully structured to create a build up of tension around what, at first, appears to be a perfectly innocent situation.

Analysis of descriptive detail

The writer's use of detail holds the reader's attention. For example, individual aspects of the dogs are highlighted, emphasizing their ferocity:

'an animal the size of a small calf'

'ferocious barking'

'tongues lolling'

'hateful eyes'

'mean and bony skull'

Exaggeration is deliberately used in the first example to make the dog seem even more intimidating, while the 'mean and bony skull' suggests a sinister monster who is desperate to attack.

Even the description of the baby at the breast seems quite sinister: 'scalp springing with hair the colour of tar' gives the child an unnatural appearance, as if it were an alien creature.

The 'insects floating atop the milk' and the 'curious giggling sound' contribute to this rather sinister atmosphere, as if we are waiting for something nasty to happen. These descriptive details play an important part in maintaining the particular atmosphere.

Evaluating effectiveness

I was totally absorbed by the way in which the author placed the two women in an unpredictable situation where their differing reactions could be seen (**PR**).

The 'I' character shows her practical side when she warns of the possibility of dogs, while Mrs Yardley shows her lack of awareness by trotting on 'regardless' (**E**). When the huge dog races towards them, the first character takes command, shouting, 'Don't move'. Bravely, she confronts the 'brute' by 'forcing (herself) to gaze into its hateful eyes' (**E**). Mrs Yardley, on the other hand, reacts pathetically by 'whimpering'. We are told she is 'trembling' and the author adds an effective image (**CV**) when she observes 'a pin-prick of blood stood on her cheek' (**E**).

Characterization (**CV**) is developed through the contrasting dialogue (**CV**). When Mrs Yardley is 'urged' by her companion to 'Think of what to give them' and asked is she has any money, she replies naively, 'Money, why do we need money?' (**E**). Clearly she is not an experienced traveller and has not worked out what to do in this kind of situation, whereas her companion thinks quickly and shows initiative. She shows her greater experience when she comments 'Nothing is for free in this world' (**E**). Her forceful character is also shown when she calls the man 'Pig' (**E**) but is clever enough to smile while she is saying it. Mrs Yardley's final sentence sums up her character very effectively, showing her rather childish reaction to what she envisages is going to happen: 'If he's going to cut its throat in front of us, I shall scream.'

Beryl Bainbridge has successfully developed two contrasting characters within the short space of this scene by skilful use of dialogue and detailed reactions (**PR**).

Demonstrating analysis and evaluation

In summary, using the building blocks approach to analysis and evaluation, several readings of this extract have revealed a clearer awareness of the following aspects:
  ◆ style
  ◆ language
  ◆ situation
  ◆ mood/atmosphere
  ◆ dialogue
  ◆ narrative voice
  ◆ character
  ◆ relationships
  ◆ personal response to all of the above

EXTRACT Ⓑ *Ned Lowry and Rita Lomasney had, one might say, been lovers from childhood. The first time they had met was when he was fourteen and she a year or two younger. It was on the North Mall on a Sunday afternoon, and she was sitting on a bench by the river under the trees; a tall, bony string of a girl with a long, obstinate jaw. Ned was a studious-looking young fellow in a blue and white college cap — thin, pale and spectacled. As he passed he looked at her owlishly, and she gave him back an impudent stare. This upset him — he had no experience of girls — so he blushed and raised his cap. At this she seemed to relent.*

'Hullo,' she said experimentally.

'Good afternoon,' he replied with a pale, prissy smile.

'Where are you off to?' she asked.

'Oh, just up the Dyke for a walk.'

'Sit down,' she said in a sharp voice, laying her hand on the bench beside her, and he did as he was told. It was a summer evening, and the white quay walls and tall, crazy, claret-coloured tenements under a blue and white sky were reflected in the lazy water, which wrinkled only at the edges and seemed like a painted carpet.

'It's very pleasant here,' he said complacently.

'Is it?' she asked with a truculence that startled him. 'I don't see anything very pleasant about it.'

'Oh, it's very nice and quiet,' he said in mild surprise as he raised his fair eyebrows and looked up and down the Mall. 'My name is Lowry,' he added politely.

'Are ye the ones that have the jeweller's shop in the Parade?' she asked.

'That's right,' he replied with modest pride.

'We have a clock we got from ye,' she said. 'Tisn't much good of an old clock either,' she added with quiet malice.

'You should bring it back to the shop,' he said with concern. 'It probably needs overhauling.'

'I'm going down the river in a boat with a couple of fellows,' she said, going off at a tangent. 'Will ye come?'

'Couldn't', he said with a smile.

'Why not?'

'I'm only left go up the Dyke for a walk,' he replied complacently. 'On Saturdays I go to Confession at St Peter and Paul's; then I go up the Dyke and come back the Western Road. Sometimes you see very good cricket matches. Do you like cricket?'

'A lot of old sissies pucking a ball!' she said shortly. 'I do not.'

'I like it,' he said firmly. 'I go up there every Saturday when it's fine. Of course, I'm not supposed to talk to anyone,' he added with mild amusement at his own audacity.

'Why not?'

'My mother doesn't like me to.'

'Why doesn't she?'

'She comes from an awfully good family,' he answered mildly, and but for his gentle smile, she might have thought he was deliberately insulting her.

From The Mad Lomasneys *by Frank O'Connor*

ACTIVITY

Now it's your turn to demonstrate what you've learnt about analysis and evaluation by exploring the extract from the short story *The Mad Lomasneys* by Frank O'Connor.

Directing discussion on analysis and evaluation

Use the following prompts to help direct your discussion of the extract.

- How does the writer's use of descriptive detail contribute to our impression of the characters as individuals? (Analysis)
- How does dialogue help to highlight the differences between the two characters? (Analysis)
- The extract is about the first meeting between two young people. How successful, do you feel, Frank O'Connor is in his handling of the situation? (Evaluation)

CHAPTER 7 *Poetry*

BUILDING BLOCKS TO UNDERSTANDING

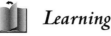 *Learning*

Introduction

Like any other form of communication, poetry needs to connect with its audience. Before the mass of the population could read, poetry developed as part of an oral tradition – it would be spoken aloud to its listeners. Later it was written down, but was still intended to be read aloud. We should remember this fact whenever we read a poem. **Sound** (of rhythm, rhyme, language and tone) is, therefore, vitally important in directing us to an understanding of a poem's meaning, as well as to an appreciation of its style.

Once a poem could be seen written down on the page, its **form** and **structure** could be more readily appreciated. People could see that poetry differed in shape and form from prose or drama. Recognizing how a poem is put together, its shape and form, is an important key to understanding the ideas the poet is trying to convey, as well as helping us to appreciate some of the techniques the poet has used to communicate those ideas.

A poet relies on skilful use of the tools of language – sound, shape and arrangement – to stimulate readers' imaginations and to arouse their senses.

One meaningful approach to furthering our understanding, analysis and evaluation of poetry, therefore, is to develop an awareness of how these key aspects interact with each other:
- Poetry as **form** and **structure**
- Poetry as **sound**
- Poetry as **language**

If we translate these into building blocks to understanding poetry, they look like this:

BLOCK A	BLOCK B
Understanding of main ideas, central concerns through: *form and structure; key words and phrases*	Understanding of significant detail through: *tone and imagery*

Let's begin with an extract from a poetry text, to see how these building blocks work in action and help to reveal meaning.

TEXT Ⓐ   **Grandmother (an extract)**

connotations of wisdom/reverence

Double underline:
time markers
help to signpost
the stages of the narrative

By the time I knew my grandmother she was dead.
Before that she was where I thought she stood,
Spectacles, slippers, venerable head,
A standard-issue twinkle in her eyes —
5 Familiar stage props of grandmotherhood.
It took her death to teach me they were lies.

short, dramatic statements startle the reader

'stage props' metaphorically convey a stereotypical picture of grandmother but this preconceived picture is a 'lie'

My sixteen-year-old knowingness was shocked
To hear her family narrate her past
In quiet nostalgic chorus. As they talked
10 Her body stiffened on the muted fast
Though well washed linen coverlet of her bed.
The kitchen where we sat, a room I knew,
Took on a strangeness with each word they said.
How she was born where wealth was **pennies**, grew
15 Into a woman before she was a girl,
From dirt and pain constructed happiness,
Shed youth's dreams in the fierce sweat of a mill,
Married and mothered in her sixteenth year,
Fed children from her own mouth's emptiness
20 In an attic rats owned half of, liked her beer.
Careless they scattered pictures: mother, wife,
Strikes lived through, hard concessions bought and sold
In a level-headed bargaining with life,
Told anecdotes in which her strength rang **gold**,
25 Her eyes were clear, her wants as plain as salt.

mocks his own cocksure attitude: he is 'shocked' to see quite a different picture of his grandmother emerge

Underline:
harsh contrasts highlight the world of reality: elsewhere contrasting words & phrases used to highlight themes

striking use of paradox

alliterated phrase emphasizes the proximity of the two events

image captures grandmother's realistic/pragmatic attitude to life: no unrealistic expectations

positive images: a realistic view of life; needs were simple

The past became a **mint** from which they struck
Small change till that room **glittered** like a **vault**.
The corpse in the other room became to me
Awesome as Pharaoh now, as if one look
30 Would show me all that I had failed to see.

words in bold refer to money, both literally and metaphorically

simile, comparing grandmother's dead body to that of an Egyptian king, captures the idea of the dramatic change in the boy's perception of her

William McIlvanney

BLOCK A

Understanding of main ideas, central concerns through: *form and structure; key words and phrases*

ACTIVITY 1

Recognizing and interpreting features of form and structure: narrative

a) The narrative begins in the immediate past with the death of his grandmother. How does it develop thereafter?

Use the following narrative signposts to help you.

'Before that ... grandmotherhood' (lines 2–5)
'To hear her family narrate ... as plain as salt.' (lines 8–25)
'till that room glittered ... failed to see' (lines 27–30)

b) There is another narrative running alongside the story of grandmother's life and death. What is that other story about? Look closely at verse one and at lines 29–30.

ACTIVITY 2
Recognizing and interpreting features of form and structure: sentence structure

a) Look at the opening and closing lines of verse one. Both are short, simple statements. How does this choice of structure help your understanding of the effect the grandmother's death had on the boy?

   Remember that simple sentences are often used to create particular effects: for example, to emphasize an important point; to shock or surprise the reader; to create tension.

b) Look at the structure of the following two sentences:

   'How she was born where wealth was pennies, grew ... liked her beer' (**lines 14–20**)

   'Careless they scattered pictures: mother, wife ... plain as salt' (**lines 21–25**)

   In what way do these particular structures help to give us a picture of the grandmother's life? Pay special attention to the effect of listing within a sentence structure.

ACTIVITY 3
Recognizing and interpreting features of form and structure: key words and phrases

Single key words

venerable	strength
lies	awesome
past	

Contrasting key words and phrases

pain/happiness	girl/woman	bought/sold
show/failed to see	married/mothered	concessions/bargaining
wealth/wants as plain as salt	youth's dreams/	teach/knowingness
gold/pennies	fierce sweat of a mill	mint/small change

Discuss what you can learn about the main ideas in the poem from these groups of contrasting key words and phrases.

ACTIVITY 4

Recognizing and interpreting features of style: tone

Try reading aloud and listening carefully to the following examples from *Grandmother*. Listen for the tones used.

'By the time I knew my grandmother she was dead.' *(line 1)*

' ... As they talked
Her body stiffened on the muted fast' *(lines 9–10)*

'Told anecdotes in which her strength rang gold' *(line 24)*

'The corpse in the other room became to me
Awesome as Pharaoh now ... ' *(lines 28–29)*

' ... as if one look
Would show me all that I had failed to see.' *(lines 29–30)*

From your listening, what do you learn of the boy's feelings?

From the boxed list, select the word or phrase which best matches the tone(s) you hear in these quoted examples. You may, of course, add a choice of your own.

awe admiration respect humility apology self-criticism regret reproach

ACTIVITY 5

Recognizing and interpreting features of style: imagery

Like key words and phrases, key images can help to unfold layers of meaning within a text. They are, after all, simply groups of words which, because of their careful selection and juxtapositioning, combine to form word pictures.

These are examples of images which help to reveal aspects of the Grandmother's life and character:

'grew into a woman before she was a girl' *(lines 14–15)*

This apparent contradiction or **paradox** highlights the unnaturally short period of her childhood: circumstances forced her to grow up before her time.

'from dirt and pain constructed happiness' *(line 16)*

Again, an apparent **paradox**: she managed to build happiness out of very unpromising raw materials – 'pain' and 'dirt'. The image reveals her courage and determination to rise above her difficulties.

What further information about character and circumstances do the following images offer?
- 'shed youth's dreams in the fierce sweat of a mill' *(line 17)*
- 'fed children from her own mouth's emptiness' *(line 19)*
- 'her strength rang gold' *(line 24)*
- 'her wants as plain as salt' *(line 25)*

CHAPTER 8 *Poetry*

BUILDING BLOCKS TO UNDERSTANDING

 *Developing*

Practice in developing understanding

In Chapter 7 you learned to recognize and interpret aspects of meaning within a poem by applying the building blocks to understanding.

With more practice, you will become more skilled, boosting your confidence in being able to apply these techniques to an unseen text.

Below you will find two complete poems with discussion questions to help you develop further confidence in recognizing and interpreting the keys to understanding.

BLOCK A

Understanding of main ideas, central concerns through: *form and structure; key words and phrases*

BLOCK B

Understanding of significant detail through: *tone and imagery*

TEXT A

The Panther
In the Jardin des Plantes, Paris

His vision, from the constantly passing bars,
    has grown so weary that it cannot hold
anything else. It seems to him there are
    a thousand bars; and behind the bars, no world.

5 As he paces in cramped circles, over and over,
    the movement of his powerful soft strides
is like a ritual dance around a centre
    in which a mighty will stands, paralysed.

Only at times, the curtain of the pupils
10   lifts, quietly —. An image enters in,
rushes down through tensed, arrested muscles,
    plunges into the heart and is gone.

Rainer Maria Rilke

ACTIVITY 1

Form and structure of poem

BLOCK A

Understanding of main ideas, central concerns through: *form and structure; key words and phrases*

The story is told from the perspective of an onlooker, but with occasional glimpses of the animal's world from the panther's perspective.

Let's take a closer look at three aspects of the poem's physical form:

a) The regular, four-line stanza where the lines visually dip in and out.

Can you see any connection between this shape and the panther's caged world?

b) The full stop at the end of every verse.

What contribution, if any, does this punctuation feature make to your findings in a)?

c) The consistent use of run-on lines, or *enjambment.*

What particular aspect of the panther's condition could be said to be emphasized by the poet's use of enjambment?

ACTIVITY 2
Structure of sentences and punctuation

a) What is significant about the sentence structure in verse two?

Can you identify the key word which holds the structure together?

How does the sentence structure in this verse heighten your awareness of the panther's condition?

b) Comment on any features of the following structure which contribute to your understanding of the panther's situation.

> *'An image enters in,*
> *rushes down through the tensed, arrested muscles,*
> *plunges into the heart and is gone.'*

c) Let's look at an example where punctuation is helping to underline an idea.

> *'It seems to him there are*
> *a thousand bars; and behind the bars no world.'*

The first part of the sentence makes a bald statement about the panther's perspective on his world, which he sees as confined by *'a thousand bars'*. The semi-colon, however, allows the poet to extend this point even more shockingly when he adds that, the *'thousand'* bars are so confining that he is totally blind to the world outside his cage. So the semi-colon has helped us to push our understanding beyond the initial fairly straightforward point, to develop into a more complex idea.

What part do the following punctuation features play in developing your understanding of ideas in the poem?
   ◆ the full stop after *'else'* in the middle of line 3
   ◆ the dash after *'quietly'* in line 10.

ACTIVITY 3
Key words and phrases
The following groups of words and phrases provide useful keys to our understanding of the panther's tragic circumstances.

Taking each group separately, discuss what part each plays in this process. Focus, in particular, on the idea of the conflict between the panther's natural life in the wild and his unnatural caged existence.

1	2	3	4
weary paralysed tensed arrested	paces rushes plunges	powerful mighty will	soft strides quietly

	5	6	
	no world cramped circles over and over a centre curtain	vision ritual dance heart	

BLOCK B

Understanding of significant detail through: *tone and imagery*

ACTIVITY 4

Tone

There is a consistent tone running throughout the poem: it is a tone which communicates how the poet feels about what people can do to a beautiful wild animal when they cage it.

Within this dominant tone, there are occasional minor shifts.

a) Look at this list of adjectives describing possible tones. Which of these would you say best describes the dominant tone of *The Panther*?

> detached   impersonal   sad   cynical   matter-of-fact   despairing
> accepting   angry

Use quoted examples to support your views.

b) Can you detect any places in the poem where you recognize a slight shift in tone?

ACTIVITY 5

Imagery

Many of the images in the poem provide us with real insight into the panther and his predicament. Discuss how each of the following examples helps our understanding of the animal's plight.

'behind the bars, no world' *(line 4)*

'a ritual dance around a centre
in which a mighty will stands paralysed' (extended image) *(lines 7–8)*

'the curtain of the pupils
lifts quietly –.' *(lines 9–10)*

'an image enters in,
rushes down through the tensed, arrested muscles,
plunges into the heart and is gone.' (extended image) *(lines 10–12)*

TEXT **B**   Mongol (an extract)

As he passes by they look away
They look over his shoulder
They stare at the sky
Or an empty window
5   Anywhere as long as their eyes don't meet his.

The tiny children run ahead and stare
And poke out their tongues
And waggle their fingers
And grin and giggle
10   And then run back in fear to their parents when he
Only grins back.

His 'friends', the eight year olds
Walk beside him and hug his coat
And say hello quite politely
15   And give him sweets
And then stand back in a corner as
He walks in.

The young wives turn away,
And clutch their children's hands
20   And pet them
And fuss them
And don't smack them that morning
Thankful that their bodies
Fit their minds so well.

25   High in his glass house
The young executive looks down
He sees the clumsy bulk in gaberdine raincoat
And fingers his Savile Row suit
And fumbles between the telephone
30   And the dictaphone
And the linguaphone

And remembers when he kicked him in school for
Not understanding the game
And snaps at his secretary.
35   The few who treat him as a neighbour and friend
Smile over-jovially
Laugh too energetically
And sigh with awkward relief when they leave.

And the rest stare at him, or away, with pity, or regret,
40   As he holds his mother's hand,
And he shoots at the windows with his water pistol,
And laughs at the sun,
And smiles at his friendly world.

Jennifer Noble

ACTIVITY 1

Form and structure

The poem takes the form of a narrative, which tells the story of a day in the life of a Down's Syndrome adult, or Mongol. (The name 'mongol' is now regarded as a derogatory term, but many people still use it, sometimes unthinkingly, sometimes knowingly.)

a) The structure of this main narrative is like a series of snapshots of scenes from a daily journey made by the man and his mother. Each scene has the same basic ingredients.

Can you identify the two main ingredients in each scene?

b) As well as the main narrative, the structure also builds in a secondary storyline.

What is this secondary narrative? In what way does it throw any light on the main narrative?

ACTIVITY 2

Structure of sentences and punctuation

a) The overall sentence structure could be said to reflect the pattern of a child's writing style. Can you find evidence to justify this statement?

Look at the following aspects of sentence structure to help you:
- length
- type
- variety
- links (conjunctions)

b) In what way does this particular pattern of sentence structure help your understanding of the poem's subject matter?

c) Is there any connection between the pattern of sentence structure and the relative absence of punctuation?

ACTIVITY 3

Key words and phrases

R = repeated

	1		2		3	4
	look away	R	stare		poke out tongues	pity
R	look over				waggle fingers	regret
	looks down			R	grin	
					giggle	
	5		**6**		**7**	**8**
	clutch	R	smile		shoots	fingers
	pet	R	laugh		laughs	fumbles
	fuss		sigh		smiles	snaps
	don't smack				friendly	

Examine each of these groups of key words and phrases to show how they have contributed to your understanding of character and/or theme. Here is an example to get you started.

Example   The adverbs *'over-jovially'* and *'energetically'* help to give us an impression of the *'few who treat him as a neighbour and friend'*. They suggest a falseness, as if these people do not feel comfortable about their relationship with the man but are too polite to let it show.

BLOCK B

Understanding of significant detail through: *tone and imagery*

ACTIVITY 4

Tone

Read the following examples from *Mongol* and listen for the dominant tone of voice.

> 'They stare at the sky
> Or an empty window
> Anywhere as long as their eyes don't meet his.' *(lines 3–5)*

> 'His "friends", the eight year olds
> Walk beside him and hug his coat
> And say hello quite politely' *(lines 12–14)*

> 'The young wives turn away,
> And clutch their children's hands' *(lines 18–19)*

> 'And fingers his Savile Row suit
> And fumbles between the telephone
> And the dictaphone . . .
> And snaps at his secretary' *(lines 28–34)*

What would you say is the dominant tone of the poem? How does the tone contribute to your appreciation of the poem's theme(s)? (See note under **Imagery** below for some help with theme, if you need it.)

ACTIVITY 5

Imagery

The poem is mainly concerned with addressing the problem of people's attitudes towards those who are different, in some way, from the norm: the main theme, therefore, is **prejudice.** The secondary theme could be said to be the theme of **innocence**: the young Down's Syndrome man does not recognize the fears and prejudices in those around him – instead, he appears happy and sees the world as 'friendly'.

Much of our understanding of theme comes from the poem's imagery. See if you can collect some evidence of images which help to reveal theme, along the lines of the following example:

> 'The young wives turn away,
> And clutch their children's hands' *(lines18–19)*

The image of the young women *'turning away'* communicates their rejection of the young man: because of their preconceived notions about handicapped people, they turn away in fear. This fear is heard in the word *'clutch'*, which suggests a desperation on the part of the mothers to protect their children from what they see as some kind of threat from the man.

Now pick out your own examples, and comment on them.

CHAPTER 9 *Poetry*

BUILDING BLOCKS TO UNDERSTANDING

Demonstrating

Chapter 8 provided you with opportunities to develop the skills of recognizing and interpreting the **building blocks to understanding.** In this chapter the focus will be on demonstrating your new confidence in applying these techniques.

Accompanying the poem *Strength Made Perfect in Weakness*, you will find a commentary on those aspects which help us to build a fuller understanding of the main, as well as the detailed, concerns of the text. Use this model to help you in your own independent exploration of the final text in this chapter.

TEXT A This poem is one of a collection called *The Alzheimer Sequence.*

Strength Made Perfect in Weakness
for Alex and Zena

You hover at the door as I arrive.
    The wave suggests you recognise me.
Not that it matters. Ward keys
    are turned. I breach the glass edge
5 of your world, scale the precipice.
    Today it's you who greets me with a kiss.
That's a surprise: the word has gone,
    but not the pleasure or the sign.

You speak of Zena many times today.
10   'Zena, dear': two words welded
in your deepest mind. 'She's coming
    soon' I say. You're in the mood
to talk. She'll be so pleased to know
    you said her name. I try to hold
15 your phrases in my head to tell her.
    'It's very lovely' and 'I've no doubt
at all of that' and, true to character,
    'We're very fortunate.'

This universe of yours is reeling
20   with abandoned souls, littered
with their verbal debris.
    But out and in among it all,
you still can say it all.
    Your undiminished song
25 and all the wordless spaces held
    between you, just like you say,
are 'good and strong.'

Christine De Luca

53

Sample commentary on *Strength Made Perfect in Weakness*

Form and structure

BLOCK A

Understanding of main ideas, central concerns through: *form and structure; key words and phrases*

BLOCK B

Understanding of significant detail through: *tone and imagery*

The poem is structured in the form of an account of an incident, which takes us through the first two verses. The use of the present tense, coupled with the direct address to 'you', give the account a sense of immediacy. The third verse forms the reflective stage of the structure, where the poet looks back on the visit and draws a conclusion about the patient's undaunted spirit in the face of Alzheimer's Disease.

The sentence structure of the first two verses, in particular, reflects the child-like state which the disease has produced in the individual. They are short, simple structures which give a simple account of events. In the third verse, the sentences become more complex, in keeping with the reflective process:

> 'Your undiminished song
> and all the wordless spaces held
> between you, just like you say,
> are "good and strong."'

Similarly, the punctuation of the first two verses reflects the individual's mental state. The lines are often interrupted midway by a full stop, comma or colon, giving the impression of interrupted thought processes or pauses, typical of the Alzheimer sufferer:

> 'That's a surprise: the word has gone
> but not the pleasure or the sign.'

> '"Zena, dear": two words welded
> in your deepest mind ... '

The use of phrases quoted from the patient's speech reinforces this idea of a haphazard mental process, full of gaps and pauses.

> 'It's very lovely'

> 'I've no doubt at all of that'

> 'We're very fortunate'

Key words and phrases

The following groups of words and phrases lead us to a greater understanding of the poem's central theme: the strength of the human spirit in the face of suffering.

1	2	3
words	hover	strength
talk	ward keys	made perfect
undiminished song	breach	kiss
wordless spaces	glass edge	pleasure
	scale	pleased
	precipice	lovely
	reeling	very fortunate
	abandoned souls	good and strong
	verbal debris	

The positive aspects of the human spirit shine through this Alzheimer-afflicted mind. Despite the weakness of the patient's mind and body, the spirit can still give out and receive what is 'good and strong'. A close study of these words does, then, provide the keys to unlocking the poem's 'central concerns'.

Tone

The optimism of the theme is also communicated through tone, as in:

> *'Your undiminished song*
> *and all the wordless spaces held*
> *between you, just like you say,*
> *are "good and strong."'*

The dominant tone, however, is one of tender compassion for the Alzheimer victim, who struggles to communicate. '*She's coming soon*' adopts the reassuring tone of an adult speaking to a frightened or unhappy child whose '*universe ... is reeling with abandoned souls*'. Despite this chaotic world, the Alzheimer sufferer '*still can say it all*' and the tone of loving admiration is heard in the poet's voice here.

Imagery

Imagery plays a central part in unlocking the main concerns of the poem. Images which capture suffering and adversity are set against others which communicate optimism and the healing strength of the human spirit.

The '*ward keys*' open into a world whose '*glass edge*' the visitor has to '*breach*'. This world is fragile and brittle: it can so easily disintegrate. Those trying to communicate with the inhabitants of this world have to climb metaphoric mountains to reach them. The word '*precipice*' suggests a sheer face from which one can so easily fall. The effort in climbing this '*precipice*' is conveyed in '*scale*'. Breaking through the barriers of communication with an Alzheimer patient is a struggle, but one which both patient and visitor are prepared to tackle.

Set against these images of struggle, there are those which capture the strength and optimism of the human spirit which can grow '*perfect in weakness*'. The image conveyed in '*the undiminished song*', still '*good and strong*', despite the difficulties, is filled with compassionate hope in which one can hear the note of optimism echoing across the barriers which Alzheimer's disease raises.

TEXT B

The Apple Ghost

A musty smell of dampness filled the room
Where wrinkled green and yellow apples lay
On folded pages from an August newspaper.

She said:
5   *'My husband brought them in, you understand,*
Only a week or two before he died.
He never had much truck with waste, and
I can't bring myself to throw them out.
He passed away so soon ... '

10   I understood then how the wonky kitchen door,
And the old Austin, settling upon its
Softened tyres in the wooden shed,
Were paying homage to the absence of his quiet hands.

In the late afternoon, I opened
15   Shallow cupboards where the sunlight leaned on
Shelf over shelf of apples, weightless with decay.
Beneath them, sheets of folded wallpaper
Showed ponies prancing through a summer field.
This must have been the only daughter's room.
20   Before she left for good.

I did not sleep well.

The old woman told me over breakfast
How the boards were sprung in that upper hall;
But I knew I had heard his footsteps in the night,
25   As he dragged his wasted body to the attic room
Where the angles of the roof slide through the walls,
And the fruit lay blighted by his helpless gaze.

I knew beside that, had I crossed to the window
On the rug of moonlight,
30   I would have seen him down in the frosted garden,
Trying to hang the fruit back on the tree.

John Glenday

ACTIVITY

Now, having worked your way through the 'model' commentary on *Strength Made Perfect in Weakness*, it's your turn to demonstrate what you've learnt about decoding meaning by exploring the final poem in this chapter, *The Apple Ghost* by John Glenday.

Use the following prompts to help direct your discussion of this text.

Form and structure
- *The Apple Ghost* is the title. What similarities in structure are there between the poem and a conventional ghost story?
- Are there any significant differences?
- How does time help to mark out the stages of the narrative?
- Comment on the significance of the positioning of the line: '*I did not sleep well.*'

Key words and phrases
How do the following groups of key words and phrases help you to understand the poem's central ideas?

1	2	3	4
apples	musty smell of dampness	died	sunlight
shelf over shelf of apples	wrinkled	passed away	summer
fruit	decay	left for good	moonlight
	wasted body	helpless	frosted
	blighted		

Tone

How would you describe the tone of the following extracts from the poem?
Use the bank of adjectives to help you with your discussion.

'A musty smell of dampness filled the room
Where wrinkled green and yellow apples lay
On folded pages from an August newspaper.' (*verse 1*)

'I can't bring myself to throw them out.
He passed away so soon ... ' (*lines 8–9*)

'I did not sleep well.' (*line 21*)

'I know beside that, had I crossed to the window
On the rug of moonlight,
I would have seen him down in the frosted garden,
Trying to hang the fruit back on the tree.' (*lines 28–31*)

Bank of adjectives describing tone:

nostalgic	grief-stricken
pathetic	uneasy
sad	weary
regretful	poignant
mournful	heavy
apologetic	distasteful

Imagery

One of the central themes running through the poem is that of life and
death; decay and renewal, **symbolized** by the apples.

The poem's imagery helps us to explore this theme.

Can you identify some of these images which set up a tension between life
and death, decay and renewal? Use this example to start your discussion:

'Shallow cupboards where the sunlight leaned on
Shelf over shelf of apples weightless with decay' (*lines 15–16*)

CHAPTER 10 *Poetry*

BUILDING BLOCKS TO ANALYSIS AND EVALUATION

 ## *Learning*

Armed with the building blocks to understanding dealt with in Chapters 7 to 9, you're now ready to extend your skills and respond more fully to poetry texts. Knowing how to **analyse** and **evaluate** a text will help you to do this.

Look at the SQA criteria for Textual Analysis at Intermediate 2.

ANALYSIS	'Responses explain in some detail **ways in which** aspects of **structure/style/language** contribute to **meaning/effect/impact**.'
EVALUATION	'Responses reveal **engagement** with the text or aspects of the text and stated or implied evaluation of **effectiveness**, using some **appropriate critical terminology** and substantiated with some **relevant evidence** from the text.'

The words in **bold** highlight key ingredients in the process of analysing and evaluating.

Some of these require further explanation.

Analysis

> **'ways in which'** simply means *how* in a technical sense
> **'style'** refers to the distinctive way in which an author uses the various tools of writing
> **'effect'** relates to the particular response(s) produced in the reader as a result of the way in which an author has used a specific writing tool

> **NB** Not to be confused with **effectiveness**. See below for note on 'effectiveness'.

Evaluation

> **'engagement'** means obvious personal involvement with the text
> **'effectiveness'** relates to the degree of success an author has had in using specific techniques to communicate effectively with the reader
> **'appropriate critical terminology'** means the special vocabulary used when discussing specific literary features: for poetry, some of these terms would be *form, structure, rhythm, rhyme, figurative language* ...
> **'relevant evidence'** indicates that whatever statement is being made about a text or aspect of a text needs to be backed up by evidence directly related to that statement.

The SQA criteria indicate the skills a candidate needs to demonstrate in order to achieve a pass at Intermediate 2 in Textual Analysis. Using these as our framework, let's see how they translate into useful **building blocks.**

Analysis in action

Using the following text, *Landscape With One Figure* by Douglas Dunn, let's explore further the **process** of analysis to see how it works in practice.

TEXT A

Landscape With One Figure

The shipyard cranes have come down again
To drink at the river, turning their long necks
And saying to their reflections on the Clyde,
'How noble we are.'

5   The fields are waiting for them to come over,
The trees gesticulate into the rain,
The nerves of grasses quiver at their tips.
Come over and join us in the wet grass!

The wings of the gulls in the distance wave
10   Like handkerchiefs after departing emigrants.
A tug sniffs up the river, looking like itself.
Waves fall from their small heights on river mud.

If I could sleep standing, I would wait here
Forever, become a landmark, something fixed
15   For tug crews or seabound passengers to point at,
An example of being a part of a place.

Douglas Dunn

As we saw when looking at prose on page 28, the process of analysis could be said to involve three key stages: making a statement about an aspect of structure/style/language; providing relevant evidence to back up that statement; and then commenting on the effect of the selected aspect. For ease of memory, this process can be reduced to a neat acronym, **SEA**:

S   **statement**

E   **evidence**   **(SEA)**

A   **analysis**

Working with a few examples from the *Landscape With One Figure*, let's look at this process in action.

Example 1   statement
The title of the poem is striking in the way in which it suggests both a literal and figurative meaning.

evidence

The '*one figure*' could refer to the only human figure in this landscape, but it could also be said to sum up the main theme of the poem.

analysis

The '*one figure*' is both a lonely human figure but it could also be seen as belonging to the landscape. It captures the idea of identity, of having a sense of belonging. The natural world of fields and trees, as well as the man-made world of the shipyard cranes which have become a part of the landscape of the Clyde because they have been there for so long, have a clear sense of identity, of being '*part of a place*'. The human figure would like to be a part of that landscape, '*something fixed*', like a piece of sculpture whose title might be '*Landscape With One Figure*'.

Example 2   **statement**

The poem opens with a fresh and arresting image.

evidence

The shipyard cranes are compared to giraffes coming down to drink at the river, '*turning their long necks*' to admire their reflections.

analysis

The metaphor brings the cranes to life, giving them a personality, showing they have a clear sense of their own identity: '*How noble we are.*' In the same way as giraffes, moving down to the river for an evening drink would seem a natural part of an African landscape, so here the shipyard cranes are being portrayed as at one with the landscape of the Clyde.

ACTIVITY 1

Using each of the following statements as your starting point, try to find evidence and analysis to support these statements, using the above examples to help you.

statement A

The poem's rich use of **figurative language** brings the landscape to life.

evidence

analysis

statement B

The final verse neatly brings together the key images of the first three verses.

evidence

analysis

Evaluation in action

Although we've separated the two areas of analysis and evaluation for teaching purposes, they are, of course, very closely related. Often your evaluative comments will be based on specific aspects which you've already analysed. The emphasis, however, will be different. If you look at **building block D** again, you'll see that the focus is on assessing the **effectiveness** of a text or aspects of a text through the following elements:

personal response
relevant evidence
appropriate critical vocabulary

> **BLOCK D** *Evaluation*
> Assessing the effectiveness of a text through personal response, supported by relevant evidence and appropriate critical vocabulary.

Let's go back to *Landscape With One Figure* to see some examples of the **evaluative process** in action.

Example 1   I found the poem captured the atmosphere of the shipbuilding areas of the Clyde very effectively **(PR)**. It does this in particular through its use of imagery and tone **(CV)**. The shipyard cranes are familiar to most of us, but to see them as long-necked giraffes coming down to drink at the river gives them a fresh appeal **(E)**. They seem graceful and proud creatures, not just bits of machinery. The familiar sight of the rain and of the gulls swooping over the river adds to the authentic atmosphere. We can hear a note of real pleasure as well as a nostalgic tone to the poem **(CV)**. There is real delight in the sound of:

> 'The shipyard cranes have come down again
> To drink at the river … '   **(E)**

But there is also a note of nostalgia for the past history of the Clyde, which has seen so many families leave Scotland for other countries:

> 'The wings of gulls in the distance wave
> Like handkerchiefs after departing emigrants.'   **(E)**

The atmosphere of this landscape seems very authentic, drawing me into the poem, helping me to understand what the poet is saying about being '*part of a place*' **(PR)**.

(PR = personal response; E = evidence; CV = critical vocabulary)

Example 2   The poem's theme seemed to develop very naturally from the description of the landscape **(PR)**. As Douglas Dunn places features of the natural landscape – the grass, trees and seagulls – alongside mechanical features such as the cranes and tug boats, we are prepared for the 'I' to come in in the last verse **(E)**. It seemed quite natural for man to want to become a permanent feature of this landscape. By careful juxtapositioning of natural and mechanical images **(CV)**, the poet prepares us for the theme of belonging, of being 'part of a place' **(PR)**.

ACTIVITY 2

The poet is successful in communicating his theme because he chooses a simple structure and striking images (PR).

Try to expand on this response, using 'relevant evidence' (E) and 'appropriate critical vocabulary' (CV) to back up what you say. Use the examples on page 61 to help you.

CHAPTER II *Poetry*

BUILDING BLOCKS TO ANALYSIS AND EVALUATION

 Developing

The next two poetry texts and extracts aim to provide you with opportunities to develop specific analytical and evaluative skills by focusing on key aspects of each text and exploring *how* individual poets have achieved particular effects as well as assessing their effectiveness.

TEXT   Maladjusted Boys

      I have made ten minutes of silence.
      I know they are afraid of silence
      And the mind's pattern of order.
      They gaze at me out of oblique faces
  5   And try to fidget away the bleak thoughts
      Simmering in the dark tangle of their minds.
      I read their unfriendly eyes, cushion
      The confused hatred, stand presumptuously
      And pretend not to be afraid.
 10   I keep at them with my eyes,
      Will them to work, and ride
      The storm in a roomful of cold attention.
      Here and there faces cringe
      And I read a future ... the dark corner
 15   Of a street hiding the cruel
      Thud of a chain or boot.
      I see a hunter mask glow on a face
      And grimy nailbitten hands bend a ruler
      To its limit ... all this in a room
 20   Yellow with June sun and music
      Of birds from a private wood.

Robert Morgan

ACTIVITY

a) Focus of interest for analysis: recreating a tense atmosphere.

How?
Areas for consideration:
  - **metaphor** (for example, '*I have made ten minutes of silence.*')
  - **harsh sound effects** (for example, '*simmering*'; '*storm*'; '*thud*'; '*boot*')
  - **contrast** (for example, between the '*dark tangle of their minds*' and the yellow of the '*June sun*' or between the strained silence in the room and the '*music of birds*')

Using the three listed areas for consideration as the basis for your discussion, explore *how* each of these areas contributes to the build up of the tense atmosphere within the classroom.

Remember to support your statements with evidence and analysis. Use the examples in Chapter 10 to remind you of the process of analysis.

b) Focus of interest for evaluation: characterization.

How successful is the poet in communicating the teacher's thoughts and feelings? To help your discussion you may wish to focus on the following areas:

- **Structure**
  How does the shape and organization of the poem reflect the way the teacher is feeling? It is written as a single, tight **verse paragraph** with a number of **end-stopped** lines (where there is a full stop at the end of a line).

- **Word choice**
  Look at the number of words with negative or aggressive **connotations**. What do these suggest about the way the teacher feels about these '*maladjusted boys*'?

- **Tone**
  Is there one tone which you hear more often than any others, which you think captures the teacher's strongest feelings about the boys? Can you hear any other tones? If so, what are they? Give some examples. How well do they communicate how the teacher feels?

Remember to show a personal response to the extract, using relevant evidence and appropriate critical vocabulary. Use the examples in Chapter 10 to remind you of the process of evaluation.

TEXT B

Follower

My father worked with a horse-plough,
His shoulders globed with a full sail strung
Between the shafts and the furrow.
The horses strained at his clicking tongue.

5 An expert. He would set his wing
And fit the bright steel-pointed sock.
The sod rolled over without breaking.
At the headrig, with a single pluck

Of reins, the sweating team turned round
10 And back into the land. His eye
Narrowed and angled at the ground,
Mapping the furrow exactly.

I stumbled in his hob-nailed wake,
Fell sometimes on the polished sod;
15 Sometimes he rode me on his back
Dipping and rising to his plod.

I wanted to grow up and plough,
To close one eye, stiffen my arm.
All I ever did was follow
20 In his broad shadow round the farm.

I was a nuisance, tripping, falling,
Yapping always. But today
It is my father who keeps stumbling
Behind me, and will not go away.

Seamus Heaney

ACTIVITY

a) Focus of interest for analysis: creating a picture of a father/son relationship.

How?
Areas for consideration:
- word choice
- imagery
- tone

Using the three listed areas for consideration as the basis for your discussion, explore *how* each of these areas plays a part in developing the relationship between father and son.

Remember to support your statements with evidence and analysis. Use the examples in Chapter 10 to remind you of the process of analysis.

b) Focus of interest for evaluation: bringing the past to life.

How convincing do you find Heaney's picture of a scene from his rural childhood? You may find it helpful to look at such aspects as:
- structure
- rhythm
- rhyme

Remember to show a personal response to the extract, using relevant evidence and appropriate critical vocabulary. Use the examples in Chapter 10 to remind you of the process of evaluation.

CHAPTER 12 *Poetry*

BUILDING BLOCKS TO ANALYSIS AND EVALUATION

 Demonstrating

Demonstrating analysis and evaluation

In Chapter 9 we explored Christine De Luca's poem, *Strength Made Perfect in Weakness*, using the building blocks to understanding in order to provide a working model as preparation for your independent study of a text.

Now we're going to apply the **building blocks of analysis and evaluation** to this same text in preparation for your own independent study of another, unseen poem.

BLOCK C *Analysis*	**BLOCK D** *Evaluation*
Examining aspects of structure, style, language to show HOW they contribute to meaning and effect.	Assessing the effectiveness of a text through personal response, supported by relevant evidence and appropriate critical vocabulary.

But first, as part of that preparation, a reminder about **denotation** and **connotation.**

Analysis of language

In Chapter 6 we discussed the difference between denotation and connotation. Words have a literal meaning (denotation) but poets rely very heavily on imagery to create effects and to convey ideas: images are created out of the powerful and often striking relationship between words. Think of an image made up of a group of words represented by a series of windows, each with a potentially different view. Opening these 'windows' one by one will not produce the same views: some will be much more interesting and far-reaching than others. The more interesting ones will lie beyond those 'windows' or words which carry associations or **connotations.** The more appropriate and striking the connotations within the context, the more effective the image.

For example:

Sun stroked (dykes) (embraced) the cropped fields,

Sheltering them from their (sudden nakedness).

In this example, when we open the circled 'windows', we find they carry additional connotations: the image of the 'dykes' – or walls – 'embracing' the fields carries associations of warmth, love, comfort, security and protection. Placed alongside the phrase 'sun stroked', some of these associations are reinforced. The phrase 'sudden nakedness' suggests exposure, vulnerability, a self-consciousness at being 'cropped' so suddenly.

Your analysis of word choice and imagery should always explore any relevant connotations.

Sample commentary on *Strength Made Perfect in Weakness*

Use the following sample commentary to help you in your own independent exploration of the second, unseen poem in this chapter.

TEXT A This poem is one of a collection called *The Alzheimer Sequence*.

Strength Made Perfect in Weakness
for Alex and Zena

You hover at the door as I arrive.
    The wave suggests you recognise me.
Not that it matters. Ward keys
    are turned. I breach the glass edge
5 of your world, scale the precipice.
    Today it's you who greets me with a kiss.
That's a surprise: the word has gone,
    but not the pleasure or the sign.

You speak of Zena many times today.
10   'Zena, dear': two words welded
in your deepest mind. 'She's coming
    soon' I say. You're in the mood
to talk. She'll be so pleased to know
    you said her name. I try to hold
15 your phrases in my head to tell her.
    'It's very lovely' and 'I've no doubt
at all of that' and, true to character,
    'We're very fortunate.'

This universe of yours is reeling
20   with abandoned souls, littered
with their verbal debris.
    But out and in among it all,
you still can say it all.
    Your undiminished song
25 and all the wordless spaces held
    between you, just like you say,
are 'good and strong.'

Christine De Luca

Analysis of structure, rhythm and rhyme in relation to mood

The poem is made up of three verses, each very similar in length. The verses are also very similar in shape with an even, regular movement in and out of the lines. The overall visual impression is of balance and composure. This seems to set the mood of the poem, which is calm and affirmative.

The rhythm reinforces this feeling of balance and composure. It moves along steadily, pausing occasionally to capture the broken thought processes, but then regaining its regular pace until the last verse, where the rhythm quickens as the final positive statement is made. Even in illness, strength and goodness shine through. This triumphant mood is reflected in the quickening pace of the rhythm.

> 'But out and in among it all,
> you still can say it all.
> Your undiminished song
> and all the wordless spaces held
> between you, just like you say,
> are "good and strong"'

(lines 22–27)

The absence of rhyme reflects the mood of quiet conversation as if the two people were, indeed, having a normal exchange in which rhyme would not feature. The end words, however, do set up their own kind of tension between the fragile and hard, clipped consonants in words such as *'precipice'*, *'edge'*, *'kiss'*, *'debris'* and *'littered'* and the long, yearning vowel sounds in *'today'*, *'hold'*, *'all'*, *'song'*, *'say'* and *'strong'*.

Analysis of language in relation to theme

The language of the title gives us an immediate insight into the poem's central theme. The **paradox** of strength being made perfect in weakness suggests that this is a poem which deals with the human spirit's response to suffering. The phrase *'made perfect'* suggests some kind of refining process, where all the flaws and weaknesses have been removed. It gives us a picture of the Alzheimer sufferer actually refining an already strong character through the testing stages of illness.

Language is used to suggest both fragility and strength, highlighting the theme. *'Hover'* and *'wave'* in the first two lines have a delicacy of sound as if the words would break if they were said too loudly. The *'glass edge'* and the *'precipice'* are both brittle-sounding expressions, again suggesting their fragility. This sense of things about to fall apart is also captured in *'I try to hold your phrases in my head'* where the phrases seem so light and delicate that they threaten to float away.

Set against this fragile language is some positive language of strength and firmness. *'Zena, dear'* is *'welded in your deepest mind'* as if the phrase is so deeply rooted in the heart that it will never be dislodged, no matter what Alzheimer's does to the mind. *'I've no doubt at all of that'*, the sufferer says, with certainty. *'You still can say it all'* rings with the strength of a belief that no matter what, the person is the same as always, despite the condition. The patient's song is *'undiminished'*: a solid, reassuring word, while the *'wordless spaces'* are still *'good and strong'*.

Evaluating effectiveness

How successful is the poet in revealing character?

The Alzheimer sufferer at the heart of the poem emerges not as a pitiful, lost soul, but as someone who, despite the nature of the disease, does still have days when a kind and generous spirit shines through. Christine De Luca treats her subject with compassion and respect, which does not encourage the reader to pity him or her as a victim but to see the sufferer as someone with strength and goodness whose illness has, in fact, refined that strength, making it *'perfect'* (**PR**).

The sensitive use of the spoken word as in *'It's very lovely'* or *'We're very fortunate'* captures the patient's positive attitude to life. These words are *'true to character'* (**E**).

Likewise, the carefully chosen images suggest a gentle and affectionate person (**CV**):

> *'Today it's you who greets me with a kiss.'*

> *'It's very lovely'* (**E**)

But above all, it is the tone of tender compassion which reveals character: the tone indicates someone who is dearly loved and admired:

> *'But out and in among it all,*
> *you still can say it all'* (**E**)

Christine De Luca communicates a very clear and touching picture of a gentle person whose strength of spirit is somehow *'made perfect'* in the face of the weakening effects of Alzheimer's disease (**PR**).

Demonstrating analysis and evaluation

In summary, using the building blocks approach to analysis and evaluation, our study of this text has revealed a clearer awareness of the **effect** and **effectiveness** of the following aspects:

- form and structure
- rhythm
- rhyme
- sound effects
- word choice and imagery
- mood/atmosphere
- tone
- personal response to all of the above

TEXT B

The Blind

On Tuesdays they walked from the school
to the public baths,

passing our window, leaving us unseen
in every weather: flecked with snow or rain.

5   They marched in pairs, a good eight hundred yards
of guesswork.

All afternoon I pictured them
swimming in silence,

> attuned to one another through the play
> 10 of water and skin,
>
> imagining some kinship with the drowned
> they might possess, unknowing how they would guess
>
> at motion and other lives
> through the palm-smooth tiles;
>
> 15 and later, through trig,
> I heard them walking back
>
> and waited for the first blithe face to show
> beyond the fence, the tap of whited canes
>
> tracing a current home, through bricks and tar:
> 20 magnetic; guided; rooting in the darkness.
>
> *John Burnside*

ACTIVITY

Now it's your turn to demonstrate what you've learnt about analysis and evaluation by exploring the poem *The Blind* by John Burnside.

Directing discussion on analysis and evaluation

Use the following prompts to help direct your discussion.

- What impression of the blind children do you get from word choice and imagery? (Analysis)
- How does the poet's choice of structure contribute to the subject matter? (Analysis)
- How effective is the poem in helping the reader to 'see' the world from the perspective of a blind person? (Evaluation)

CHAPTER 13 *Drama*

BUILDING BLOCKS TO UNDERSTANDING

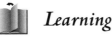 *Learning*

Introduction

A play is designed to be performed on a stage in front of an audience. Whenever this happens, a whole range of people, including the director, the actors, and set, costume and lighting designers, will come together to help communicate the playwright's ideas as effectively as possible. When we read a drama text, rather than watch it acted out on stage, therefore, we do not have the full benefit of these aids to understanding and appreciation, which an audience has. What we do have, however, is the same raw material as a director has when he or she first sets out to produce a play — the text.

In the same way as a director will examine the text carefully for helpful clues to aid interpretation of character and theme, you will explore a variety of extracts from drama texts, learning how to build on your skills of understanding, analysis and evaluation. Successive chapters will focus on developing and demonstrating these skills, using a similar building blocks approach to the one which you've already seen in action in the Prose and Poetry chapters.

Understanding is the most important building block. Picture an arched, stone-built bridge. The keystone (or keystane in Scots) is the central stone which connects and supports the whole structure. Similarly, **understanding** is the keystone in building a bridge to a full appreciation of a piece of literature.

Building blocks to understanding drama

BLOCK A	BLOCK B
Understanding of main ideas, central concerns through: *structure; dialogue; key words and phrases*	Understanding of significant detail through: *stage directions; punctuation; dramatic conflict*

Let's begin with a specific extract from the drama text, *Death of a Salesman* by Arthur Miller, to see how these building blocks work in action to help reveal meaning.

EXTRACT (A) (Willy, a travelling salesman, is staying in a Boston hotel. His son, Biff, has come to ask him to persuade his teacher, Mr Birnbaum, to give him a pass mark in Maths. Just after Biff arrives, however, he is confronted with the awful truth that Willy is having an affair.)

(Willy **laughs** and The Woman joins in offstage)

Willy	(*without hesitation*): Hurry downstairs and —	laughter sets up a false atmosphere which jars, in the context of what follows
Biff:	Somebody in there?	
Willy:	No, that was next door.	

(The Woman **laughs** offstage)

Biff: Somebody got in your bathroom!

Willy: No, it's the next room, there's a party —

The Woman (*enters, laughing. She lisps this*): Can I come in? There's something in the bathtub, Willy, and it's moving! (*Willy looks at Biff, who is staring **open-mouthed** and **horrified** at The Woman*) — captures Biff's reaction

Willy: Ah — you better go back to your room. They must be finished painting by now. They're painting her room so I let her take a shower here. Go back, go back … (*He pushes her*) — appears to lie with ease

The Woman (*resisting*): But I've got to get dressed. Willy, I can't —

Willy: Get out of here! Go back, go back … (*Suddenly striving for the ordinary.*) This is Miss Francis, Biff, she's a buyer. They're painting her room. Go back, Miss Francis, go back …

The Woman: But my clothes. I can't go out naked in the hall! — aggressive language and behaviour

Willy (*pushing her offstage*): **Get outa here!** Go back, go back!

(Biff slowly sits down on his suitcase as the argument continues offstage)

The Woman: Where's my stockings? You promised me stockings, Willy!

Willy: I have no stockings here!

The Woman: You had two boxes of size nine sheers for me, and I want them!

Willy: Here for God's sake, will you get outa here!

The Woman (*enters holding a box of stockings*): I just hope there's nobody in the hall. That's all I hope. (*to Biff*) Are you **football or baseball**? — play on literal and metaphoric meanings

Biff: Football.

The Woman (*angry, humiliated*): That's me too. G'night. (*She snatches her clothes from Willy, and walks out*)

Willy (*after a pause*): Well better get going. I want to get to the school first thing in the morning. Get my suits out of the closet. I'll get my valise. (*Biff doesn't move*) What's the matter? (*Biff remains motionless, tears falling*) She's a buyer. Buys for J.H. Simmons. She lives down the hall — they're painting. You don't — tries to regain control of the situation by issuing orders

imagine — (*He breaks off. After a pause*) Now listen, pal, she's just a buyer. She sees merchandise in her room and they have to keep it looking just so ... (*Pause, assuming command*) <u>All right, get my suits.</u> (*Biff doesn't move*) <u>Now, stop crying and do as I say. I gave you an order, Biff. I gave you an order!</u> Is that what you do when I give you an order? How dare you cry? (*Putting his arm around Biff*) <u>Now look, Biff, when you grow up you'll understand about these things.</u> You mustn't — you mustn't over-emphasise a thing like this. I'll see Birnbaum first thing in the morning.

further orders

patronising tone: treats Biff like a child

Biff: Never mind.

Willy   (*getting down beside Biff*): Never mind! He's going to give you these points. <u>I'll see to it.</u>

supremely confident

disillusionment

Biff: <u>He wouldn't listen to you.</u>

Willy: <u>He certainly will listen to me.</u> You need those points for the U. of Virginia.

boastful, even arrogant

Biff: I'm not going there.

Willy: Heh? If I can't get him to change that mark you'll make it up in summer school. You've got all summer to —

Biff   (*his weeping breaking from him*): Dad ...

Willy   (*infected by it*): Oh my boy ...

Biff: Dad ...

vocabulary of stage direction highlights powerful nature of Biff's feelings

Willy: She's nothing to me, Biff. I was **lonely**, I was **terribly lonely**.

series of dots indicates broken nature of dialogue

Biff: <u>You — you gave her Mama's stockings.</u> (*His tears break through and he rises to go*)

finally tries to confront the truth

Willy   (**grabbing** for Biff): I gave you an order!

Biff: Don't touch me, you — liar!

theme of betrayal

Willy: Apologise for that!

Biff: You **fake**! You **phoney little fake**! You **fake**!

again, note violence of action

exclamations play an important role in building pace and tension

(*Overcome, he turns quickly and, weeping fully, goes out with his suitcase. <u>Willy is left on the floor on his knees</u>*)

From Death of a Salesman *by Arthur Miller*

symbolic significance of stage direction?

ACTIVITY 1

Recognizing and interpreting structure of extract

The structure of the scene has many of the characteristics of a classic 'bedroom farce': hotel bedroom; woman in a state of undress; 'gifts' in the form of stockings; a sudden intrusion; a list of excuses to cover the affair.

a) At what point in the extract does this element of farce begin to turn into something much nearer to tragedy?

b) What do you learn about the character of Willy from the way in which he handles:
- ◆ the farcical moments of the scene?
- ◆ the potentially tragic moments of the scene?

c) Reread the section from Biff's '*Never mind*' to the end of the extract. Here the scene builds to a powerful climax. What does the structure of this section tell you about the relationship between Biff and Willy?

ACTIVITY 2
Recognizing and interpreting structure of dialogue
Look closely at the structure of Willy's dialogue down to the point where The Woman exits *(She snatches her clothes from Willy ...)*. It is made up of a series of short sentences, often in the form of commands.

a) What does the structure of this section of dialogue tell you about how Willy is feeling at this point?

b) Look at Biff's dialogue. It is made up of a series of very short sentences, often unfinished, and one-word responses. What does the structure of Biff's dialogue tell you about his feelings?

ACTIVITY 3
Recognizing and interpreting key words and phrases
The repetition of specific words or phrases within an extract can help the reader to grasp main ideas.

For example, the word 'stockings' is repeated four times in the extract. By the time Biff says: '*You — gave her Mama's stockings*' we realize that they are not simply a 'gift' which Willy is using as 'payment' for The Woman, but that, for Biff, they carry far greater significance as a symbol of his father's betrayal of his wife.

Look at these groups of repeated or similar key words and phrases from the extract.

Try to suggest what contribution is made by individual words or phrases to your understanding of character, situation or theme.

The letter **R** indicates a repeated word or phrase.

R	get outa here		liar	**R**	painting her room	**R**	gave you an order
R	go back	**R**	fake	**R**	buyer		never mind
						R	(wouldn't) listen

ACTIVITY 4

Recognizing and interpreting features of stage directions

Stage directions are the playwright's instructions to the director about a character's actions and reactions, sometimes indicating facial expression and tone of voice. They are recognizable as 'directions' by their distinctive font and by their separation, usually by brackets, from the scripted dialogue.

The information contained in stage directions can add significantly to our understanding of any or all of the following: situation; atmosphere; character; relationships and themes.

For example, in the *Death of a Salesman* extract, the second stage direction, referring to Willy, reads: *(without hesitation)*. This shows that Willy intervenes quickly when The Woman's laughter is heard. It suggests that he is perhaps quite experienced at having to cover up his actions and has become a good actor, quick to deceive.

Look closely at the following stage directions as they are used in context.

The Woman *(enters, laughing. She lisps this)*

(Willy looks at Biff, who is staring open-mouthed and horrified at the Woman.)

(Suddenly striving for the ordinary)

(Pause, assuming command)

(Overcome, he turns quickly and, weeping fully, goes out with his suitcase)

How does each of these directions help your understanding of any of the following:
- situation
- atmosphere
- character
- relationships
- theme?

ACTIVITY 5

Recognizing and interpreting features of punctuation

Willy's dialogue is regularly punctuated by the exclamation mark, the dash or a series of dots, indicating unfinished or interrupted speech. For example:

'Ah – you better get back to your room.'   'Get out of here!'
'Go back, Miss Francis, go back … '   'I have no stockings here!'
'You don't imagine –'   'I gave you an order!'

How does this pattern of punctuation help you to understand Willy's mood?

ACTIVITY 6

Recognizing and interpreting features of dramatic conflict

At the heart of all drama is conflict: between people; between ideas; within relationships; within individuals. Being able to identify and understand how these conflicts affect plot and character is an important skill of textual analysis.

In this extract, there are three main areas of conflict:

◆ between Willy and The Woman	**The Woman:**	*Where's my stockings? You promised me stockings, Willy!*	
	Willy:	*I have no stockings here!*	
◆ between Biff and Willy	**Biff:**	*Never mind.*	
	Willy:	*Never mind! He's going to give you these points. I'll see to it.*	
	Biff:	*He wouldn't listen to you.*	
◆ between truth and lies	**Willy:**	*She lives down the hall — they're painting.*	
	Biff:	*Don't touch me, you — liar!*	

Find some other examples to illustrate each of these areas of conflict. What contribution do these examples of dramatic conflict make to the atmosphere of the scene?

CHAPTER 14 *Drama*

BUILDING BLOCKS TO UNDERSTANDING

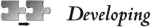 *Developing*

Practice in developing understanding

In Chapter 13 you learned to recognize and interpret aspects of meaning within an extract from a drama text by applying the building blocks to understanding.

With more practice, you will become more skilled, boosting your confidence in being able to apply these techniques to an unseen text.

Below you will find two further drama extracts with discussion questions to help you develop confidence in recognition and interpretation of the keys to understanding.

EXTRACT A (The scene is set against the background of war-torn Belfast. Cassie's husband, Joe, is in prison, her mother Nora's husband, Sean, is dead; and Marie's husband, Michael, has been killed.)

Nora: Listen to her and wasn't she desperate to marry the man?
Cassie: I was desperate to marry David Essex as well. My brains hadn't grown in yet.
Nora: And him with his own business and good money coming in. There's plenty would've been glad to be in your shoes, Cassie. 5
Cassie *(kicking her own shoes off)*: They can have them, anytime they like.
Nora: I don't know what you thought marriage would be, but you should've learned by your age. You've a job to do bringing up that family and making a decent home for you and your man, so get on with it.
Cassie: I'll start crocheting a new house for us tomorrow. 10
Nora: And he never lifted a finger to her, Marie. Not once.
Cassie: Oh I should've thanked him for that should I? Thank you Joe for not taking the poker to me every Saturday.
Nora: Well you should know what it could've been like. You of all people should've been able to see when you were well off. 15
Cassie: What's that supposed to mean?
Marie: Does anyone want some fruit loaf?
Nora: As if you didn't know.
Marie: I'll get some crisps out, we can have crisps with our drinks.
Cassie: No, I don't know. 20
Nora: Because you don't want to know, you never did. *(Marie pauses on her way back to the kitchen, looking nervously from one to the other)* Not even when you saw it with your own eyes. *(Cassie doesn't say anything)* I would say to him, 'Would you hit your own wife in front of your wains?' Sure I never got any answer at all but bruises. Sean was never much for conversation. 25
Cassie *(in a low voice)*: That hardly ever happened.
Nora: That happened every time he had enough drink in him.

Cassie: You should've left him alone.

Nora: Oh right, I shouldn't have thrown myself in the way of his fists like that. 30

Cassie: I couldn't sleep for you nagging on and on at him, that stupid wee shrill complaining, complaining, on and on.

Nora: She'd come down in the morning, Marie, and find me crying on the floor with the bruises going black on my face and all she'd say was, 'Have you been upsetting daddy again?' Go and fix herself a cup of tea. 35

Cassie: He never beat you that bad. You'd all of us terrified with your squealing and carrying on.

Nora: Eight years old, Marie, and all I saw on her face was hatred, of me. Of *me*. There's something wrong with this girl's heart.

Cassie: He was the gentlest man! The gentlest man if you'd just given him peace! 40

From Bold Girls *by Rona Munro*

BLOCK A

Understanding of main ideas, central concerns through: *structure; dialogue; key words and phrases*

ACTIVITY 1

Structure of extract

The extract is structured in the form of an argument between Nora and her daughter, Cassie. Marriage and men is the subject of the argument.

a) There are three definite stages in the development of the argument. Where do you think the turning points come in the extract?

b) Which character seems to be provoking, controlling and directing the shape of the argument? Support your view with evidence.

c) The exchanges between Nora and her daughter form the main focus of the scene. What role does the third character, Marie, play in the structure of the argument?

ACTIVITY 2

Structure of dialogue

Cassie says of her mother:

'I couldn't sleep for you nagging on and on at him, that stupid wee shrill complaining, complaining, on and on.' *(lines 31–32)*

a) Is there anything in the structure of Nora's dialogue to suggest a nagging, complaining character? Give some examples to support your view.

b) Look at these two groups of examples of Cassie's dialogue.

Group I

'*(kicking her own shoes off)* They can have them, anytime they like.' *(line 6)*
'I'll start crocheting a new house for us tomorrow.' *(line 10)*
'Oh I should've thanked him for that should I? Thank you Joe for not taking a poker to me every Saturday.' *(lines 12–13)*

Group 2

'You should've left him alone.' *(line 28)*

'He never beat you that bad. You'd all of us terrified with your squealing and carrying on.' *(lines 36–37)*

'He was the gentlest man! The gentlest man if you'd just given him peace!' *(lines 40–41)*

The examples in **Group 1** are all structured in the form of what we might call 'throwaway' lines: they are not directed straight at Nora but to a more general audience, including Marie.

The examples in **Group 2** suggest a shift in the focus of her dialogue. In what way?

ACTIVITY 3

Key words and phrases

The following key words and phrases contribute to our understanding of some of the main ideas running through the extract. What specific ideas are highlighted by these examples?

1	2	3
own business	marriage	hit
good money	bringing up that family	drink
well off	decent home	fists
		beat
		terrified
		hatred
	4	
	never lifted a finger to her	
	gentlest man	
	just given him peace	

ACTIVITY 4

Stage directions

There are only four stage directions in this extract, but each one contributes to our understanding of characters' feelings. Look at each of the examples and try to indicate what you think it suggests about how the character is feeling.

Cassie *(kicking her own shoes off)* *(line 6)*

(Marie pauses on her way to the kitchen, looking nervously from one to the other) *(lines 21–22)*

(Cassie doesn't say anything) *(line 23)*

Cassie *(in a low voice)* *(line 26)*

■ **ACTIVITY 5**

Punctuation

There are a number of places in the extract where the question mark is used, sometimes to indicate a rhetorical question ('*Oh I should've thanked him for that should I?*'), sometimes to mark a direct question ('*Does anyone want some fruit loaf?*')

What do these questions contribute to your awareness of the atmosphere of the scene?

■ **ACTIVITY 6**

Dramatic conflict

There are two main areas of conflict in this extract, both of which arise from a common conflict between ideas on marriage and the behaviour of men.
  ◆ The conflict between Nora and Cassie – mother and daughter
  ◆ The conflict between Nora and her husband, Sean

What part does each of these conflicts play in helping you to understand character?

EXTRACT Ⓑ (Rita, a hairdresser from Liverpool, has embarked on an Open University course with Frank as her tutor.)

Frank: Rita! Sit down!
(Rita goes to her usual chair and sits)
Frank *(going to the side of her)*: When you were so late I phoned the shop.
Rita: Which shop?
Frank: The hairdresser's shop. Where you work. Or, should I say, worked.   5
Rita: I haven't worked there for a long time. I work in a bistro now.
Frank: You didn't tell me.
Rita: Didn't I? I thought I did. I was telling someone.
Frank: It wasn't me.
Rita: Oh. Sorry. *(After a pause)* What's wrong?   10
Frank *(after a pause)*: It struck me that there was a time when you told me everything.
Rita: I thought I had told you.
Frank: No. Like a drink?
Rita: Who cares if I've left hairdressin' to work in a bistro?   15
Frank: I care. *(He goes to the bookshelves and takes a bottle from an eye-level shelf)* You don't want a drink? Mind if I do?
Rita: But why do you care about details like that? It's just boring, insignificant detail.
Frank *(getting a mug from the small table)*: Oh. Is it?   20
Rita: That's why I couldn't stand being in a hairdresser's any longer; boring, irrelevant detail all the time, on and on ... Well I'm sorry but I've had enough of that. I don't wanna talk about irrelevant rubbish anymore.
Frank: And what do you talk about in your bistro? Cheers.
Rita: Everything.   25
Frank: Everything.
Rita: Yeh.

Frank: Ah.

Rita: We talk about what's important, Frank, and we leave out the boring details for those who want them. 30

Frank: Is Mr Tyson one of your customers?

Rita: A lot of students come in; he's one of them. You're not gonna give me another warning are y', Frank?

Frank: Would it do any good?

Rita: Look, for your information I do find Tiger fascinatin', like I find a lot 35 of the people I mix with fascinating; they're young, and they're passionate about things that matter. They're not trapped — they're too young for that. And I like to be with them.

Frank *(moving DR of the desk and keeping his back to her)*: Perhaps — perhaps you don't want to waste your time coming here any more? 40

Rita: Don't be stupid. I'm sorry I was late. *(After a pause she gets up)* Look, Frank, I've got to go. I'm meeting Trish at seven. We're going to see a production of *The Seagull.*

Frank: Yes. *(He turns to face her)* Well. When Chekhov* calls …

Rita: Tch. 45

Frank: You can hardly bear to spend a moment here can you?

Rita *(moving towards him a little)*: That isn't true. It's just that I've got to go to the theatre.

Frank: And last week you didn't turn up at all. Just a phone call to say you had to cancel. 50

Rita: It's just that — that there's so many things happening now. It's harder.

Frank: As I said, Rita, if you want to stop com —

Rita *(going right up to him)*: For God's sake, I don't want to stop coming here. What about my exam?

Frank: Oh I wouldn't worry about that. You'd sail through it anyway. You 55 really don't have to put in the odd appearance out of sentimentality; *(he moves round to the other side of the desk)* I'd rather you spared me. *(Frank goes to drink)*

Rita: If you could stop pouring that junk down your throat in the hope that it'll make you feel like a poet you might be able to talk about things 60 that matter instead of where I do or don't work; an' then it might be worth comin' here.

Frank: Are you capable of recognising what does or does not matter, Rita?

Rita: I understand literary criticism, Frank. When I come here that's what we're supposed to be dealing with. 65

Frank: You want literary criticism? *(He looks at her for a moment and then goes to the top drawer of his desk and takes out two slim volumes and some typewritten sheets of poetry and hands them to her)* I want an essay on that lot by next week.

Rita: What is it?

Frank: No sentimentality, no subjectivity. Just pure criticism. A critical 70 assessment of a lesser known English poet. Me.

* Anton Chekhov is the author of the play, *The Seagull*

From Educating Rita *by Willy Russell*

ACTIVITY 1

Structure of extract

The extract is structured as a series of questions and answers, sparked by an apparently minor issue, Rita's change of job, but building to something more serious.

a) What does the way the structure develops tell us about:
- ◆ the relationship between the two characters?
- ◆ the atmosphere of the scene?

b) Look at the closing section of the extract from Frank's question, '*Are you capable of recognising what does or does not matter, Rita?*' to the end.

How does the structure of this closing section help your understanding of the phrase '*things that matter*'?

ACTIVITY 2

Structure of dialogue

Look at the structure of the dialogue of both characters. Frank's tends to be short, often in question form.

a) What does this suggest about Frank's mood?

b) What does it contribute to the overall atmosphere of the scene?

c) As the scene develops, Rita's dialogue is rather different in structure from Frank's. What differences do you notice? What does this suggest about Rita's mood?

ACTIVITY 3

Key words and phrases

Often contrasting key words and phrases can give us some insight into a character's thoughts and feelings. Look at the following groups and discuss what insights these give you into Rita's thoughts and feelings.

A	A	B	B
what's important things that matter	irrelevant details rubbish	trapped waste your time	everything fascinatin' young passionate so many things happening

ACTIVITY 4

Stage directions

There are only a few stage directions in this extract, some of which relate directly to actions. There are a number, however, which do contribute to our understanding of such aspects as situation, character, mood and atmosphere.

Look at the following stage directions in the context of the dialogue, and suggest what each contributes to any one of those aspects.

(He goes to the bookshelves and takes a bottle from an eye-level shelf) **(line 16)**

(… keeping his back to her) **(line 39)**

(He turns to face her) **(line 44)**

(moving towards him a little) **(line 47)**

(going right up to him) **(line 53)**

(Frank goes to drink) **(line 58)**

(He looks at her for a moment) **(line 66)**

ACTIVITY 5
Punctuation

The extract features a high proportion of question marks, introducing both rhetorical and conventional questions. These imply an awkward tension in Rita and Frank's relationship. The dash and series of dots, indicating interrupted or unfinished statements, also feature quite regularly.

Look at the following examples and indicate what each one contributes to your understanding of any of the following:
- situation
- characters' feelings/attitudes/behaviour
- atmosphere.

Rita: That's why I couldn't stand being in a hairdresser's any longer; boring, irrelevant detail all the time, on and on … *(lines 21–22)*

Frank: Perhaps — perhaps you don't want to waste your time coming here any more? *(lines 39–40)*

Frank: When Chekhov calls … *(line 44)*

Rita: It's just that — that there's so many things happening now. *(line 51)*

Frank: As I said, Rita, if you want to stop com — *(line 52)*

ACTIVITY 6
Dramatic conflict

There are a number of conflicts running through this extract:
- conflict between Rita and Frank
- conflict within Frank — between the would-be poet and the drunk
- conflict within Rita — between her dependence on Frank and her desire to break free
- conflict of ideas — between what are perceived as 'boring' matters and what are seen as 'important' issues

Identify one area in the extract where you can see evidence of each of these conflicts. What contribution does each make to your understanding of any of the following:
- situation
- character
- theme?

CHAPTER 15 *Drama*

BUILDING BLOCKS TO UNDERSTANDING

Demonstrating

So far you've been concentrating on learning to identify and interpret the building blocks of meaning. In this chapter, you will be given an opportunity to demonstrate that you are now able to explore an unseen drama extract, using the tools of textual analysis to uncover what may be several layers of meaning.

Below is an extract from *A Doll's House* by the Norwegian playwright, Henrik Ibsen. Following this, you will find a full commentary, showing how the key elements of building blocks A and B have helped the reader to an understanding of this extract. Use this sample commentary to help you in your own independent exploration of the final extract in this chapter.

EXTRACT A

(Nora and the children play, laughing and shrieking, in this room and in the adjacent room on the right. Finally Nora hides under the table; the children come rushing in to look for her but cannot find her; they hear her stifled laughter, rush to the table, lift up the tablecloth and find her. Tremendous shouts of delight. She creeps out and pretends to frighten them. More shouts. Meanwhile there has been a knock at the front door, which nobody has heard. The door half opens and Krogstad can be seen. He waits a little; the game continues.)

Krogstad: I beg your pardon, Mrs Helmer ...
Nora *(turns with a stifled cry and half jumps up)*: Oh! What do you want?
Krogstad: Excuse me. The front door was ajar. Someone must have forgotten to shut it ...
Nora *(standing up)*: My husband is not at home, Mr Krogstad.   5
Krogstad: I know.
Nora: Well ... what are you doing here, then?
Krogstad: I want a word with you.
Nora: With ... ? *(Quietly, to the children)* Go inside to Anne-Marie. What? No, the strange man won't do anything to hurt Mummy. When he's   10 gone we'll have another game. *(She leads the children into the room, left, and shuts the door after them; tense and uneasy.)* You want to speak to me?
Krogstad: Yes, I do.
Nora: Today? But it's not the first of the month yet ...
Krogstad: No, it's Christmas Eve. Whether or not you have a merry Christmas   15 depends on you.
Nora: What do you want? I can't give you anything today ...
Krogstad: Let's not talk about that for the moment. There's something else. You have a moment to spare?
Nora: Oh, yes. Yes, I suppose so; though ...   20
Krogstad: Good. I was sitting in the cafe down below and I saw your husband cross the street ...
Nora: Did you?
Krogstad: With a lady.
Nora: Well?   25

Krogstad:	Might I be so bold as to ask: was not that lady a Mrs Linde?	
Nora:	Yes.	
Krogstad:	Recently arrived in town?	
Nora:	Yes, today.	
Krogstad:	And she's a good friend of yours, is she not?	30
Nora:	Yes, she is. But I still don't see ...	
Krogstad:	I used to know her too once.	
Nora:	I know.	
Krogstad:	Oh? So you know all about it? Yes, I thought as much. Well then, may I ask you a straight question: is Mrs Linde to be employed at the bank?	35
Nora:	How dare you presume to cross-examine me, Mr Krogstad? You, one of my husband's employees? But since you ask, you shall have an answer. Yes, Mrs Linde is to be employed by the bank. And I arranged it, Mr Krogstad. Now you know.	40
Krogstad:	I guessed right, then.	
Nora	(*walking up and down*): Oh, one has a little influence, you know. Just because one's a woman it doesn't necessarily mean that ... When one is in a humble position, Mr Krogstad, one should think twice before offending someone who ... hm ...	45
Krogstad:	... has influence?	
Nora:	Exactly.	
Krogstad	(*changing his tone*): Mrs Helmer, will you have the kindness to use your influence on my behalf?	
Nora:	What? What do you mean?	50
Krogstad:	Will you be so good as to see that I keep my humble position at the bank?	
Nora:	What do you mean? Who is thinking of removing you from your position?	
Krogstad:	Oh you don't need to play the innocent with me. I realise it can't be very pleasant for your friend to risk bumping into me; and I now realise whom I have to thank for being hounded out like this.	55
Nora:	But I assure you ...	
Krogstad:	Look, let's not beat about the bush. There's still time, and I'd advise you to use your influence to stop it.	60
Nora:	But Mr Krogstad, I have no influence!	
Krogstad:	Oh? I thought you just said ...	
Nora:	But I didn't mean it like that! Me? How on earth could you imagine that I would have any influence over my husband?	
Krogstad:	Oh, I've known your husband since we were students together. I imagine he has his weaknesses like other married men.	65
Nora:	If you speak disrespectfully of my husband like that, I'll show you the door.	
Krogstad:	You're a bold woman, Mrs Helmer.	
Nora:	I'm not afraid of you any longer. After the New Year, I'll soon be finished with the whole business.	70
Krogstad	(*controlling himself*): Now, listen to me, Mrs Helmer. If I'm forced to, I shall fight for my little job at the bank as if I were fighting for my life.	

From A Doll's House *by Henrik Ibsen*

Sample commentary on extract from *A Doll's House*

Structure of extract

The main part of the extract is structured as a mock parallel of the game which Nora is playing with her children. In the game she hides under the table while she is being 'hunted' by her children. When they discover her, she '*creeps out and pretends to frighten them*'.

In the more sinister 'game' acted out with Krogstad, Nora feels threatened by this '*strange man*' who intrudes unannounced into her domestic playtime. She tries to protect herself by 'hiding' behind her husband's position as Krogstad's employer but, by the end of the scene, she claims she is no longer afraid of the intruder who has spent much of the scene playing a teasing question-and-answer game with her.

Structure of dialogue

Much of the dialogue is made up of a series of short, direct questions and answers which create a tense, uneasy atmosphere. For example:

> **Nora:**   Well … what are you doing here, then? *(line 7)*
> **Krogstad:** I want a word with you. *(line 8)*
> **Nora:**   … You want to speak to me? *(line 12)*
> **Krogstad:** Yes, I do. *(line 13)*
> **Nora:**   Today? But it's not the first of the month yet … *(line 14)*
> **Krogstad:** No, it's Christmas Eve … *(line 15)*
> **Nora:**   What do you want? I can't give you anything today. *(line 17)*

Krogstad controls the direction of the dialogue until Nora attempts to regain some of that control when she demands:

> 'How dare you presume to cross-examine me, Mr Krogstad? You, one of my husband's employees?' *(lines 37–38)*

But control is once again regained by Krogstad when he puts pressure on Nora:

> 'Look, let's not beat about the bush. There's still time, and I'd advise you to use your influence to stop it.' *(lines 59–60)*

Despite Nora's statement that she is no longer afraid of Krogstad, it is he who has the last word when he threatens that:

> 'If I'm forced to, I shall fight for my little job at the bank as if I were fighting for my life.' *(lines 72–74)*

The way Krogstad manipulates the direction of the dialogue reinforces the impression of him as a sinister figure who has some power over Nora, possibly as a blackmailer because of the clues we get about the bank and payments to be made on the first of the month.

Key words and phrases

If we look closely at the following groups of words and phrases, many of which are repeated (**R**), some of which share elements of meaning (**S**), we can see that they give us significant clues about the main concerns running through the extract.

R	bank	S	employee		strange man	R	a woman
R	influence	S	humble position	S	hurt	S	bold
		S	little job		game	S	not afraid
				S	fight		
		S	question				
		S	cross-examine				

The word 'influence' is repeated six times during the course of the extract, clearly indicating that one of the main themes is that of power: the power which comes from one's position in society. The opposite idea of powerlessness is captured in 'little job', 'humble position' and 'employee'.

Other concerns picked up in these key words and phrases are the position of women in society and the intimidating power of the desperate blackmailer who will question and cross-examine to get information which will help him 'fight' to protect his position.

Stage directions
The detailed stage directions which open the extract are very important because they set up a happy, carefree tone which is then abruptly broken by the arrival of Krogstad. The children are 'laughing and shrieking'; Nora's 'stifled laughter' can be heard and there are 'tremendous shouts of delight'.

There is dramatic irony in the direction 'She creeps out and pretends to frighten them'. This is a game but it foreshadows what happens thereafter for real; only it is Nora, not the children, who is being frightened.

Other examples of stage directions give us an insight into the mood of the two characters. For example, Nora's fear is registered in 'turns with a stifled cry' while her nervousness is conveyed in 'walking up and down'.

Something of Krogstad's character is suggested in the direction 'changing his tone'. This comes just after Nora has mentioned the word 'influence'. Krogstad is clever enough to realize that if he is going to get what he wants, he will have to sound more humble and less aggressive. But he has difficulty maintaining that tone as can be heard in the stage direction 'controlling himself', which suggests that he has to fight to keep his aggression in check.

Punctuation
The question mark dominates this extract, contributing to our awareness of the tense atmosphere, as well as to our understanding of character and theme. Krogstad asks the questions that matter, while many of Nora's questions arise out of her confusion:

'What do you want?'

'What are you doing here, then?'

Controlling and directing the questions gives the character power, in this case a frightening hold over Nora.

The series of dots reinforces the atmosphere of uneasiness, while the exclamation mark in Nora's lines:

'But Mr Krogstad, I have no influence!' *(line 61)*

'But I didn't mean it like that!" *(line 63)*

underline Nora's nervous confusion.

Dramatic conflict

The main source of dramatic conflict in the extract arises from the struggle for power. This determines several conflicts:
- between Nora and Krogstad
- between Krogstad and Nora's husband as employee and employer
- between Nora as a woman and society

Each of these conflicts helps us to understand one of the main themes of the extract, as well as the relationship between the individual characters.

Demonstrating understanding

In summary, using the building blocks approach, several readings of this extract have revealed in terms of meanings a clearer understanding of the following aspects:
- situation
- mood/atmosphere
- character
- relationships
- theme(s)

EXTRACT B (Stanhope is a Company Captain in the front line during the First World War. In this scene, a young officer, Hibbert, tries to persuade Stanhope that he is too ill to carry on with his duties.)

(Hibbert comes quietly into the dug-out from the tunnel leading from his sleeping quarters.)

Stanhope: Hullo, I thought you were asleep.

Hibbert: I just wanted a word with you, Stanhope.

Stanhope: Fire away.

Hibbert: This neuralgia of mine. I'm awfully sorry. I'm afraid I can't stick it any longer —

Stanhope: I know. It's rotten, isn't it? I've got it like hell —

Hibbert *(taken aback): You* have?

Stanhope: Had it for weeks.

Hibbert: Well, I'm sorry, Stanhope. It's no good. I've tried damned hard; but I must go down —

Stanhope: Go down — where?

Hibbert: Why, go sick — go down the line. I must go into hospital and have some kind of treatment. *(There is a silence for a moment. Stanhope is looking at Hibbert — till Hibbert turns away and walks towards his dug-out.)* I'll go right along now, I think —

Stanhope *(quietly):* You're going to stay here.

Hibbert:	I'm going down to see the doctor. He'll send me to hospital when he understands —
Stanhope:	I've seen the doctor. I saw him this morning. He won't send you to hospital, Hibbert; he'll send you back here. He promised me he would. *(There is silence)* So you can save yourself a walk.
Hibbert	*(fiercely):* What the hell — !
Stanhope:	Stop that!
Hibbert:	I've a perfect right to go sick if I want to. The men can — why can't an officer?
Stanhope:	No man's sent down unless he's very ill. There's nothing wrong with you, Hibbert. The German attack's on Thursday; almost for certain. You're going to stay here and see it through with the rest of us.
Hibbert	*(hysterically):* I tell you, I *can't* — the pain's nearly sending me mad. I'm going now — you can't stop me! *(He goes excitedly into the dug-out. Stanhope walks slowly towards the steps, turns, and undoes the flap of his revolver holster. He takes out his revolver, and stands casually examining it. Hibbert returns with his pack slung on his back and a walking-stick in his hand, He pauses at the sight of Stanhope by the steps.)*
Hibbert:	Let's get by, Stanhope.
Stanhope:	You're going to stay here and do your job.
Hibbert:	Haven't I *told* you? I *can't.* Don't you understand? Let — let me get by.
Stanhope:	Now look here, Hibbert. I've got a lot of work to do and no time to waste. Once and for all, you're going to stay here and see it through with the rest of us.
Hibbert:	I shall die of this pain if I don't go!
Stanhope:	Better die of the pain than be shot for deserting.
Hibbert	*(in a low voice):* What do you mean?
Stanhope:	You know what I mean —
Hibbert:	I've a right to see the doctor!
Stanhope:	Good God! Don't you understand! — he'll send you back here. Dr Preston's never let a shirker pass him yet — and he's not going to start now — two days before the attack —
Hibbert	*(pleadingly):* Stanhope — if you only *knew* how awful I feel — Please do let me go by — *(He walks round behind Stanhope. Stanhope turns and thrusts him roughly back. With a lightning movement Hibbert raises his stick and strikes blindly at Stanhope, who catches the stick, tears it from Hibbert's hands, smashes it across his knee, and throws it on the ground.)*
Stanhope:	God! — you little swine. You know what that means — don't you? Striking a superior officer! *(There is silence. Stanhope takes hold of his revolver as it swings from its lanyard. Hibbert stands quivering in front of Stanhope.)* Never mind, though. I won't have you shot for that —

From Journey's End *by R. C. Sheriff*

ACTIVITY

Now it's your turn to demonstrate what you've learnt about decoding meaning by exploring the extract from the play *Journey's End* by R. C. Sherriff.

Use the following prompts to help direct your discussion of the extract.

Structure of extract

The extract builds to a number of mini-climaxes before the final climax of the assault. Where do these mini-climaxes occur? What contribution do they make to atmosphere?

Structure of dialogue

What information does the structure of each character's dialogue give you about personality and mood?

Key words and phrases

Make a list of key words and phrases used by a) Stanhope and b) Hibbert. How is your understanding of each of the characters developed by the key words and phrases they use?

Stage directions

Taking each stage direction in turn, discuss what contribution it makes to your understanding of any of the following:

- character
- mood
- atmosphere
- theme.

Punctuation

Look closely at the contexts in which the exclamation mark is used. What part does it play in establishing character and/or atmosphere?

Dramatic conflict

Apart from the final physical conflict between Stanhope and Hibbert, what other conflicts can you detect running through the extract?

Which aspects of the extract do these help to develop:

- character
- mood
- theme?

CHAPTER 16 *Drama*

BUILDING BLOCKS TO ANALYSIS AND EVALUATION

 *Learning*

Armed with the building blocks to understanding dealt with in Chapters 13 to 15, you're now ready to extend your skills to enable you to respond more fully to extracts from drama texts. Knowing how to **analyse** and **evaluate** such extracts will help you to do this.

Look at the SQA criteria for Textual Analysis at Intermediate 2.

ANALYSIS	'Responses explain in some detail **ways in which** aspects of **structure/style/language** contribute to **meaning/effect/impact**.'
EVALUATION	'Responses reveal **engagement** with the text or aspects of the text and stated or implied evaluation of **effectiveness**, using some **appropriate critical terminology** and substantiated with some **relevant evidence** from the text.'

The words in **bold** highlight key ingredients in the process of analysing and evaluating. Some of these require further explanation.

Analysis

'**ways in which**' simply means *how* in a technical sense
'**style**' refers to the distinctive way in which an author uses the various tools of writing
'**effect**' relates to the particular response(s) produced in the reader as a result of the way in which an author has used a specific writing tool

NB Not to be confused with **effectiveness**. See below for note on 'effectiveness'.

Evaluation

'**engagement**' means obvious personal involvement with the text
'**effectiveness**' relates to the degree of success an author has had in using specific techniques to communicate effectively with the reader
'**appropriate critical terminology**' means the special vocabulary used when discussing specific features relating to that genre: for drama, some of these terms would be *character, dialogue, stage directions, dramatic conflict, climax, set design, sound and lighting effects*
'**relevant evidence**' indicates that whatever statement is being made about a text or aspect of a text, this needs to be backed up by evidence directly related to that statement.

The SQA criteria indicate the skills a candidate requires to demonstrate in order to achieve a pass at Intermediate 2 in Textual Analysis. Using these as our framework, let's see how they translate into useful **building blocks**.

Analysis in action

Using the following extract from *All My Sons* by Arthur Miller, let's explore further the **process** of analysis to see how it works in practice.

EXTRACT Ⓐ (Joe Keller has manufactured a batch of faulty aircraft parts and allowed them to be installed on fighter planes being used during the Second World War, resulting in the death of twenty-one men. In this extract, his son, Chris, makes him tell the truth about the incident for the first time.)

Chris: Dad ... Dad, you killed twenty-one men!

Keller: What, killed?

Chris: You killed them, you murdered them.

Keller *(as though throwing his whole nature open before Chris)*: How could I kill anybody?   5

Chris: Dad! Dad!

Keller *(trying to hush him)*: I didn't kill anybody!

Chris: Then explain it to me. What did you do? Explain it to me or I'll tear you to pieces!

Keller *(horrified at his overwhelming fury)*: Don't, Chris, don't –   10

Chris: I want to know what you did, now what did you do?

Keller: If you're going to hang me then I –

Chris: I'm listening. God Almighty, I'm listening!

Keller *(their movements now are those of subtle pursuit and escape. Keller keeps a step out of Chris's range as he talks)*: You're a boy, what could I do? I'm in business,   15
a man is in business; a hundred and twenty cracked, you're out of business; you got a process, the process don't work you're out of business; you don't know how to operate, your stuff is no good; they close you up, they tear up your contracts, what the hell's it to them? You lay forty years into a business and they knock you out in five   20
minutes, what could I do, let them take forty years, let them take my life away? *(His voice is cracking)* I never thought they'd install them. I swear to God. I thought they'd stop 'em before anybody took off.

Chris: Then why'd you ship them out?

Keller: By the time you could spot them I thought I'd have the process going   25
again, and I could show them they needed me and they'd let it go by. But weeks passed and I got no kick-back, so I was going to tell them.

Chris: Then why didn't you tell them?

Keller: It was too late. The paper, it was all over the front page, twenty-one went down, it was too late. They came with handcuffs into the shop,   30
what could I do? *(He sits on bench)* Chris, I did it for you, it was a chance and I took it for you. I'm sixty-one years old, when would I get another chance to make something for you? Sixty-one years old you don't get another chance, do ya?

Chris: You even knew they wouldn't hold up in the air.   35

Keller: I didn't say that.

Chris: But you weren't going to warn them not to use them —

Keller: But that don't mean —

Chris: It means you knew they'd crash.

Keller: It don't mean that. 40

Chris: Then you *thought* they'd crash.

Keller: I was afraid maybe —

Chris: You were afraid maybe! God in heaven, what kind of a man are you? Kids were hanging in the air by those heads. You knew that!

Keller: For you, a business for you! 45

Chris *(with burning fury)*: For me! Where do you live, where have you come from? For me! — I was dying every day and you were killing my boys and you did it for me? What the hell do you think I was thinking of, the goddam business? Is that as far as your mind can see, the business? What is that, the world — the business? What the hell do you mean, 50 you did it for me? Don't you have a country? Don't you live in the world? What the hell are you? You're not even an animal, no animal kills his own, what are you? What must I do to you? I ought to tear the tongue out of your mouth, what must I do? *(With his fist he pounds down on his father's shoulder. He stumbles away, covering his face as he weeps)* 55 What must I do, Jesus God, what must I do?

Keller: Chris ... My Chris ...

From All My Sons *by Arthur Miller*

As we saw when looking at prose on page 28 and poetry on page 59, the process of analysis could be said to involve three key stages: making a statement about an aspect of structure/style/language; providing relevant evidence to back up that statement; and then commenting on the effect of the selected aspect. For ease of memory, this process can be reduced to a neat acronym, **SEA**:

S   **statement**

E   **evidence**   (SEA)

A   **analysis**

Working with a few examples from the extract from *All My Sons*, let's look at this process in action.

Example 1   **statement**

Chris's horror at his father's actions is conveyed in the violence of his language.

evidence

He uses words such as '*killed*' and '*murdered*' and expressions such as '*tear you to pieces*' and '*tear the tongue out of your mouth*'.

analysis

'*Killed*' and '*murdered*' are both very emotive words, rousing in us a sense of horror and revulsion. The expression '*tear you to pieces*' has violent animal connotations, suggesting a wild creature savagely attacking its prey. Chris's emotions are so powerful at this point that he seems out of control, and threatening to behave like a wild animal. Similarly, when he says he ought to tear his father's tongue out, he sounds like a character from a barbaric scene where primitive torture methods are being used.

Example 2   **statement**

Stage directions help to underline the powerful emotions at work in this scene.

evidence

> (*horrified at his overwhelming fury*) (**line 10**)
> (*their movements now are those of subtle pursuit and escape. Keller keeps a step out of Chris's range as he talks*) (**lines 14–15**)
> (*His voice is cracking*) (**line 22**)
> (*with burning fury*) (**line 46**)
> (*With his fist he pounds down on his father's shoulder. He stumbles away, covering his face as he weeps*) (**lines 54–55**)

analysis

Father and son are seen as hunter and hunted, the one '*pursuing*', the other trying to '*escape*'. '*Keller keeps a step out of Chris's range*' because he senses the strength of his emotion which is obviously running at a dangerously high level. His fury is described as '*burning*' as if it threatens to consume him. This fury is also caught in his actions as he '*pounds*' his father. The violence and pain implied in this stage direction breaks him and he '*stumbles*' away, overcome with grief.

Example 3   **statement**

The structure of Keller's dialogue tells us a good deal about his character.

evidence

> 'How could I kill anybody?' (*lines 4–5*)
> 'I didn't kill anybody!' (*line 7*)
> 'I'm in business … what the hell's it to them?' (*lines 15–19*)

analysis

The first rhetorical question is meant as an appeal, suggesting that Keller is playing the innocent here, trying to persuade his son that he is not capable of killing. When this doesn't work, he tries to convince by saying quite firmly that he didn't kill anyone, again in the hope that Chris will believe him. He seems to be a man in denial who is unable to face what he has done. It is only when Chris threatens to 'tear him to pieces' that he breaks.

The long, loose structure, beginning, 'I'm in business … ' is punctuated by repeated semi-colons and finishes with a rhetorical question. The effect is disjointed, full of stops and starts as if he is thinking on his feet, piling one excuse on top of another. He is presenting himself as a man with no other options; he needed to do as he did for his son's sake.

ACTIVITY 1

Now try to provide **evidence** and **analysis** to support the following statements, using the above examples to help you.

statements

1   Repetition plays an important part in building the dramatic tension.

2   The structure of Chris's dialogue tells us a good deal about his feelings.

3   Keller and Chris both use the rhetorical question, but with different effects.

Evaluation in action

Although we've separated the two areas of analysis and evaluation for teaching purposes, they are, of course, very closely related. Often your evaluative comments will be based on specific aspects which you've already analysed. The emphasis, however, will be different. If you look at building block D again, you'll see that the focus is on assessing the **effectiveness** of a text or aspects of a text through the following elements:

personal response
relevant evidence
appropriate critical vocabulary

> **BLOCK D** *Evaluation*
> Assessing the effectiveness of a text through personal response, supported by relevant evidence and appropriate critical vocabulary.

Let's go back to the extract from *All My Sons* to see some examples of the **evaluative process** in action.

Example 1   Arthur Miller very effectively draws the reader into this powerful scene **(PR)**. Dramatic tension is created in the dialogue as well as through stage directions **(CV)**. Chris is seen as the accuser, and his father the accused. The force and directness of questions such as: '*What did you do?*' and '*Why didn't you tell them?*' heightens the tension, while Keller's explanation in phrases such as '*I'm in business*' and '*I never thought they'd install them*' **(E)** sound weak and unconvincing.

The powerful force of the characters' emotions, sometimes expressed in the stage directions **(CV)**, kept my attention **(PR)**. When we are told that Keller's voice is '*cracking*', we feel his guilt at the awfulness of what he has done. Likewise, when Keller is '*horrified at his* (Chris's) *overwhelming fury*', **(E)** we are made aware of the sheer force of Chris's emotion: he is consumed by his feeling of rage at his father and the frightening power of that emotion comes across to the reader, drawing him into the drama.

(**PR** = personal response; **E** = evidence; **CV** = critical vocabulary)

Example 2   The playwright has presented us with a very convincing picture of a father/son relationship **(PR)**. The two characters act as foils **(CV)** to each other: Keller is defensive, trying hard to convince Chris that he had no option but to do as he did, whereas his son is forceful and direct, determined to get at the truth, whatever the cost. Keller tries to find excuses for his actions: '*what could I do, let them take forty years?*' and '*They came with handcuffs into the shop, what could I do?*' (E) while his son demands the truth: '*Then why didn't you tell them?*' (E) This reverses the way in which we would normally expect to see a father/son relationship portrayed. More usually, it would be the father asking the direct questions, and the son looking for convincing explanations or excuses.

The intensity of the emotion adds to the convincing picture. This is a very painful situation where a son is hearing an awful truth about his father's guilt. Phrases such as '*cracking*', '*overwhelming fury*' and '*burning fury*' (E) all help to underline the pain, confusion and anger felt by the two characters. Miller communicates very effectively the terrible grief which a son must experience when he feels betrayed by his own father (PR).

ACTIVITY 2

I feel that the playwright is particularly skilled in the way in which he handles dialogue (PR).

Try to expand on this response, using 'relevant evidence' (E) and 'appropriate critical vocabulary' (CV) to back up what you say. Use the examples on page 95 to help you.

CHAPTER 17 *Drama*

BUILDING BLOCKS TO ANALYSIS AND EVALUATION

 *Developing*

Practice in developing the skills of analysis and evaluation

The next two extracts aim to provide you with opportunities to develop specific analytical and evaluative skills by focusing on key aspects of each text, and exploring *how* individual playwrights have achieved particular effects and assessing their effectiveness.

EXTRACT A (Sir Thomas More has been imprisoned by Henry VIII because he has refused on principle to agree to what the King has done in order to divorce himself from Queen Catherine of Aragon. His daughter, Margaret, and his wife, Alice, visit him in prison).

More:	Now listen, you must leave the country. All of you must leave the country.
Margaret:	And leave you here?
More:	It makes no difference, Meg; they won't let you see me again. *(Breathlessly, a prepared speech under pressure.)* You must all go on the same day, but not on the same boat; different boats from different ports.
Margaret:	After the trial, then.
More:	There'll be no trial, they have no case. Do this for me I beseech you?
Margaret:	Yes.
More:	Alice? *(She turns her back.)* Alice, I command it!
Alice	*(harshly)*: Right!
More	*(looks into her basket)*: Oh, this is splendid; I know who packed this.
Alice	*(harshly)*: I packed it.
More:	Yes. *(Eats a morsel.)* You still make superlative custard, Alice.
Alice:	Do I?
More:	That's a nice dress you have on.
Alice:	It's my cooking dress.
More:	It's very nice, anyway. Nice colour.
Alice	*(turns. Quietly)*: By God, you think very little of me. *(Mounting bitterness.)* I know I'm a fool. But I'm no such fool as at this time to be lamenting for my dresses! Or to relish complimenting on my custard!
More	*(regarding her with frozen attention. He nods once or twice)*: I am well rebuked. *(Holds out his hands.)* Al—!
Alice:	No! *(She remains where she is, glaring at him.)*
More	*(he is in great fear of her)*: I am faint when I think of the worst that they may do to me. But worse than that would be to go, with you not understanding why I go.
Alice:	I don't.
More	*(just hanging onto his self-possession)*: Alice, if you can tell me that you understand, I think I can make a good death, if I have to.

Alice:	Your death's no 'good' to me!
More:	Alice, you must tell me that you understand!
Alice:	I don't. *(She throws it straight at his head.)* I don't believe this had to happen.
More	*(his face is drawn)*: If you say that, Alice, I don't see how I'm to face it.
Alice:	It's the truth!
More	*(gasping)*: You're an honest woman.
Alice:	Much good may it do me! I'll tell you what I'm afraid of; that when you've gone, I shall hate you for it.
More	*(turns from her: his face working)*: Well, you mustn't, Alice, that's all. *(Swiftly she crosses the stage to him; he turns and they clasp each other fiercely).* You mustn't, you —
Alice	*(covers his mouth with her hand)*: S–s–sh … As for understanding, I understand you're the best man that I ever met or am likely to; and if you go — well God knows why I suppose — though as God's my witness God's kept deadly quiet about it! And if anyone wants my opinion of the King and his Council they've only to ask for it!
More:	Why, it's a lion I married! A lion! A lion! *(he breaks away from her his face shining)*

From A Man for All Seasons *by Robert Bolt*

ACTIVITY

a) Focus of interest for analysis: tonal effects.

How?
Areas for consideration:
- word choice
- stage directions
- punctuation

Using the three listed areas for consideration as the basis for your discussion, explore *how* each of these areas helps the writer to communicate the various tonal changes.

Remember to support your statements with evidence and analysis (SEA). Use the examples in Chapter 16 to remind you of the process of analysis.

Here are some examples from each of the areas for consideration, to help start the discussion.

Example 1   **effect of word choice on tone**
'*splendid*' and '*nice dress*': More is using a conciliatory tone: he's trying to humour Alice but, in fact, his tone comes across as rather patronizing, as if he is addressing a child.

Example 2   **effect of stage directions on tone**
(harshly) (mounting bitterness): Alice is clearly angry with her husband and this comes out in her tone, which becomes progressively more resentful.

Example 3   **effect of punctuation on tone**

The exclamation mark in the following:

> **Alice:** But I'm no such fool ... dresses!
> **Alice:** Your death's no 'good' to me!

The punctuation reinforces the tone of bitter anger in the first example, and the scathing note in the second example.

b) Focus of interest for evaluation: effectiveness of characterization.

How successful do you feel the dramatist is in giving us some idea of the relationship between More and Alice?

It may help you to consider such aspects as:
- what each says to the other and how it is said
- how each reacts to the other
- how the extract ends

Remember to show a personal involvement with the extract, using appropriate critical vocabulary when making your evaluation. Use the examples in Chapter 16 to remind you of the process of evaluation.

EXTRACT B   (The Boyle family are going through hard times: the father, Jack Boyle, is unemployed and the son, Johnny, is an invalid. But daughter Mary arrives with a Mr Bentham, who has some good news for the family.)

(Mary enters with Charlie Bentham; he is a young man of twenty-five, tall, good-looking, with a very high opinion of himself generally. He is dressed in a brown coat, brown knee-breeches, grey stockings, a brown sweater, with a deep blue tie; he carries gloves and a walking stick.)

Mrs Boyle *(fussing round)*:	Come in, Mr Bentham; sit down, Mr Bentham, in this chair; it's more comfortable than that, Mr Bentham. Himself'll be here in a minute; he's just takin' off his trousers.
Mary:	Mother!
Bentham:	Please don't put yourself to any trouble, Mrs Boyle – I'm quite all right here, thank you.
Mrs Boyle:	An' to think you knowin' Mary, an' she knowin' the news you had for us, an' wouldn't let on; but it's all the more welcomer now, for we were on our last lap!
Johnny *(inside)*:	What are you kickin' up all the racket for?
Boyle *(roughly)*:	I'm takin' off me moleskin trousers!
Johnny:	Can't you do it, then, without lettin' th' whole house know you're takin' off your trousers? What d'ye want puttin' them on an' takin' them off again?
Boyle:	Will you let me alone, will you let me alone? Am I never goin' to be done thryin' to please the whole o' yous?
Mrs Boyle *(to Bentham)*:	You must excuse th' state o' th' place, Mr Bentham; th' minute I turn me back that man o' mine always makes a litther o' th' place, a litther o' th' place.
Bentham:	Don't worry, Mrs Boyle; it's all right, I assure ...
Boyle *(inside)*:	Where's me braces; where in th' name o' God did I leave me braces?

Johnny	*(inside, calling out)*: Ma, will you come in here an' take da away out o' this or he'll dhrive me mad.
Mrs Boyle	*(going towards door)*: Dear, dear, dear, that man'll be lookin' for somethin' on th' day o' Judgement. *(Looking into room and calling to Boyle)* Look at your braces, man, hangin' round your neck!
Boyle	*(inside)*: Aw, Holy God!
Mrs Boyle	*(calling)*: Johnny, Johnny, come out here for a minute.
Johnny:	Ah leave Johnny alone, an' don't be annoyin' him.
Mrs Boyle:	Come on, Johnny, till I inthroduce you to Mr Bentham. *(To Bentham)* Me son, Mr Bentham; he's after goin' through the mill. He was only a chiselur of a Boy Scout in Easter Week, when he got hit in the hip; and his arm was blew off in the fight in O'Connell Street.* *(Johnny comes in)* Here he is, Mr Bentham; Mr Bentham, Johnny. None can deny he done his bit for Irelan', if that's goin' to do him any good.
Johnny	*(boastfully)*: I'd do it agen, ma, I'd do it agen; for a principle's a principle.
Mrs Boyle:	Ah, you lost your best principle, me boy, when you lost your arm; them's the only sort o' principles that's any good to a workin' man.
Johnny:	Ireland only half free'll never be at peace while she has a son left to pull a trigger.
Mrs Boyle:	To be sure, to be sure — no bread's a lot betther than half a loaf.

* refers to the Easter Rising of 1916, when a group of Irish revolutionaries rose up in an attempt to end English rule. During the uprising they occupied the General Post Office in Dublin's O'Connell Street.

From Juno and the Paycock *by Sean O'Casey*

ACTIVITY 1

Focus of interest for analysis: humour.

How?

Areas for consideration:

◆ setting
◆ situation
◆ dialogue

Using the three listed areas for consideration as the basis for your discussion, explore *how* each of these areas contributes to the scene's comic effect.

Remember to support your statements with evidence and analysis (SEA). Use the examples in Chapter 16 to remind you of the process of analysis.

Here is one example from each of the areas for consideration to help start the discussion.

Example 1   **an aspect of setting which contributes to comic effect**

Mrs Boyle: You must excuse th' state o' th' place.

> The room appears to be in a state of chaos, which provides a comic setting for the immaculately dressed Mr Bentham.

Example 2   **an aspect of situation which contributes to comic effect**

Mr Boyle is offstage struggling to change his trousers while Mrs Boyle is trying very hard to entertain Mr Bentham.

> The contrast between these two situations is amusing.

Example 3   **an aspect of dialogue which contributes to comic effect**

Voice of Johnny inside: What are you kickin' up all the racket for?
Boyle (*roughly*): I'm takin' off me moleskin trousers!

> The directness of this exchange, in contrast to Mrs Boyle's attempts at politeness, provides humour.

ACTIVITY 2

Focus of interest for evaluation: humour.

The scene is set in the 1920s. How effective is the humour of this extract to a modern-day audience?

It may help you to consider such aspects as:
- characterization
- contrast
- stage layout

Remember to show a personal involvement with the extract, using appropriate critical vocabulary when making your evaluation. Use the examples in Chapter 16 to remind you of the process of evaluation.

CHAPTER 18 *Drama*

BUILDING BLOCKS TO ANALYSIS AND EVALUATION

 ## *Demonstrating*

Demonstrating analysis and evaluation

In Chapter 13 we explored an extract from *Death of a Salesman* using the **building blocks to understanding** in order to provide a working model as preparation for your independent study of a text.

Now we're going to apply the **building blocks of analysis and evaluation** to this same extract in preparation for your own independent study of another, unseen extract.

BLOCK C *Analysis*	**BLOCK D** *Evaluation*
Examining aspects of structure, style, language to show HOW they contribute to meaning and effect.	Assessing the effectiveness of a text through personal response, supported by relevant evidence and appropriate critical vocabulary.

But first, as part of that preparation, a reminder about **denotation** and **connotation**.

Analysis of language

Look back at what was said on this important aspect in Chapter 6 of the Prose section (page 36).

Dramatists, like novelists and poets, rely heavily on their ability to tap into the connotative layers of language.

For example:

>**Child:** But Grandpa, what will I be when I grow up?
>
>**Grandpa:** I hope you'll be ⟨yourself⟩; ⟨light of heart⟩, ⟨free of spirit⟩ and honest as ⟨a clear blue sky⟩.

In this example, when we unlock the circled words we find they carry additional **connotations**: '*yourself*' suggests someone natural and honest, with no pretensions; '*light of heart*' implies carrying no burdens, cheerful, with a positive attitude to life. Generosity, openness, independence of mind are all possible connotations of the phrase '*free of spirit*', while comparing honesty to '*a clear blue sky*' captures the idea of complete openness, an unclouded approach to the truth, hiding nothing, in the same way as a clear blue sky reveals everything set against it.

Your analysis of language features should always explore any relevant connotations.

Sample commentary on *Death of a Salesman*

Use the sample commentary which follows this extract to help you in your own independent exploration of the second, unseen extract in this chapter.

EXTRACT A (Willy, a travelling salesman, is staying in a Boston hotel. His son, Biff, has come to ask him to persuade his teacher, Mr Birnbaum, to give him a pass mark in Maths. Just after Biff arrives, however, he is confronted with the awful truth that Willy is having an affair.)

(Willy laughs and The Woman joins in offstage)

Willy	*(without hesitation)*: Hurry downstairs and –
Biff:	Somebody in there?
Willy:	No, that was next door.

(The Woman laughs offstage)

Biff:	Somebody got in your bathroom!
Willy:	No, it's the next room, there's a party –
The Woman	*(enters, laughing. She lisps this)*: Can I come in? There's something in the bathtub, Willy, and it's moving! *(Willy looks at Biff, who is staring open-mouthed and horrified at The Woman)*
Willy:	Ah – you better go back to your room. They must be finished painting by now. They're painting her room so I let her take a shower here. Go back, go back … *(He pushes her)*
The Woman	*(resisting)*: But I've got to get dressed. Willy, I can't –
Willy:	Get out of here! Go back, go back … *(Suddenly striving for the ordinary.)* This is Miss Francis, Biff, she's a buyer. They're painting her room. Go back, Miss Francis, go back …
The Woman:	But my clothes. I can't go out naked in the hall!
Willy	*(pushing her offstage)*: Get outa here! Go back, go back!

(Biff slowly sits down on his suitcase as the argument continues offstage)

The Woman:	Where's my stockings? You promised me stockings, Willy!
Willy:	I have no stockings here!
The Woman:	You had two boxes of size nine sheers for me, and I want them!
Willy:	Here for God's sake, will you get outa here!
The Woman	*(enters holding a box of stockings)*: I just hope there's nobody in the hall. That's all I hope. *(to Biff)* Are you football or baseball?
Biff:	Football.
The Woman	*(angry, humiliated)*: That's me too. G'night. *(She snatches her clothes from Willy, and walks out)*
Willy	*(after a pause)*: Well better get going. I want to get to the school first thing in the morning. Get my suits out of the closet. I'll get my valise. *(Biff doesn't move)* What's the matter? *(Biff remains motionless, tears falling)* She's a buyer. Buys for J.H. Simmons. She lives down the hall – they're painting. You don't imagine – *(He breaks off. After a pause)* Now listen, pal, she's just a buyer. She sees merchandise in her room and they have to keep it looking just so … *(Pause, assuming command)* All right, get my suits. *(Biff doesn't move)* Now, stop crying and do as I say. I gave you an order, Biff. I gave you an order! Is that what you do when I give you an order? How dare you cry? *(Putting his arm around Biff)* Now look, Biff, when you grow up you'll understand about these things. You mustn't – you mustn't over-emphasise a thing like this. I'll see Birnbaum first thing in the morning.

Biff:	Never mind.
Willy	(*getting down beside Biff*): Never mind! He's going to give you these points. I'll see to it.
Biff:	He wouldn't listen to you.
Willy:	He certainly will listen to me. You need those points for the U. of Virginia.
Biff:	I'm not going there.
Willy:	Heh? If I can't get him to change that mark you'll make it up in summer school. You've got all summer to –
Biff	(*his weeping breaking from him*): Dad …
Willy	(*infected by it*): Oh my boy …
Biff:	Dad …
Willy:	She's nothing to me, Biff. I was lonely, I was terribly lonely.
Biff:	You – you gave her Mama's stockings. (*His tears break through and he rises to go*)
Willy	(*grabbing for Biff*): I gave you an order!
Biff:	Don't touch me, you – liar!
Willy:	Apologise for that!
Biff:	You fake! You phoney little fake! You fake!

(*Overcome, he turns quickly and, weeping fully, goes out with his suitcase. Willy is left on the floor on his knees*)

From Death of a Salesman *by Arthur Miller*

BLOCK C *Analysis*

Examining aspects of structure, style, language to show HOW they contribute to meaning and effect.

Analysis of character through language

We are given an insight into certain aspects of Willy's character through the style of language he uses. In particular, he speaks in the language of orders, commanding both Biff and The Woman to do things. For example, in the first half of the extract, he repeats the words '*go back*' or '*get outa here*' on several occasions, indicating an aggressive, bullying side to his character. Biff, too, is spoken to in commanding language: '*get my suits*' and '*stop crying*'. When Biff does not respond to these orders, Willy repeats the line, '*I gave you an order*', underlining the idea that Willy feels he is someone who should be obeyed. Towards the end of the extract, when Biff breaks down completely, Willy seems to cling desperately to this same line as if he thinks he can get out of a situation by simply repeating the order.

Not only does he come across here as bullying but also as arrogant: he says that Mr Birnbaum '*certainly will listen to me*', as if he is overly confident that he will be able to overrule the teacher's decision about Biff's examination mark.

In addition, Willy's language choice shows him up as a liar: as he tries to build up a feeble explanation for the woman's presence in his room, he repeats the same phrase '*painting her room*' several times, as if trying to convince himself that this is, in fact, the true explanation.

The only time we feel we see through the false Willy to the real person is when he reacts to his son's tears by admitting '*I was lonely, I was terribly lonely*'. The word 'lonely' captures what seems to be a real side of Willy's character: we suspect that underneath the arrogance and the bullying, there is a pathetic, lonely man.

Analysis of mood through stage directions

The extract opens on a relaxed note with the direction '*Willy laughs and The Woman joins in offstage*'. But the mood becomes more nervous when '*The Woman laughs offstage*' once again, and we begin to realize that there is something wrong with the situation.

There is a more dramatic mood change when we are told Biff '*is staring open-mouthed and horrified at The Woman*'. This darker mood is reinforced by Willy's desperate attempts to remove The Woman. '*He pushes her*' and '*pushing her offstage*' create a mood of panic. Willy tries to recover the mood of normality, '*suddenly striving for the ordinary*', but is prevented from doing so by the appearance of The Woman who is '*angry, humiliated*'.

From the point where '*Biff remains motionless, tears falling*' to the end when Biff '*overcome, turns quickly and, weeping fully, goes out with his suitcase*' the mood takes on a poignant, even tragic note. Biff has been devastated by seeing his father lie and cheat while Willy has lost his son through his own deceitful actions.

BLOCK D *Evaluation*

Assessing the effectiveness of a text through personal response, supported by relevant evidence and appropriate critical vocabulary.

Evaluating effectiveness in communicating theme

Arthur Miller presents us with a very powerful scene in which the idea of deception is dramatically communicated through a variety of techniques, including action and dialogue (**PR**). The pattern of events effectively illustrates the theme: The Woman is discovered in a state of undress in Willy's hotel room. He tries to concoct a laughable excuse to explain her presence in his bathroom by saying her room is being painted (**E**). When she will not go, Willy is forced to produce the boxes of stockings. It is this act of handing over what Biff sees as '*Mama's stockings*' which captures the theme: Willy has deceived his wife, his son, The Woman (by treating her like a '*football*') and himself.

The thread of lies and deception is conveyed through the dialogue (**CV**). When Willy repeatedly denies The Woman's presence, saying '*No, that was next door*' and '*No, it's the next room*' (**E**), he is clearly lying. And when he repeats the line '*They're painting her room*' (**E**), he is trying hard to convince Biff, and us, of the explanation, but it does not ring true.

Biff's final words to Willy, however, communicate the theme most clearly when he calls his father a '*liar*' and a '*phoney little fake*' (**E**). These words, in particular, brought home to me the terrible consequences of Willy's deceitful behaviour, both for others and for himself (**PR**).

Demonstrating analysis and evaluation

In summary, using the building blocks approach to analysis and evaluation, several readings of this extract have revealed a clearer awareness of the following aspects:

- ◆ style
- ◆ language
- ◆ situation
- ◆ mood/atmosphere

- ◆ dialogue
- ◆ character
- ◆ theme
- ◆ personal response to all of these

EXTRACT B (Stanhope is a Company Captain in the front line during the First World War. In this scene, he threatens to shoot a young officer, Hibbert, because he wants to go down the line 'sick'. This extract is a continuation of the one on pages 88–89 of Chapter 15.)

Hibbert: Let me go —

Stanhope: If you went, I'd have you shot — for deserting. It's a hell of a disgrace — to die like that, I'd rather spare you the disgrace. I give you half a minute to think. You either stay here and try to be a man — or you try to get out of that door — to desert. If you do that, there's going to be an accident. D'you understand? I'm fiddling with my revolver, d'you see? — cleaning it — and it's going off by accident. It often happens out here. It's going off, and it's going to shoot you between the eyes.

Hibbert (in a whisper): You daren't —

Stanhope: You don't deserve to be shot by accident — but I'd save you the disgrace of the other way. I give you half a minute to decide. (He holds up his wrist to look at his watch) Half a minute from now.

(There is a silence; a few seconds go by. Suddenly Hibbert bursts into a high-pitched laugh)

Hibbert: Go on, then, shoot! You won't let me go to hospital. I swear I'll never go into those trenches again. Shoot! — and thank God —

Stanhope (with his eyes on his watch): Fifteen more seconds —

Hibbert: Go on! I'm ready —

Stanhope (He looks up at Hibbert, who has closed his eyes): Five.

(Again Stanhope looks up. After a moment he quietly drops his revolver into its holster and steps towards Hibbert, who stands with lowered head and eyes tightly screwed up, his arms stretched stiffly by his sides, his hands tightly clutching the edges of his tunic. Gently Stanhope places his hands on Hibbert's shoulders. Hibbert starts violently and gives a little cry. He opens his eyes and stares vacantly into Stanhope's face. Stanhope is smiling)

Stanhope: Good man, Hibbert. I liked the way you stuck that.

Hibbert (hoarsely): Why didn't you shoot?

Stanhope: Stay here, old chap — and see it through.

(Hibbert stands trembling, trying to speak. Suddenly he breaks down and cries. Stanhope takes his hands from his shoulders and turns away)

Hibbert: Stanhope! I've tried like hell — I swear I have. Ever since I came out here I've hated and loathed it. Every sound up there makes me all — cold and sick. I'm different to — the others — you don't understand. It gets worse and worse, and now I can't bear it any longer. I'll never go up those steps again — into the line — with the men looking at me — and knowing — I'd rather die here. (He is sitting on Stanhope's bed, crying without effort to restrain himself)

Stanhope (pouring out a whisky): Try a drop of this, old chap —

Hibbert: No thanks.

Stanhope: Go on. Drink it. (Hibbert takes the mug and drinks. Stanhope sits down beside Hibbert and puts an arm round his shoulder) I know what you feel, Hibbert. I've known all along —

Hibbert: How *can* you know?

Stanhope: Because I feel the same — exactly the same! Every little noise up there makes me feel — just as you feel. Why didn't you tell me instead of talking about neuralgia? We all feel like you do sometimes, if you only knew. I hate and loathe it all. Sometimes I feel I could just lie down on this bed and pretend I was paralysed

or something – and couldn't move – and just lie there till I died –
or was dragged away.

From Journey's End *by R. C. Sherriff*

ACTIVITY

Now it's your turn to demonstrate what you've learnt about analysis and
evaluation by exploring the drama extract from *Journey's End* by
R. C. Sherriff.

Directing discussion on analysis and evaluation

Use the following prompts to help direct your discussion of the extract.

- ◆ What effect do any of the following have on the build up of tension
  in the scene?
  - actions
  - dialogue
  - stage directions   (Analysis)
  - tone
  - punctuation
  - language

- ◆ How does Hibbert's language help to convey his feelings about being
  in the trenches? (Analysis)

- ◆ How successful is the dramatist in putting across the idea of duty? In
  particular, consider Stanhope's words and actions. (Evaluation)

HIGHER

CHAPTER 19 *Prose*

BUILDING BLOCKS TO UNDERSTANDING

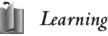 *Learning*

What? Why? How?

Textual Analysis is introduced on page 1 of the Intermediate 2 section of this book. Read this page to help you to understand **what** is meant by the term, **why** you should study it and **how** you can develop the skills you will need to tackle this aspect of the Higher course in English.

Building blocks to understanding prose

BLOCK A	BLOCK B
Understanding of main ideas through: *structure; key words and phrases*	Understanding of significant detail through: *punctuation and tone*

Block A shows us that one of the most important building blocks to understanding that we need to learn to recognize and interpret is **structure**; in other words, the way a piece of writing is arranged and organized on the page. Any piece of literature will have:

- an outer shape or structure (for example, a novel may be arranged in chapters which may have linked titles)
- an inner structure made up of connected paragraphs and sentences.

The recognition and accurate interpretation of these structures is vital to our understanding of meaning. Let's look at a specific example to see structure in action.

EXTRACT A (Young Denis has decided to run away from home, but he needs to get to a post office to withdraw some money.)

I stood for ten minutes outside the post office, wondering wildly if one of the clerks would turn up. I felt that I simply couldn't return home. And then the idea struck me that the city was only twenty miles away, and that the post office there was bound to be open. I had been to the city a couple of times with Mother, so there was nothing very unfamiliar or frightening in the idea of it. When I got my money I could either stay the night at a hotel or cycle on through the dark. I was attracted by the latter idea. It would be good fun to cycle through the sleeping villages and towns, and see the dawn break over Dublin, and arrive at Auntie May's door, in the Shelbourne Road, while she was lighting the fire. I could imagine how she would greet me — 'Child of Grace, where did you come from?' 'Ah, just cycled,' I would reply, without any fuss. [Paragraph 1]

It was very pleasant, but it wasn't enough. I cycled slowly and undecidedly out the familiar main road and where we walked on Sunday, past the seminary and the little suburban houses. I was still uncertain that I should go on. Then something happened. Suddenly the countryside struck me as strange. I got off my bicycle and looked around. The town had sunk back into its black, bushy hills, with little showing of it but the spire of the church and the ruined tower of the abbey. It was as though it had accompanied me so far and then silently left me and returned. I found myself in a new country, with a little, painted town sprawled across a river, and beyond it, bigger, smoother, greener hills. It was a curious sensation, rather like the moment when you find yourself out of your depth and two inclinations struggle in you — one to turn back in panic to the shallows, the other to strike out boldly for the other side. [Paragraph 2]

The mere analogy was enough for me. It was like a challenge, and that moment of panic gave new energy to my cycling. The little town, the big red-brick mansion at the end of a beech avenue, the hexagonal brown building on top of the smooth hill before me, and the glimpses I caught of the river were both fascinating and frightening. I was aware of great distances, of big cloud masses on the horizon, of the fragility of my tyres compared with the rough surface of the road, and everything disappeared in the urgent need to get to the city, to draw out my money, to find myself food and a bed for the night. [Paragraph 3]

From the short story Masculine Protest *by Frank O'Connor*

ACTIVITY 1

Recognizing and interpreting structure: paragraphing

a) Look at the **length** of the paragraphs in this extract in relation to each other. Is there any recognizable pattern? If so, how does this help meaning?

b) Look more closely at the **content** of each paragraph. How does paragraphing divide up the content? (Look for any signs of logical progression.)

c) Examine the opening and closing sentences of each paragraph. How are they **linked** to each other? Explain how these links contribute to our understanding of content.

ACTIVITY 2

Recognizing and interpreting sentence structure

Below are three of the most commonly used types of sentence structures, and a reminder of what each type looks like.

- **Simple:** contains a single main point. Used to emphasize a key point or emotion; to surprise/startle/shock the reader; to create a humorous/comic effect; to underline an ending
- **Compound:** contains two or more linked main points
- **Complex:** contains a main point, plus one or more subordinate points. Used to develop or explain points/emotions; to add details (for example, of time/place/manner); to vary pace.

Identify those occasions when the writer is using simple or compound or complex sentences. How does the writer's use of each of these three varieties of structure help to convey meaning? Consider such aspects as:

- the need to convey information
- the need to reveal thoughts and feelings
- the need to move the narrative on.

ACTIVITY 3

Recognizing and interpreting key words and phrases

The repetition of specific words or phrases within an extract can help the reader to grasp main ideas.

For example, look at the repetition of the word '*city*' in this extract. On one level, it helps us to understand the challenge of the young boy's physical journey, but more importantly, on another level, it highlights the importance of his metaphoric journey from the shelter of his home town to the excitement and possible dangers of the adult city.

Similarly, the setting up of an opposition between contrasting words or phrases can highlight important areas for understanding.

For example, in paragraph 2 of the extract, we begin to understand something of the confusion in the boy's mind when '*undecidedly*' (in the first line) is contrasted with the word '*boldly*' (in the last line).

Pick out 3 or 4 pairs of contrasting words or phrases. What contribution does each of these contrasts make to our understanding of the boy's feelings and reactions?

ACTIVITY 4

Recognizing and interpreting features of punctuation

BLOCK B
Understanding of significant detail through: *punctuation and tone*

Accurate reading for understanding depends on our ability to interpret the various functions of punctuation marks. Commas, inverted commas, colons, semi-colons, question marks, exclamation marks, brackets and dashes can all impact on meaning. By this stage in your school career, you should be familiar with the different functions of all key forms of punctuation. If you're still uncertain about any of these, now is the time to check them out.

The comma is used frequently in the extract from *Masculine Protest*. Reread the last paragraph, from, '*The little town*' to the end. Remember that commas can be used for a range of purposes such as: to separate items in a list; to build up pace as the sentence moves towards a climax; to reproduce a feeling of confusion by piling several items/feelings/pieces of information one on top of the other; to separate non-essential information from the main part of the sentence.

- ◆ For what main purpose is the comma being used here?
- ◆ What contribution does its use make to our understanding of the content of this paragraph?

ACTIVITY 5

Recognizing and interpreting features of tone

The **tone** which a writer adopts is another important tool shaping meaning and refining understanding. By tone, we mean the 'speaking' voice of the writer or character. In the same way as our predominant conversational tones will change and range widely, depending on the situation and the individuals to whom we are speaking, written tones will also vary across a wide spectrum from sympathetic to aggressive, from mocking to amused, and so on.

If you feel uncertain about your ability to identify tone, speak the written words aloud and listen carefully to catch the rhythm and emphasis of the words, both of which help to determine tone.

In this particular extract the writer uses the first person narrator, the 'I' voice. What effect does this have on the overall tone of the extract?

Paragraph 1 could be said to build on a tone of cheerful optimism: '*only twenty miles away*'; '*the post office there was **bound** to be open*'; '***nothing** very unfamiliar or frightening*'; '*it would be **good fun**'*; '*I would reply, **without any fuss**'*.

Identify the predominant tone in each of paragraphs 2 and 3, quoting some evidence to support your findings, along the lines of this example.

Comments on structure, key words/phrases, punctuation and tone

Now compare your responses to Activities 1 to 5 with the following comments to see what you can add to your answers.

Paragraph structure

The paragraphs are quite similar in length and look accessible on the page. Each deals with a stage in the narrative of the boy's journey from his familiar town to the unfamiliar city.

- Paragraph 1 reflects on alternative plans for his journey, prompted by the fact that he cannot access his money in the local post office.
- Paragraph 2 takes the reader through the uncertain phase where, confronted by the turning point of a changing landscape — '*Then something happened*' — the boy has to resolve the conflict between turning back or heading onwards to the city.
- The final, shorter paragraph quickens the pace, bringing the narrative to a climax.

This structure helps the reader to mark out the clearly defined, chronological stages of the boy's journey, leading to a better understanding of his metaphoric journey to the 'other side' of boyhood.

Paragraph links

- The opening sentence of paragraph 2 links back to the last sentence of paragraph 1 through the word '*it*', which refers to the boy's imagined reaction to his aunt's greeting. '*But*' then looks forward to the conflicting emotions expressed in the remainder of the paragraph.
- The simile contained in the last sentence of paragraph 2 links forward to paragraph 3, picked up in the phrase '*mere analogy*'. In the second sentence, '*challenge*' echoes the simile of paragraph 2 with its choice between '*two inclinations*' which '*struggle in you*'.
- The extract closes with a list of three priorities: '*to get to the city*'; '*to draw out money*'; and '*to find food and a bed*'. These link back to key expressions in the opening paragraph: '*the city was only twenty miles away*'; '*when I got my money*'; and '*I could ... stay the night at a hotel*'.

By recognizing these as links in the structure, the reader is encouraged to look back and re-examine areas of the text, thereby refining understanding.

EXTRACT Ⓐ **Sentence structure**

I stood for ten minutes outside the post office, wondering wildly if one of the clerks would turn up. I felt that I simply couldn't return home. And then the idea struck me that the city was only twenty miles away, and that the post office there was bound to be open. I had been to the city a couple of times with Mother, so there was nothing very unfamiliar or frightening in the idea of it. When I got my money I could either stay the night at a hotel or cycle on through the dark. I was attracted by the latter idea. It would be good fun to cycle through the sleeping villages and towns, and see the dawn break over Dublin, and arrive at Auntie May's door, in the Shelbourne Road, while she was lighting the fire. I could imagine how she would greet me — 'Child of Grace, where did you come from?' 'Ah, just cycled,' I would reply, without any fuss.

It was very pleasant, but it wasn't enough. I cycled slowly and undecidedly out the familiar main road and where we walked on Sunday, past the seminary and the little suburban houses. I was still uncertain that I should go on. Then something happened. Suddenly the countryside struck me as strange. I got off my bicycle and looked around. The town had sunk back into its black, bushy hills, with little showing of it but the spire of the church and the ruined tower of the abbey. It was as though it had accompanied me so far and then silently left me and returned. I found myself in a new country, with a little, painted town sprawled across a river, and beyond it, bigger, smoother, greener hills. It was a curious sensation, rather like the moment when you find yourself out of your depth and two inclinations struggle in you — one to turn back in panic to the shallows, the other to strike out boldly for the other side.

The mere analogy was enough for me. It was like a challenge, and that moment of panic gave new energy to my cycling. The little town, the big red-brick mansion at the end of a beech avenue, the hexagonal brown building on top of the smooth hill before me, and the glimpses I caught of the river were both fascinating and frightening. I was aware of great distances, of big cloud masses on the horizon, of the fragility of my tyres compared with the rough surface of the road, and everything disappeared in the urgent need to get to the city, to draw out my money, to find myself food and a bed for the night.

Annotations (left margin): simple sentence, complex sentence, simple sentence, simple sentence, compound sentence

Annotations (right margin): compound sentence, complex sentence

Line numbers: 5, 10, 15, 20, 25, 30

The narrator is a young boy who is running away from home as part of his transition into adulthood. Sentence structure reflects this transition: a mix of simple, complex and compound structures, many loosely linked by the conjunction 'and', imitating the speech patterns of a young boy. For example, the simple sentence '*I felt I simply couldn't return*' has a child-like directness about it while the long, list-like final compound sentence allows time to show the boy's maturing awareness, but, at the same time, builds pace.

Key words and phrases

I stood for ten minutes outside the post office, wondering **wildly** [1] *if one of the clerks would turn up. I felt that I simply couldn't return home. And then the idea struck me that the city was only twenty miles away, and that the post office there was bound to be open. I had been to*

*the city a couple of times with Mother, so there was nothing very **unfamiliar** [3] or **frightening** [1] in the idea of it. When I got my money I could either stay the night at a hotel or cycle on through the **dark** [13]. I was attracted by the latter idea. It would be **good fun** [2] to cycle through the **sleeping** [13] villages and towns, and see the **dawn** [14] break over Dublin, and arrive at Auntie May's door, in the Shelbourne Road, while she was **lighting the fire** [14]. I could imagine how she would greet me — 'Child of Grace, where did you come from?' 'Ah, just cycled,' I would reply, **without any fuss** [2].*

*It was very **pleasant** [2], but it wasn't enough. I cycled **slowly and undecidedly** [5] out the **familiar** [4] main road and where we walked on Sunday, past the seminary and the **little** [7] suburban houses. I was still **uncertain** [5] that I should **go on** [9]. Then something happened. Suddenly the countryside struck me as **strange** [3]. I got off my bicycle and looked around. The town had sunk back into its **black** [13], bushy hills, with little showing of it but the spire of the church and the ruined tower of the abbey. It was as though it had **accompanied me** [11] so far and then silently **left me** [12] and returned. I found myself in **a new country** [3], with a **little** [7], painted town sprawled across a river, and beyond it, **bigger** [8], smoother, greener hills. It was a **curious** [3] sensation, rather like the moment when you find yourself **out of your depth** [1] and **two inclinations struggle** [5] in you — one to **turn back** [10] in **panic** [1] to the shallows, the other to **strike out boldly** [6] for the other side.*

*The mere analogy was enough for me. It was like a challenge, and that moment of **panic** [1] gave **new energy** [6] to my cycling. The **little** [7] town, the **big** [8] red-brick mansion at the end of a beech avenue, the hexagonal brown building on top of the smooth hill before me, and the glimpses I caught of the river were both fascinating and **frightening** [1]. I was aware of **great** [8] distances, of **big** [8] cloud masses on the horizon, of the **fragility** [15] of my tyres compared with the **rough** [16] surface of the road, and everything disappeared in the **urgent** need to get to the city, to draw out my money, to find myself food and a bed for the **night** [13].*

Words and phrases suggesting some degree of contrast are numbered in pairs: 1 and 2; 3 and 4, etc.

These key words and phrases set up a tension which reflects the young boy's inner struggle to cope with his situation.

Punctuation

The comma is used frequently throughout the extract, sometimes to link sections of longer, loosely connected complex and compound-complex sentences. For example:

> *'It would be good fun to cycle through the sleeping villages and towns, and see the dawn break over Dublin, and arrive at Auntie May's door, in the Shelbourne Road, while she was lighting the fire.'* **(lines 7–10)**

Here the punctuation helps the reader to identify with the young boy as narrator, breathlessly running ahead of himself in his eager imaginings.

> *'I was aware of great distances, of big cloud masses on the horizon, of the fragility of my tyres compared with the rough surface of the road, and everything disappeared in the urgent need to get to the city, to draw out my money, to find myself food and a bed for the night.'* **(lines 30–34)**

In this example, the comma is used to separate items on a list, helping the reader to understand the boy's confusion at being assaulted by so many changing aspects of his journey as well as conveying the urgency of his new-found 'adult' priorities: getting money, food and shelter.

Tone

The use of the first person narrator gives an honesty and child-like intimacy to the overall tone. For example:

'I felt that I simply couldn't return home.' *(line 2)*

'It would be good fun to cycle through sleeping villages and towns ... while she was lighting the fire.' *(lines 7–10)*

' ... and the glimpses I caught of the river were both fascinating and frightening.' *(lines 29–30)*

The predominant tone of paragraph 2 is one of uncertainty: it suggests doubt, hesitancy, even fear. For example:

'I cycled slowly and undecidedly.' *(line 13)*

'I was still uncertain that I should go on.' *(lines 15–16)*

'It was as though it had accompanied me so far and then silently left me and returned.' *(lines 19–20)*

'It was a curious sensation, rather like the moment when you find yourself out of your depth and two inclinations struggle in you — one to turn back in panic to the shallows ... ' *(lines 22–24)*

In paragraph 3 there is a tone of increasing confidence and urgency. For example:

'like a challenge' *(line 26)*

'and that moment of panic gave new energy' *(lines 26–27)*

'both fascinating and frightening' *(line 30)*

'in the urgent need to get ... to draw out ... to find ... ' *(lines 32–33)*

CHAPTER 20 *Prose*

BUILDING BLOCKS TO UNDERSTANDING

 *Developing*

BLOCK A

Understanding of main ideas, central concerns through: *structure; key words and phrases*

BLOCK B

Understanding of significant detail through: *punctuation and tone*

Practice in developing understanding

Chapter 19 showed you how the keystone of understanding of meaning connects and supports all the elements which combine to create a text. Hopefully, you may be already feeling more confident because you are beginning to see how the building blocks work.

With further practice, you will gain in confidence as your skills develop. Work your way through the following two extracts and feel your confidence grow.

EXTRACT A (Mr Stevens, butler to Lord Darlington of Darlington Hall during the 1920s, recalls a conversation he had with the housekeeper of the time, Miss Kenton.)

'I was just thinking earlier, Miss Kenton. It's rather funny to remember now, but you know, only this time a year ago, you were still insisting you were going to resign. It rather amused me to think of it.' I gave a laugh, but behind me Miss Kenton remained silent. When I finally turned, she was gazing through the glass at the great expanse of fog outside.

'You probably have no idea, Mr Stevens,' she said eventually, 'how seriously I really thought of 5
leaving this house. I felt so strongly about what happened. Had I been anyone worthy of any respect at all, I dare say I would have left Darlington Hall long ago.' She paused for a while, and I turned my gaze back out to the poplar trees down in the distance. Then she continued in a tired voice: 'It was cowardice, Mr Stevens. Simple cowardice. Where could I have gone? I have no family. Only my aunt. I love her dearly, but I can't live with her for a day without feeling 10
my whole life is wasting away. I did tell myself, of course, I would soon find some new situation. But I was so frightened, Mr Stevens. Whenever I thought of leaving, I just saw myself going out there and finding nobody who knew or cared about me. There, that's all my high principles amount to. I feel so ashamed of myself. But I just couldn't leave, Mr Stevens. I just couldn't bring myself to leave.' 15

Miss Kenton paused again and seemed to be deep in thought. I thus thought it opportune to relate at this point, as precisely as possible, what had taken place earlier between myself and Lord Darlington. I proceeded to do so and concluded by saying:

'What's done can hardly be undone. But it is at least a great comfort to hear his lordship declare so unequivocally that it was all a terrible misunderstanding. I just thought you'd like to know, 20
Miss Kenton, since I recall you were as distressed by the episode as I was.'

'I'm sorry, Mr Stevens,' Miss Kenton said behind me in an entirely new voice, as though she had just been jolted from a dream. 'I don't understand you.' Then as I turned to her, she went on: 'As I recall, you thought it was only right and proper that Ruth and Sarah be sent packing. You were positively cheerful about it.' 25

'Now really, Miss Kenton, that is quite incorrect and unfair. The whole matter caused me great concern, great concern indeed. It is hardly the sort of thing I like to see happen in this house.'

'Then why, Mr Stevens, did you not tell me so at the time?'

I gave a laugh, but for a moment was rather at a loss for an answer. Before I could formulate one, Miss Kenton put down her sewing and said: 30

'Do you realise, Mr Stevens, how much it would have meant to me if you had thought to share your feelings last year? You knew how upset I was when the girls were dismissed. Do you realise how much it would have helped me? Why, Mr Stevens, why, why, why do you always have to **pretend**?'

I gave another laugh at the ridiculous turn the conversation had suddenly taken. 'Really, Miss 35 Kenton,' I said, 'I'm not sure I know what you mean. Pretend? Why really ... '

'I suffered so much over Ruth and Sarah leaving us. And I suffered all the more because I believed I was alone.'

'Really, Miss Kenton ... ' I picked up the tray on which I had gathered the used crockery. 'Naturally, one disapproved of the dismissals. One would have thought that quite self-evident.' 40

She did not say anything, and as I was leaving I glanced back towards her. She was again gazing out at the view, but it had by this point grown so dark inside the summerhouse, all I could see of her was her profile outlined against a pale and empty background. I excused myself and proceeded to make my exit.

From The Remains of the Day *by Kazuo Ishiguro*

ACTIVITY 1
Structure of narrative
Although part of a much longer section of the novel, this exchange could stand on its own as a mini-narrative.

a) Outline what you see as the beginning, turning point and end point of this 'narrative'.
   What does the structure of the conversation tell you about the nature of the relationship between the two characters?

b) Mr Stevens is the first-person narrator here. Why might this use of first-person narrative affect the reader's view of the situation?

ACTIVITY 2
Structure of dialogue
Consider the length of individual speeches and type of sentence structure used. What do you learn from these structural features of the character of:

a) Miss Kenton

b) Mr Stevens?

ACTIVITY 3
Structure of sentences

'Then why, Mr Stevens, did you not tell me so at the time?' *(line 28)*

'Do you realise, Mr Stevens, how much it would have meant to me if you had thought to share your feelings last year? (lines 31–32)*

'Why, Mr Stevens, why, why, why do you always have to **pretend**?' *(lines 33–34)*

What contribution does the structure of these sentences make to our understanding of how Miss Kenton is feeling at this point in the conversation?

ACTIVITY 4
Key words and phrases
Listed below are some of the key words and phrases used by each of the characters during this exchange.

Look at both lists carefully, then try to suggest what contribution is made by individual words or phrases to your understanding of character and/or situation.

The letter **R** indicates a repeated word or phrase.

Miss Kenton

no idea
how seriously
leaving/leave/left   **R**
so strongly
worthy
respect
cowardice
wasting away
so frightened
finding nobody who knew or cared
high principles
ashamed
don't understand
sent packing
why   **R**
do you realise?   **R**
share your feelings
upset
dismissed
helped me
pretend
suffered   **R**
alone

Mr Stevens

I was just thinking
rather funny
resign
gave a laugh   **R**
I just thought
what's done
hardly be undone
as distressed as I was
now really   **R**
incorrect

unfair
great concern   **R**
not sure I know what you mean
pretend?
one   **R**
disapproved
dismissals
quite self-evident

ACTIVITY 5
Punctuation

> *'I'm not sure I know what you mean. Pretend? Why, really … '* **(line 36)**

> *'Really, Miss Kenton … '* **(line 39)**

What do these examples of unfinished sentences (indicated by the series of dots) suggest about the way Mr Stevens is feeling at this point?

ACTIVITY 6
Tone

Mr Stevens attempts to set a light, relaxed tone for this exchange.

> *'It's rather funny to remember now … '* **(line 1)**

> *'It rather amused me to think of it.'* **(lines 2–3)**

> *'I gave a laugh.'* **(line 3)**

But as soon as Miss Kenton speaks, the tone changes.

a) Examine paragraph two, and indicate what you consider to be the dominant tone of this paragraph. What do you learn of Miss Kenton's character from the tone she adopts during this speech?

b) Look closely at the rest of Miss Kenton's dialogue. What does the shifting tone tell you about of the nature of the relationship between Miss Kenton and Mr Stevens?

EXTRACT **B** (Jack Firebrace, a tunneller during the trench warfare of the First World War, is accused of falling asleep on duty, a court martial offence which could carry the death penalty.)

He had thought himself immune to death; he thought he had hardened himself against it, but it was not so. If they found him guilty they would take him alone at daybreak to some secluded place behind the lines — a glade in a forest, a yard behind a farm wall — and shoot him dead. They would ask members of his own unit, miners and diggers, men who had not even been trained to fire on the enemy, to do the job. Some would have blanks and some would not; no one would know whether the fatal shot had been fired by Tyson or Shaw or Wheeler or Jones. He would fall like the millions of the dead who had gone down into the mud: baker's boys from Saxony, farm labourers from France and factory workers from Lancashire, so much muscle and blood in the earth.

          5

He could not look on this possibility without shaking. When there was a battle or a raid, they   10
expected to die; it was the losses through sniper fire, through shells and mortars, the blowing of
the tunnel, the continuous awareness that any moment could bring death in a number of different
ways that had been harder to understand. Slowly Jack had become accustomed to even this. It
took him a day of sleep each time they went into rest before he could adjust to not being in
constant fear; then he would begin to laugh and tell stories in the surging relief that overcame   15
them. The indifference he had cultivated, however, was to the extermination of the enemy, his
colleagues and his friends; he was not, he now admitted to himself, indifferent to the prospect of
his own death.

He held his face in his hands and prayed to God to save him. There was no task he wanted to
complete, no destiny by which he felt impelled: he merely wanted to see Margaret again. He   20
wanted to touch John's hair. My son, he thought, as he sat in the rain, my darling boy. It
would make no difference to the outcome of the war whether he himself lived or died; it made no
difference whether today it was Turner whose head was blown from his body, or whether
tomorrow it was his or Shaw's or Tyson's. Let them die, he prayed shamefully; let them die, but
please God let me live.   25

From Birdsong *by Sebastian Faulks*

ACTIVITY 1

Structure of extract

Much of this extract is structured in the form of what we call an **interior monologue**, where the reader listens to a character's innermost thoughts and feelings.

Explain what role this structure plays in giving some shape and order to Jack Firebrace's confused thoughts and feelings.

ACTIVITY 2

Structure of paragraph links

Examine the opening and closing sentences of each paragraph as linking sentences. Explain how these links help to clarify the reader's understanding of the subject matter.

ACTIVITY 3

Structure of sentences

a) Many sentences are quite long, complex structures, broken up by the use of the comma, semi-colon and colon.
   Why do you think the writer tends to use these longer, looser structures? (Your response should focus on content and meaning.)

b) *'He wanted to touch John's hair.'* Is meaning affected by the length of this sentence?

ACTIVITY 4

Key words and phrases

The words *'death'*, *'dead'* and *'die'* are repeated several times, giving the reader a clear indication that this is the main focus of Jack's thoughts.

Identify other key words/phrases which are repeated. Can you pick out any key words/phrases which share some similarities of meaning?

Show what further understanding develops from recognition of these key elements.

ACTIVITY 5
Punctuation

'*He had thought himself immune to death; he thought he had hardened himself against it, but it was not so.*' (*lines 1–2*)

'*Some would have blanks and some would not; no one would know whether the fatal shot had been fired by Tyson or Shaw or Wheeler or Jones.*' (*lines 5–6*)

'*He would fall like the millions of the dead who had gone down into the mud: baker's boys from Saxony, farm labourers from France and factory workers from Lancashire, so much muscle and blood in the earth.*' (*lines 7–9*)

What is the relationship in terms of meaning between the various parts of these sentences?

ACTIVITY 6
Tone

The extract opens on a note of fear which, by the end, has built to an anguished tone of desperation.

Explain how this tonal development helps the reader to a better understanding of what is going on inside Jack's head and heart.

Demonstrating

You can do it!

So far you've been concentrating on learning to identify and interpret the building blocks of meaning. You are gaining confidence with every new activity. Now you will need to draw on this new-found confidence to demonstrate that you are able to explore an unseen prose extract, using the tools of textual analysis to uncover what may be several layers of meaning.

Below is an extract from the 1999 Booker Prize winning novel, *Disgrace* by the South African writer J. M. Coetzee. Following this, you will find a full commentary, showing how the key elements of building blocks A and B have helped the reader to an understanding of this extract.

EXTRACT Ⓐ (The central character, David Lurie, teaches poetry at the University of Cape Town. In this extract he has been summoned to the Vice-Rector's office to be questioned about his relationship with Melanie Isaacs, one of his female students.)

He calls the Vice-Rector's office and is given a five o'clock appointment, outside regular hours.

At five o'clock he is waiting in the corridor. Aram Hakim, sleek and youthful, emerges and ushers him in. There are already two persons in the room: Elaine Winter, chair of his department, and Farodia Rassool from Social Sciences, who chairs the university-wide committee on discrimination.   5

'It's late, David, we know why we are here,' says Hakim, 'so let's get to the point. How can we best tackle this business?'

'You can fill me in about the complaint.'

'Very well. We are talking about a complaint laid by Ms Melanie Isaacs. Also about' — he glances at Elaine Winter — 'some pre-existing irregularities that seem to involve Ms Isaacs.   10 *Elaine?'*

Elaine Winter takes her cue. She has never liked him; she regards him as a hangover from the past, the sooner cleared away the better. 'There is a query about Ms Isaac's attendance, David. According to her — I spoke to her on the phone — she has attended only two classes in the past month. If that is true, it should have been reported. She also says she missed the mid-term test.   15 *Yet' — she glances at the files in front of her — 'according to your records, her attendance is unblemished and she has a mark of seventy for the mid-term.' She regards him quizzically. 'So, unless there are two Melanie Isaacs ... '*

'There is only one,' he says. 'I have no defence.'

Smoothly Hakim intervenes. 'Friends, this is not the time or place to go into substantial issues.   20 *What we should do' — he glances at the other two — 'is clarify procedure. I need barely say, David, the matter will be handled in the strictest confidence, I can assure you of that. Your name will be protected, Ms Isaac's name will be protected too. A committee will be set up. Its function will be to determine whether there are grounds for disciplinary measures. You or your legal representative will have an opportunity to challenge its composition. Its hearings will be held in camera. In the meantime, until the committee has made its recommendation to the Rector and the Rector has acted, everything goes on as before. Ms Isaacs has officially withdrawn from the course she takes with you, and you will be expected to refrain from all contact with her. Is there anything I am omitting, Farodia, Elaine?'* 25

Tight-lipped, Dr Rassool shakes her head. 30

'It's always complicated, this harassment business, David, complicated as well as unfortunate, but we believe our procedures are good and fair, so we'll just take it step by step, play it by the book. My one suggestion is, acquaint yourself with the procedures and perhaps get legal advice.'

He is about to reply, but Hakim raises a warning hand. 'Sleep on it, David,' he says.

He has had enough. 'Don't tell me what to do, I'm not a child.' 35

He leaves in a fury.

From Disgrace *by J. M. Coetzee*

Sample commentary on extract from *Disgrace*

Structure of extract

Overall, the extract has the structure of a brief conventional narrative which begins at the beginning when we sense that normal events are about to be interrupted, moves through a working out of the situation when the reader gathers more background information and learns something of the relationship between the characters, and ends quite dramatically with David's angry exit. This simple, chronological structure should help clarify meaning.

Structure of paragraphs

The extract opens with a short, single-sentence paragraph which arouses the reader's interest because it sets up questions in the mind: why does he have an appointment with the Vice-Rector, and is there any significance in it being *'outside regular hours'*?

The majority of the remaining paragraphs are short, except where the two members of the interview panel, Elaine Winter and Aram Hakim, speak. This seems to suggest that these are the ones who are in control here: they dominate the scene, using their power to direct the interview. The third member of the panel, Farodia Rassool, is dismissed in a single-sentence paragraph and says nothing, reinforcing our understanding of who holds the power in this scene.

Structure of sentences

Sentences tend to be short and direct, reflecting the official and serious nature of the interview. For example:

'It's late, David, we know why we are here ... so let's get to the point.' (line 6)

These short, direct and rather tense sentence structures also help to convey some idea of the strained relationship between David Lurie and the others.

Structure of sentences

There is a repetitive quality to the sentences spoken by Aram Hakim in paragraph 8 (from *'What we should do ... '*). The relentless pace of these lines, piling one piece of official information on top of another, helps to reinforce the notion that David Lurie is powerless against this official force.

This powerlessness is further suggested by the fact that David speaks on only three occasions in very brief, monosyllabic statements:

> *'You can fill me in about the complaint.'* (**line 8**)

> *'There is only one ... I have no defence.'* (**line 19**)

> *'Don't tell me what to do, I'm not a child.'* (**line 35**)

Key words and phrases

The letter **R** indicates a repeated word or phrase.

1	2	3
discrimination	this business	committee **R**
	complaint	disciplinary measures
	irregularities	hearings
	this harassment business	

4	5
strictest confidence	defence
protected	legal representative
in camera	challenge
	legal advice

A careful study of these key groups of words shows that they provide a useful guide to the central concerns of this extract. From these we can gather the following:

> *'this harassment business'*, *'complaint'* and *'irregularities'* indicate the background to the interview

> *'committee'*, *'disciplinary measures'* and *'hearings'* tell us the official consequences of the complaint

> *'strictest confidence'*, *'protected'* and *'in camera'* help us to understand the secretive nature of the whole affair

> *'defence'*, *'legal representative'*, *'challenge'*, and *'legal advice'* all highlight the fact that the proceedings are like a court case with a prosecutor and defence.

Punctuation

The comma after *'appointment'* in the opening sentence helps to emphasize the fact that this is an unusual meeting outside regular hours. This alerts the reader to expect something extraordinary.

The recurring use of dashes to indicate interrupted speech suggest something of the awkwardness of the situation, helping us towards a clearer understanding of the relationship between the characters:

'Also about' — he glances at Elaine Winter — 'some pre-existing irregularities that seem to involve Ms Isaacs.' *(lines 9–10)*

'What we should do' — he glances at the other two — 'is clarify procedure.' *(line 21)*

The second half of this sentence, introduced by the semi-colon, sums up very neatly and clinically why Elaine Winter 'has never liked him':

She has never liked him; she regards him as a hangover from the past, the sooner cleared away the better. *(lines 12–13)*

The series of dots which indicate an unfinished sentence 'So, unless there are two Melanie Isaacs … ', sets the tone of this sentence, thereby adding to our understanding of Elaine Winter as a rather unpleasant character who already despises David and hence is not likely to give him a fair hearing.

Aram Hakim's speech is characterized by a series of question marks, from which we can deduce quite a lot about his approach to the situation:

'How can we best tackle this business?' *(lines 6–7)*

'Elaine?' *(line 11)*

'Is there anything I am omitting, Farodia, Elaine?' *(lines 28–29)*

These examples give us a picture of a man who 'plays it by the book', someone who likes to be seen to be open and fair when, in fact, we suspect that the outcome of this interview will be anything but fair because we know that at least one of the group is prejudiced against David.

Tone
The tone of the short, direct sentences helps to build an awareness of the mood of the situation as well as developing an understanding of character. For example, Aram Hakim's character is conveyed in the brusque opening tone of:

'It's late, David, we know why we are here, . . . so let's get to the point.' *(line 6)*

The phrase 'pre-existing irregularities' captures an awkward tone, suggesting that Hakim feels a little reluctant to use anything more direct than this description; he wants to smooth things over.

This desire to smooth things over is heard at a later point in the soothing, conciliatory tone of:

'Friends, this is not the time or place to go into substantial issues.' *(line 20)*

A final condescending, even arrogant voice is heard as he tells David:

' … we believe our procedures are good and fair, so we'll just take it step by step, play it by the book. My one suggestion is, acquaint yourself with the procedures and perhaps get legal advice.' *(lines 32–33)*

Elaine Winter's voice shifts from a cold, officious tone — 'If that is true, it should have been reported' *(line 15)* — to a mocking, sneering one: 'So, unless there are two Melanie Isaacs … ' *(lines 17–18)*

David Lurie's frank but rather wearied, even submissive, tone in the early stages of the interview suggests that he can't be bothered with the proceedings; he just wants to end the interview and escape.

'There is only one', he says, 'I have no defence.' (**line 19**)

His final outburst, however, shows a different side to his character as he explodes:

'Don't tell me what to do, I'm not a child.' (**line 35**)

Demonstrating understanding

In summary, using the building blocks approach, several readings of this extract have revealed in terms of meanings a clearer understanding of the following aspects:

- ◆ situation
- ◆ mood/atmosphere
- ◆ character
- ◆ relationships
- ◆ theme(s).

EXTRACT Ⓑ (In 1943 Hanna Schmitz had joined the SS and worked as a prison guard in Auschwitz and elsewhere. Years later she, together with a number of others, is standing trial, accused of a number of crimes against those prisoners she had been instructed to guard. The narrator, the 'I' in this extract, is a young lawyer who has had a very special relationship with Hanna but who has known nothing of her past life as a prison guard.)

'You stated that you knew you were sending the prisoners to their deaths — that was only true of you, wasn't it? You cannot know what your colleagues knew. Perhaps you can guess, but, in the final analysis you cannot judge, is that not so?' Hanna was asked by one of the other defendants' lawyers.

'But we all knew ... '   5

'Saying "we", "we all" is easier than saying "I", or "I alone", isn't it? Isn't it true that you and only you had special prisoners in the camp, young girls, first one for a period, and then another one?'

Hanna hesitated. 'I don't think I was the only one who ... '

'You dirty liar! Your favourites — all that was just you, no one else!' Another of the accused, a   10 coarse woman, not unlike a fat, broody hen but with a spiteful tongue, was visibly worked up.

'Is it possible that when you say "knew", the most you can actually do is assume, and that when you say "believe", you are actually making things up?' The lawyer shook his head, as if disturbed by her acknowledgement of this. 'And is it also true that once you were tired of your special prisoners, they all went back to Auschwitz with the next transport?'   15

Hanna did not answer.

'That was your special, your personal selection, wasn't it? You don't want to remember, you want to hide behind something that everyone did, but ... '

'Oh God!' The daughter, who had taken a seat in the public benches after being examined, covered her face with her hands. 'How could I have forgotten?' The presiding judge asked if she   20 wished to add anything to her testimony. She did not wait to be called to the front. She stood up and spoke from her seat among the spectators.

'Yes, she had favourites, always one of the young ones who was weak and delicate, and she took them under her wing and made sure that they didn't have to work, got them better barracks space and took care of them and fed them better, and in the evenings she had them brought to her. And the girls were never allowed to say what she did with them in the evening, and we assumed she was ... also because they all ended up on the transports, as if she had had her fun with them and then she got bored. But it wasn't like that at all, and one day one of them finally talked, and we learned that the girls read aloud to her, evening after evening. That was better than if they ... and better than working themselves to death on the building site. I must have thought it was better, or I couldn't have forgotten it. But was it better?' She sat down.

Hanna turned and looked at me. Her eyes found me at once, and I realised that she had known the whole time I was there. She just looked at me. Her face didn't ask for anything, beg for anything, assure me of anything or promise anything. It simply presented itself. I saw how tense and exhausted she was. She had circles under her eyes, and there were lines on each cheek that ran from top to bottom that I'd never seen before, that weren't yet deep, but already marked her like scars. When I turned red under her gaze, she turned away and back to the judge's bench.

The presiding judge asked the lawyer who had cross-examined Hanna if he had any further questions for the defendant. He also asked Hanna's lawyer. Ask her, I thought. Ask her if she chose the weak and delicate girls, because they could never have stood up to the work on the building site anyway, because they would have been sent on the next transport to Auschwitz in any case, and because she wanted to make their last month bearable. Say it Hanna.

From The Reader *by Bernhard Schlink*

ACTIVITY

Now it's your turn to demonstrate what you've learnt about decoding meaning by exploring the prose extract from the novel *The Reader* by Bernhard Schlink.

Use the following prompts to help direct your discussion of the extract.

Structure

How does the overall structure of the extract help to shape the reader's understanding of the situation? Identify any significant features of paragraph and sentence structure which aid understanding.

Key words and phrases

Identify any key words and phrases. What contribution do they make to your understanding of the situation and/or of character?

Punctuation

Are there any features of punctuation which you recognize as contributing to your understanding? If so, show what contribution is made.

Tone

Tone plays a very important role in helping us to decode meaning. By listening to the voices in this extract, trace the tonal changes, explaining what you learn from each of them about situation, atmosphere, character and relationships.

Apply what you've learnt so far and you'll prove to yourself (and to your teacher) that you can do it.

CHAPTER 22 *Prose*

BUILDING BLOCKS TO ANALYSIS AND EVALUATION

 Learning

Armed with the building blocks to understanding dealt with in the last three chapters, you're now ready to extend your skills to enable you to respond more fully to prose texts. Knowing how to **analyse** and **evaluate** a text will help you to do this.

Look at the SQA criteria for Textual Analysis at Higher.

ANALYSIS | 'Responses explain accurately and in some detail **ways in which** aspects of **structure/style/language** contribute to **meaning/effect/impact**.'

EVALUATION | 'Responses reveal **clear engagement** with the text or aspects of the text and stated or implied evaluation of **effectiveness**, using **appropriate critical terminology** and substantiated with **detailed and relevant evidence** from the text.'

The words in **bold** highlight key ingredients in the process of analysing and evaluating. Some of these require further explanation.

Analysis

'**ways in which**' simply means *how* in a technical sense

'**style**' refers to the distinctive way in which an author uses the various tools of writing

'**effect**' relates to the particular response(s) produced in the reader as a result of the way in which an author has used a specific writing tool

NB Not to be confused with **effectiveness**. See below for note on 'effectiveness'.

Evaluation

'**clear engagement**' means obvious personal involvement with the text

'**effectiveness**' relates to the degree of success an author has had in using specific techniques to communicate effectively with the reader

'**appropriate critical terminology**' means the special vocabulary used when discussing specific literary features: for prose, some of these terms would be *genre, structure, pace, setting, characterization*

'**detailed and relevant evidence**' indicates that whatever statement is being made about a text or aspect of a text, this needs to be backed up by ample evidence which is directly related to that statement

The SQA criteria indicate the skills a candidate needs to demonstrate in order to achieve a pass at Higher in Textual Analysis. Using these as our framework, let's see how they translate into useful building blocks.

BLOCK C *Analysis*	BLOCK D *Evaluation*
Examining aspects of structure, style, language to show HOW they contribute to meaning and effect.	Assessing the effectiveness of a text through personal response, supported by relevant evidence and appropriate critical vocabulary.

Analysis in action

Using the following extract from George Mackay Brown's short story, *Andrina*, let's explore further the **process** of analysis to see how it works in practice.

EXTRACT Ⓐ (An elderly retired sea captain, living on a remote Scottish island, has fallen ill and, during a night-time fever, is haunted by memories of his past.)

I woke tremblingly, like a ghost in a hollow stone. It was a black night. Wind soughed in the chimney. There was, from time to time, spatters of rain against the window. It was the longest night of my life. I experienced, over again, some of the dull and sordid events of my life; one certain episode was repeated again and again like an ancient gramophone record being put on time after time, and a rusty needle scuttling over worn wax. The shameful images broke and 5 *melted at last into sleep. Love had been killed but many ghosts had been awakened.*

When I woke up I heard, for the first time in four days, the sound of a voice. It was Stanley the postman speaking to the dog of Bighouse. 'There now, isn't that loud big words to say so early? It's just a letter for Minnie, a drapery catalogue. There's a good boy, go and tell Minnie I have a love letter for her ... Is that you, Minnie? I thought old Ben here was going to tear 10 *me in pieces then. Yes, Minnie, a fine morning, it is that ... '*

I have never liked that postman — a servile lickspittle to anyone he thinks is of consequence in the island — but that morning he came past my window like a messenger of light. He opened the door without knocking (I am a person of small consequence). He said, 'Letter from a distance, skipper.' He put the letter on the chair nearest the door. I was shaping my mouth to say, 'I'm 15 *not very well. I wonder ... ' If words did come out of my mouth, they must have been whispers, a ghost appeal. He looked at the dead fire and the closed window. He said, 'Phew! It's fuggy in here, skipper. You want to get some fresh air ... ' Then he went, closing the door behind him. (He would not, as I had briefly hoped, be taking word to Andrina, or the doctor down in the village.)* 20

I imagined, until I drowsed again, Captain Scott writing his few last words in the Antarctic tent.

From Andrina *by George Mackay Brown*

The process of analysis could be said to involve three key stages: making a statement about an aspect of structure/style/language; providing relevant evidence to back up that statement, and then commenting on the effect of the selected aspect. For ease of memory, this process can be reduced to a neat acronym, **SEA**:

S   **statement**

E   **evidence**   **(SEA)**

A   **analysis**

Working with a few examples from the *Andrina* extract, let's look at this process in action.

Example 1

statement

The structure of the extract helps to reinforce the idea of a fevered, troubled dream.

evidence

The opening paragraph describes his long night as he slips in and out of wakefulness and sleep, the second paragraph brings us back into the real daylight world, but the final, single sentence paragraph takes us back into the dream world as he drowses once more.

analysis

These movements in and out of the world of dream and the real world contribute to the tense, uneasy atmosphere.

Example 2

statement

The choice of imagery intensifies this uneasy atmosphere.

evidence

For example, the image of a *'ghost in a hollow stone'* is an eerie one.

analysis

The ghost suggests death while the *'hollow stone'* suggests imprisonment. The skipper has awakened from his troubled sleep, feeling as if he has experienced death but cannot rest at peace because something is troubling his spirit, like the restless ghost which is trapped in the *'hollow stone'*.

Example 3

statement

Later images also disturb the reader.

evidence

The *'rusty needle scuttling over worn wax'* or Captain Scott *'writing his few last words in the Antarctic tent'*.

analysis

The *'rusty needle'* refers to the 'needle' of memory going over and over the same episode from his past and leaving behind painful emotions just as a worn needle on a gramophone would scratch the record's surface, damaging it. The word *'rusty'* suggests that he has avoided looking at the episode for a long time while *'scuttling'* conveys the idea of a quick, secretive movement as if he does not really want to look closely at the memory.

Example 4

statement

George Mackay Brown manages to give the reader a lively thumb-nail sketch of the character of Stanley, the postman.

evidence

For example, something of Stanley's teasing humour is conveyed in his words to the dog: *'There's a good boy, go and tell Minnie I have a love letter for her ... '*

analysis

Stanley has already indicated that he's delivering a drapery catalogue but he playfully changes that to a love letter, giving us a glimpse of one aspect of his personality.

evidence

We get a less flattering view of Stanley from the skipper who describes him as '*a servile lickspittle*' who does not bother to knock because he sees the skipper as '*a person of small consequence*'.

analysis

The phrase conveys a picture of someone who's ready to literally lick the boots of someone he regards as socially important in the hope that it's going to get him somewhere. The sound of the word '*lickspittle*' reproduces the sound of Stanley gathering saliva on his tongue ready to grovel before his social superiors.

Example 5   **statement**

Word choice makes a very important contribution to atmosphere.

evidence

The combination of '*tremblingly*', '*ghost*', '*black*', '*night*', '*soughed*', and '*spatters*' creates an uneasy atmosphere.

analysis

The stormy black night provides an appropriate setting for the ghosts of past memories to resurface: the natural world is troubled, like the man's mind. '*Tremblingly*' reinforces the ominous mood, helping the reader to sense the disturbing nature of his dreams.

ACTIVITY 1

Now try to provide **evidence** and **analysis** to support the following statements, using the examples above to help you.

statements

1   The sentence structure of paragraph one reflects the dramatic nature of the night's events.

2   The extract partly relies for effect on the element of contrast.

3   Word choice and imagery make a significant contribution to the mood of the extract.

Evaluation in action

Although we've separated the two areas of analysis and evaluation for teaching purposes, they are, of course, very closely related. Often your evaluative comments will be based on specific aspects which you've already analysed. The emphasis, however, will be different. If you look at **building block D** again, you'll see that the focus is on assessing the **effectiveness** of a text or aspects of a text through the following elements:

personal response
relevant evidence
appropriate critical vocabulary

Assessing the effectiveness of a text through personal response, supported by relevant evidence and appropriate critical vocabulary.

Let's go back to the *Andrina* extract to see some examples of the **evaluative process** in action.

Example 1

(PR) I feel that George Mackay Brown is particularly skilled in creating an atmosphere (CV) which draws the reader into the narrative (CV). The weather conditions are described in such a way that we can hear the storm blowing outside: the onomatopoeic (CV) '*soughed*' and '*spatter*' are especially effective (E). The night is described as '*the longest of my life*', giving us an accurate picture of the man's distressed mood. Repetition (CV) within the phrases '*again and again*' and '*time after time*' underline this idea of a never-ending night haunted by a recurring bad dream (E). Here, I feel a real sense of pity for the skipper who is clearly tortured by his memories which he describes as '*dull and sordid events*' (PR).

(PR = personal response; E = evidence; CV = critical vocabulary)

Example 2

(PR) The author successfully heightens the significance of the incident for me by using a series of contrasts (CV). The stormy black night passes into '*a fine morning*' which brings the postman '*like a messenger of light*' (E). His cheerful voice breaks the human silence of the previous four days. Similarly, the images of death in the form of the ghost, the '*dead fire*' and the reference to Captain Scott's last words, are contrasted with lively images (CV) of Ben's loud barking and the postman's cheery remarks (E). There seems to be extra significance in the contrasts in the line:

'*Love had been killed but many ghosts had been awakened.*' (E)

This effective use of contrasts (CV) helps me to understand something of the man's emotional turmoil: I see him tossing on his bed throughout the stormy night, haunted by ghosts from the past and feeling he may not see the morning (PR).

ACTIVITY 2

I found myself drawn into the story right from the start because the first-person narrative helped me to empathize with the character's predicament (PR).

Try to expand on this response, using 'relevant evidence' (E) and 'appropriate critical vocabulary' (CV) to back up what you say. Use the examples above to help you.

CHAPTER 23 *Prose*

BUILDING BLOCKS TO ANALYSIS AND EVALUATION

 *Developing*

Practice in developing the skills of analysis and evaluation

The next two extracts aim to provide you with opportunities to develop specific analytical and evaluative skills by focusing on key aspects of each text and exploring *how* individual writers have achieved particular effects and assessing their effectiveness.

EXTRACT A (Anna finds an old rocking horse stored in her grandfather's garden shed. She longs to free it from the winter ice which has coated it during its stay in the freezing shed.)

In her dream the ice horse was silver, his ice coat shone through with a million stars. Anna swept a cloth across his side and the shell melted in an instant. She climbed on his back and lay there, felt the surface beneath start to prick like pins and needles in the rising warmth. His carved mane was transformed into soft strands, which she gripped as the horse began to move. He picked up speed and they galloped across a huge expanse of sand, ghost-white under a clouded moon. Anna clung to his back. She could hear his harsh breath, see steam issue from his nostrils. Suddenly he stopped dead and she shot over his neck, the mane wrenched from her fingers, damp sand burning her limbs as she slid along the beach; then she woke, sitting up in bed, soaked with sweat.

From The Ice Horse *by Anne Donovan*

ACTIVITY

a) Focus of interest for analysis: creation of appropriate mood/atmosphere.

How?

Areas for consideration:
- structure (narrative structure and sentence structure)
- language (particularly language of colour and language which appeals to the senses)
- contrast.

How would you describe the mood or atmosphere of this paragraph?

Using the three listed areas for consideration as the basis for your discussion, explore *how* each of these areas helps the writer to build atmosphere.

Remember to support your statements with evidence and analysis (SEA). Use the examples in Chapter 22 to remind you of the process of analysis.

b) Focus of interest for evaluation: the creation of a child's dream world.

How effective?

How successful do you feel the writer has been in recreating the dream world of a child?

Remember to show a personal response to the extract, using relevant evidence and appropriate critical vocabulary when making your evaluation. Use the examples in Chapter 22 to remind you of the process of evaluation.

EXTRACT **B** (Twelve-year-old Owen has been sent to a Borstal Home in a remote part of Ireland run by a religious order. Michael, one of the Brothers at the Home, decides to take Owen away from what he regards as a brutal and unloving environment. In this scene they are on the run in London.)

Michael couldn't help feeling slightly annoyed at the boy, annoyed that Owen had not once thanked him for any of the presents that he had bought — the watch, nothing. He argued with himself that the boy had never been **taught** *to thank people, that he had rarely, if ever, been given presents before. Nevertheless he felt irked that the boy had not the spontaneous goodwill to say thanks.* 5

The ceilidh music drummed in his ear. The tunes all seemed to be the same.

'Is there no good music on that thing?' said Owen, as if echoing Michael's thought.

'Hold it,' said Michael, getting up into a sitting position. He took a piece of still tacky Sellotape from the wrapping round one of the parcels, and stuck it on to the perspex waveband of the radio to coincide with the pointer at Radio Eireann. 10

'Now we'll never get lost,' he said and twiddled the knob until he heard sounds of rock music.

'That's better,' said Owen.

Michael gathered up the litter they had created and stuffed it into a bag. He was on his knees and pretending to jive to the music.

'Hey, Michael.' 15

'What?' It was the first time Owen had used his real name.

'Here's something for you.'

The boy extended his hand to Michael. In it was a cardboard and cellophane pack. It was a Papermate pen. He broke open the cellophane and took it out.

'It's a beauty. Thanks.' The boy grinned. Michael's voice suddenly dropped a tone. 'Where did you get it? You have no money.' 20

'In the shop. Where you bought the cash book.'

'But you have no money.'

The boy shrugged and smiled.

'You can wipe that smile off your face,' shouted Michael. 'Do you realise the risk you took? Jesus, Owen, if you're caught at that game and hauled into the manager's office it's the police. COPS. They'll be swarming all over us asking questions and THAT'S IT. Prison for me and an express trip back to the Home for you.' 25

Michael shook his head in disbelief and shuddered at what had nearly happened to them. When he looked at the boy he saw he was crying. It was the first time he had ever seen him cry. Not 30 *even the beatings in the Home, or the time his collar bone was broken had he seen tears come out of his eyes.*

He fiddled with the pen, not knowing what to do. The boy came towards him and Michael put his arms around him. He was still kneeling and the boy came to the height of his head. He encircled him with his arms and hugged him. He felt Owen relax into his hug and cry more bitterly, shuddering with each breath. 35

'O.K., Mister,' Michael said. 'It's the nicest present I ever got. But why didn't you nick a better one?'

The boy laugh-cried into his shoulder. Michael groped for a hanky and gave it to him. He noticed a park keeper walking in their direction. He held the boy at arm's length. 40

'Dry up and let's go,' he said. Owen stopped crying and turned to watch the uniformed keeper walk past them.

'Never again?' asked Michael.

'Never again,' said Owen. 'Your chin is rough.'

From Lamb *by Bernard MacLaverty*

ACTIVITY

a) Focus of interest for analysis: development of a relationship.

How?
Areas for consideration:
- dialogue
- tone
- word choice
- authorial voice
- symbolism.

Using the listed areas for consideration as the basis for your discussion, explore how each of these areas helps the writer to convey the development of the relationship between Michael and Owen.

Remember to support your statements with evidence and analysis (SEA). Use the examples in Chapter 22 to remind you of the process of analysis.

b) Focus of interest for evaluation: characterization.

How effective?
Based on what you learn of him from this extract, how convincing do you find Michael as a character?

Remember to show a personal response to the extract, using relevant evidence and appropriate critical vocabulary when making your evaluation. Use the examples in Chapter 22 to remind you of the process of evaluation.

CHAPTER 24 *Prose*

BUILDING BLOCKS TO ANALYSIS AND EVALUATION

 ## *Demonstrating*

Demonstrating analysis and evaluation

In Chapter 21 we explored an extract from *Disgrace* using the building blocks to understanding in order to provide a working model as preparation for your independent study of a text.

Now we're going to apply the **building blocks of analysis and evaluation** to this same extract in preparation for your own independent study of another unseen extract.

BLOCK C *Analysis*	**BLOCK D** *Evaluation*
Examining aspects of structure, style, language to show HOW they contribute to meaning and effect.	Assessing the effectiveness of a text through personal response, supported by relevant evidence and appropriate critical vocabulary.

But first, as part of that preparation, a reminder about **denotation** and **connotation**.

Analysis of language

To ensure that writing is to be effective, a writer makes certain of using the tools of language with care and precision. Word choice not only communicates literal meaning (**denotation**) but, in many cases, it sets up a range of additional associations in the reader's mind. These associations, or **connotations** as they are correctly known, are what gives a piece of writing its rich layers.

Imagine a group of words represented by a row of coins, each with a different value: some words do not 'buy' you very much meaning while others can 'buy' you a rich range of meanings. Look at this example.

The car (choked) on the dense fog, (puffing) out great clouds of (breathy) fumes.

The word '*car*' has only a literal or denotative meaning. The words '*choked*', '*puffing*', and '*breathy*', however, have several interesting connotations: '*choked*' is being used figuratively as personification, which sets up a picture in our minds of the car as a person struggling to breathe in the polluted air, coughing as he is overwhelmed by the fumes. '*Puffing*' develops this figurative meaning to give us a picture of the car blowing out exhaust fumes as a person might blow out polluted air. '*Breathy*' continues to develop meaning by suggesting the kind of panting rhythm which might accompany this blowing out of air.

In your analysis of language features you should look out for words with connotative value and know how to explore any relevant **connotations.**

Sample commentary on *Disgrace* extract

Use the sample commentary which follows this extract to help you in your own independent exploration of the second, unseen extract in this chapter.

EXTRACT A (The central character, David Lurie, teaches poetry at the University of Cape Town. In this extract he has been summoned to the Vice-Rector's office to be questioned about his relationship with Melanie Isaacs, one of his female students.)

He calls the Vice-Rector's office and is given a five o'clock appointment, outside regular hours.

At five o'clock he is waiting in the corridor. Aram Hakim, sleek and youthful, emerges and ushers him in. There are already two persons in the room: Elaine Winter, chair of his department, and Farodia Rassool from Social Sciences, who chairs the university-wide committee on discrimination. 5

'It's late, David, we know why we are here,' says Hakim, 'so let's get to the point. How can we best tackle this business?'

'You can fill me in about the complaint.'

'Very well. We are talking about a complaint laid by Ms Melanie Isaacs. Also about' — *he glances at Elaine Winter* — *'some pre-existing irregularities that seem to involve Ms Isaacs.* 10 *Elaine?'*

Elaine Winter takes her cue. She has never liked him; she regards him as a hangover from the past, the sooner cleared away the better. 'There is a query about Ms Isaac's attendance, David. According to her — I spoke to her on the phone — she has attended only two classes in the past month. If that is true, it should have been reported. She also says she missed the mid-term test. 15 *Yet'* — *she glances at the files in front of her* — *'according to your records, her attendance is unblemished and she has a mark of seventy for the mid-term.' She regards him quizzically. 'So, unless there are two Melanie Isaacs ...'*

'There is only one,' he says. 'I have no defence.'

Smoothly Hakim intervenes. 'Friends, this is not the time or place to go into substantial issues. 20 *What we should do'* — *he glances at the other two* — *'is clarify procedure. I need barely say, David, the matter will be handled in the strictest confidence, I can assure you of that. Your name will be protected, Ms Isaac's name will be protected too. A committee will be set up. Its function will be to determine whether there are grounds for disciplinary measures. You or your legal representative will have an opportunity to challenge its composition. Its hearings will be held* 25 *in camera. In the meantime, until the committee has made its recommendation to the Rector and the Rector has acted, everything goes on as before. Ms Isaacs has officially withdrawn from the course she takes with you, and you will be expected to refrain from all contact with her. Is there anything I am omitting, Farodia, Elaine?'*

Tight-lipped, Dr Rassool shakes her head. 30

'It's always complicated, this harassment business, David, complicated as well as unfortunate, but we believe our procedures are good and fair, so we'll just take it step by step, play it by the book. My one suggestion is, acquaint yourself with the procedures and perhaps get legal advice.'

He is about to reply, but Hakim raises a warning hand. 'Sleep on it, David,' he says.

He has had enough. 'Don't tell me what to do, I'm not a child.'

35

He leaves in a fury.

From Disgrace *by J. M. Coetzee*

Analysis of language: word choice

In paragraph I Aram Hakim is described as *'sleek and youthful'*. *'Sleek'* has animal **connotations**, as it is often used to describe an animal's silky coat. The sound of the word suggests a smooth, even sly character: the adverb *'smoothly'* is also used at a later point to describe Hakim's actions; its similarity to the word 'slick' helps to reinforce these associations. *'Youthful'* sets up a deliberate tension between Hakim and David, whose age is not disclosed but we guess that he is an older man.

Hakim *'ushers'* rather than simply 'shows' David into the interview room: the word suggests a formal setting where someone in charge is showing the way. There is an official briskness about the expression.

The word *'discrimination'* here carries **ironic** overtones: David finds himself being questioned by people who seem to disapprove of him. They are already prejudiced against him and yet indicate that their procedures are *'good and fair'*. We suspect, however, that their procedures will discriminate against David.

Hakim uses the terms *'this business'*, *'irregularities'*, *'substantial issues'*, all of which are **euphemisms** (indirect terms) which seem to suggest a character who lacks courage — he hides behind these bland terms, unwilling to confront the issue directly.

In paragraph 6, Elaine Winter *'takes her cue'* (**line 12**): she is like an actress waiting to come on stage and perform; the suggestion is that she has rehearsed her lines for her part in this 'drama'.

The **metaphor** *'a hangover from the past'* captures Elaine Winter's attitude to David: *'hangover'* carries **connotations** of a lingering feeling of nausea, of a bad taste left in the mouth, of listlessness and an aching head. To Elaine, David is all of these things and, like an alcoholic hangover, *'the sooner cleared away the better'*.

Hakim uses a particular **register**, the language of officialese, which points to a man who is at home in the world of bureaucratic red tape: *'clarify procedure'*; *'strictest confidence'*; *'committee'*; *'disciplinary measures'*; *'legal representative'*; *'hearings held in camera'*; *'officially withdrawn'* are all expressions that support this view of him as someone who does things *'by the book'*.

David's use of the expression *'no defence'* carries with it the idea of a trial in which he stands as the accused with no defence lawyer to speak for him against his prosecutors.

His use of the word *'child'* helps to reinforce this suggestion of his vulnerability, of being at the mercy of powerful forces.

Analysis of style

The overall impression of the **style** of this extract is of writing which is economical in its use of language with no decorative descriptions. The **pace** of the **narrative** and of the **dialogue** is brisk, in keeping with the dominant **tone**, which is business-like, at times, even brusque.

Similarly, the **narrative voice** is cool and detached, in the style of **reportage**.

The **setting** is anonymous, a nondescript office somewhere in the university. This anonymity of setting heightens the impact of the human drama, because there are no details of setting to distract the reader.

Evaluating effectiveness

The extract sets out to show a character, David Lurie, against whom a complaint has been made by one of his female students, being questioned by a panel of fellow university academics. It is a tense and difficult situation for all parties concerned. How successful is J. M. Coetzee in recreating the awkwardness and tension of such a situation?

The opening sentence effectively places the reader on edge:

' ... *a five o'clock appointment, outside regular hours.*' (**E**)

This is no ordinary meeting, it is an '*appointment*' with no less a person than the Vice-Rector and it has been scheduled outside normal working hours.

Thereafter the **pace**, **language**, **tone** and **character** (**CV**) all play a part in creating an uneasy, strained atmosphere. I feel the author is particularly successful in the way in which he presents the interview panel as the people with the power and David as the vulnerable accused who is given little opportunity to speak and to whom very little sympathy or loyalty is shown by his colleagues (**PR**). The character Elaine Winter comes across as vindictive, regarding David as '*a hangover from the past*' (**E**) and simply wanting to clear him away as soon a possible, like so much litter. She adds to the tension (**CV**) by pointing up discrepancies in his record keeping and by addressing him in mocking tones:

'*So, unless there are two Melanie Isaacs* ... ' (**E**)

Aram Hakim's language and behaviour also contribute to the feeling that the panel, not David, is in control of the meeting: he '*ushers*' him in at the start of the proceedings and then takes command of the situation, listing every detail of the '*procedure*', thereby building tension until David can take no more and reacts angrily: '*Don't tell me what to do, I'm not a child.*'

The '*sleek*' Hakim becomes quite a threatening figure when he tries to stop David from speaking by raising a '*warning hand*'. You can feel the sinister power of this man under his smooth exterior and this underlying threat heightens the tension (**PR**).

Finally, the brisk pace (**CV**) of the event makes me feel uneasy: it seems to be a question of getting the uncomfortable matter over with as quickly as possible (**PR**). From the moment when Hakim opens the interview with the words: '*It's late, David, we know why we are here … so let's get to the point*' (**E**), there is a sense of this being a rehearsed event with each member of the panel knowing his/her lines and coming in on '*cue*' so that David does not seem to have an opportunity to interrupt the performance.

J. M. Coetzee gets inside the situation and communicates a strong sense of the tensions and discomfort which one would expect to find under these circumstances.

Demonstrating analysis and evaluation

In summary, using the building blocks approach to analysis and evaluation, several readings of this extract have revealed a clearer awareness of the following aspects:

- style
- language
- situation
- mood/atmosphere
- dialogue
- narrative voice
- character
- relationships
- personal response to all of the above.

EXTRACT Ⓑ

It was a grand old house, the Ayemenem House, but aloof-looking. As though it had little to do with people that lived in it. Like an old man with rheumy eyes watching children play, seeing only transience in their shrill elation and their wholehearted commitment to life.

The steep, tiled roof had grown dark and mossy with age and rain. The triangular wooden frames fitted into the gables were intricately carved, the light that slanted through them and fell in patterns on the floor was full of secrets. Wolves, Flowers, Iguanas. Changing shape as the sun moved through the sky. Dying punctually, at dusk. 5

The doors had not two, but four shutters of panelled teak so that in the old days, ladies could keep the bottom half closed, lean their elbows on the ledge and bargain with visiting vendors without betraying themselves below the waist. Technically, they could buy carpets, or bangles, with their breasts covered and their bottoms bare. Technically. 10

Nine steep steps led from the driveway up to the front verandah. The elevation gave it the dignity of a stage and everything that happened there took on the aura and significance of performance. It overlooked Baby Kochamma's ornamental garden, the gravel driveway looped around it, sloping down towards the bottom of the slight hill that the house stood on. 15

It was a deep verandah, cool even at midday, when the sun was at its scorching best.

When the red cement floor was laid, the egg white from nearly nine hundred eggs went into it. It took a high polish.

Below the stuffed, button-eyed bison head, with the portraits of her father-in-law and mother-in-law on either side, Mammachi sat in a low wicker chair at a wicker table on which stood a 20 *green glass vase with a single stem of purple orchids curving from it.*

The afternoon was still and hot. The air was waiting.

From The God of Small Things *by Arundhati Roy*

ACTIVITY

Now it's your turn to demonstrate what you've learnt about analysis and evaluation by exploring the prose extract from the novel *The God of Small Things* by Arundhati Roy.

Directing discussion on analysis and evaluation

Use the following prompts to help direct your discussion of the extract.

◆ How do word choice and imagery help to create a detailed picture of setting? (Analysis)

◆ Comment on the effect of sentence structure and rhythm on the atmosphere of the scene. (Analysis)

◆ How effective is the writer in communicating to the reader something of the exotic character of the setting for the Ayemenem House? (Evaluation)

CHAPTER 25 *Poetry*

BUILDING BLOCKS TO UNDERSTANDING

 Learning

Introduction

A poet relies on skilful use of the tools of language – **sound**, **form** and **structure** – to stimulate readers' imaginations and to arouse their senses.

One meaningful approach to furthering our understanding, analysis and evaluation of poetry, therefore, is to develop an awareness of how these key aspects interact with each other:

- ◆ Poetry as **form** and **structure**
- ◆ Poetry as **sound**
- ◆ Poetry as **language**.

If we translate these into building blocks to understanding poetry, they look like this:

BLOCK A	BLOCK B
Understanding of main ideas, central concerns through: *form and structure; key words and phrases*	Understanding of significant detail through: *tone and imagery*

Let's begin with a specific poetry text, to see how these building blocks work in action to help reveal meaning.

TEXT A

title taken from Shakespeare's <u>Macbeth</u>, who begins a famous speech with the words: 'Out, out, brief candle . . .' (the extinguished candle symbolizes the end of life)

'Out, Out —'

(effect of run-on lines or <u>enjambment</u> on rhythm of opening section?)

    The buzz saw snarled and rattled in the yard
    And made dust and dropped stove-length sticks of wood,
    Sweet-scented stuff when the breeze drew across it.
    And from there those that lifted eyes could count
5   Five mountain ranges one behind the other
    Under the sunset far into Vermont.
    And the saw snarled and rattled, snarled and rattled,
    As it ran light, or had to bear a load.
    And nothing happened: day was all but done.
10   Call it a day, I wish they might have said
    To please the boy by giving him the half hour
    That a boy counts so much when saved from work.
    His sister stood beside them in her apron
    To tell them 'Supper'. At the word, the saw,
15   As if to prove saws knew what supper meant,

sensuous imagery helps to establish atmosphere

poem starts with a specific incident of cutting wood . . . set against a clearly visualized landscape

ominous note sounded

menacing repetition breaks the tranquil mood of the opening five lines

irony in the normality of the domestic scene

145

sinister
personification
of the saw

end of line positioning
exclamation mark
emphasize the horror

Leaped out at the boy's hand, or seemed to leap —
He must have given the hand. However it was,
Neither refused the meeting. But the hand!
The boy's first outcry was a rueful laugh,

20 As he swung toward them holding up the hand
Half in appeal, but half as if to keep
The life from spilling. Then the boy saw all —
Since he was old enough to know, big boy
Doing a man's work, though a child at heart —

25 He saw all spoiled. 'Don't let him cut my hand off —
The doctor, when he comes. Don't let him sister!'
So. But the hand was gone already.
The doctor put him in the dark of ether.
He lay and puffed his lips out with his breath.

30 And then — the watcher at his pulse took fright.
No one believed. They listened at his heart.
Little — less — nothing! — and that ended it.
No more to build on there. And they, since they
Were not the one dead, turned to their affairs.

sympathy aroused by t
highlighted contrast
between the boy's
age and the man's wor
he was doing

matter of fact
tone shocks

tone of desperation
captured in direct spee

imagery of the hospital
scene has a nightmarish
quality

impersonal,
anonymous
term

conclusion captures the
poem's theme: that life
carries on, even after
a tragedy of this natu

Poem is structured as a single verse paragraph in narrative form and bearing the
hallmarks of storytelling (e.g. the frequent use of the conjunction, 'and'). Stages of the
story clearly marked off, using the passage of time ('under the sunset' etc.). The
informal, conversational feel to the language effectively reinforces the narrative genre.

Robert Frost

ACTIVITY 1

Recognizing and interpreting features of form and structure:
narrative

a) This poem is in the form of a narrative structured as a single verse
paragraph but divided into clear stages, each stage marked off by time.
Identify each of these stages, quoting the time phrases which act as
turning points in the story.

b) Tracing the shape of the narrative will help you to understand the central
concerns of the poem. It begins with an apparently ordinary, everyday
event, sawing firewood. What happens to the shape of the narrative after
this specific starting point? Concentrate on the idea of where the story
narrows its focus and where it opens out. Try to draw out this shape on
paper. Use the annotations to help you.

ACTIVITY 2

Recognizing and interpreting features of form and structure: sentence
structure

Look at the pattern of sentence structure in the first eight lines (down to '*bear
a load*'). Pay particular attention to length and punctuation features.

Then look at the pattern of sentence structure in the last eight lines from '*So*' to the end. Again, pay particular attention to length and punctuation features.

How do these patterns help your understanding of what the poet is trying to communicate at each of these key points in the narrative?

ACTIVITY 3

Recognizing and interpreting features of form and structure: key words and phrases
Pick out the key words and phrases, using the annotations to help you.

a) What contribution do these key words/phrases make to your understanding of the poem's central concerns?

b) Pick out two or three **groups** of key words/phrases and indicate what they add to your understanding of events and/or ideas in the poem.

c) There are a number of contrasting words/phrases set up in the text. Identify at least one of these examples and comment on its contribution to meaning.

ACTIVITY 4

BLOCK B

Understanding of significant detail through: *tone and imagery*

Recognizing and interpreting features of style: tone
The changes in tone parallel the developing stages in the narrative, contributing significant detail to the general meaning. After the noise of the opening line, the poem takes on a gentle, peaceful note, reflecting the setting '*under the sunset of Vermont*'. Thereafter there are a number of significant shifts in tone.

Using the annotations to help you, comment on the tone of each of the following quotes and indicate what you learn from each example:

'*And nothing happened*'	*(line 9)*
'*Call it a day, I wish they might have said*'	*(line 10)*
'*But the hand!*'	*(line 18)*
'*Then the boy saw all —*'	*(line 22)*
'*So. But the hand was gone already.*'	*(line 27)*
'*The doctor put him in the dark of ether.*'	*(line 28)*
'*And then — the watcher at his pulse took fright.*'	*(line 30)*
'*No one believed.*'	*(line 31)*
'*And they, since they* *Were not the one dead, turned to their affairs.*'	*(lines 33–34)*

ACTIVITY 5

Recognizing and interpreting features of style: imagery

Like key words and phrases, key images can help to unfold layers of meaning within a text. They are, after all, simply groups of words which, because of their careful selection and juxtapositioning, combine to form word pictures.

In this case, the imagery uncovers the significance of the various aspects of the story, such as the peaceful setting:

'*Under the sunset far into Vermont*' (**line 6**)

and the aggressive saw, which becomes a central 'character' in the narrative:

' *... At the word, the saw ...*
Leaped out at the boy's hand ... ' (**lines 14–16**)

Other aspects of the story are listed below. See if you can find and quote a central image or images which could be said to contribute towards your understanding of each of these aspects.

- the innocent characters of the boy and his sister
- the theme of spoiling, of something ruined
- the chilling, matter of fact tone of reporting
- the detached, impersonal description of the hospital scene.

CHAPTER 26 *Poetry*

BUILDING BLOCKS TO UNDERSTANDING

 Developing

BLOCK A

Understanding of main ideas, central concerns through: *form and structure; key words and phrases*

BLOCK B

Understanding of significant detail through: *tone and imagery*

Practice in developing understanding

In Chapter 25 you were learning to recognize and interpret aspects of meaning within a poem by applying the building blocks to understanding.

With more practice, you will become even more skilled, boosting your confidence in being able to apply these techniques to an unseen text.

Below you will find two complete poems with discussion questions to help you develop further confidence in recognizing and interpreting the keys to understanding.

TEXT A Twice Shy

Her scarf *à la* Bardot
In suede flats for the walk,
She came with me one evening
For air and friendly talk.
5 We crossed the quiet river
Took the embankment walk.

Traffic holding its breath,
Sky a tense diaphragm:
Dusk hung like a backcloth
10 That shook where a swan swam,
Tremulous as a hawk
Hanging deadly, calm.

A vacuum of need
Collapsed each hunting heart
15 But tremulously we held
As hawk and prey apart,
Preserved classic decorum,
Deployed our talk with art.

Our juvenilia
20 Had taught us both to wait,
Not to publish feeling
And regret it all too late —
Mushroom loves already
Had puffed and burst in hate.

25 So chary and excited
As a thrush linked on a hawk,
We thrilled to the March twilight
With nervous childish talk:
Still waters running deep
30 Along the embankment walk.

Seamus Heaney

BLOCK A

Understanding of main ideas,
central concerns through: *form
and structure; key words and
phrases*

ACTIVITY 1

Form and structure of poem

Twice Shy is written in the form of a mini-narrative, an account of an incident which has taken place between a young man and a woman.

In what way is your understanding of the situation helped by the poet's chosen form and structure?

In your discussion you may find it helpful to focus on some or all of the following areas:

- number and length of verses
- line length
- staging points in the narrative
- narrative links such as '*but*' and '*so*'
- the regular rhyme scheme
- pace of rhythm
- repeat pattern in the opening and closing couplets
- significance of title – note the proverb 'Once bitten, twice shy'.

ACTIVITY 2

Structure of sentences and punctuation

> *'Her scarf* à la *Bardot*
> *In suede flats for the walk,*
> *She came with me one evening*
> *For air and friendly talk.'*

Here the inversion of the normal order of the sentence structure highlights the importance the poet wishes to attach to the dress details of the scarf and shoes.

Are there any other features of sentence structure and/or punctuation which bring out significant details of meaning?

You may wish to focus your discussion, in particular, but not exclusively, on the sentence structures in verses two and four.

ACTIVITY 3

Key words and phrases

Key rhyming words, as well as oppositional words/phrases, capture the mood which, in turn, leads us to a better understanding of the young couple's conflicting emotions.

A	B
holding its breath	hawk
tense	deadly
shook	hunting
tremulous	prey
excited	thrush
thrilled	

a) What contribution do these two groups of key words/phrases make to your understanding of the relationship between the two young people?

b) Pick out two or three other individual key words/phrases, or groups of key words/phrases, and indicate what they add to your understanding of this relationship.

c) A number of contrasting words/phrases are set up in the text. Identify two examples of such contrasting expressions. Comment on their contribution to the development of your understanding of the conflicting emotions experienced by the two young people.

ACTIVITY 4

Tone

BLOCK B
Understanding of significant detail
through: *tone and imagery*

Listening to the tonal shifts in *Twice Shy* helps us to understand the complex emotional currents between the two people. For example, the first verse establishes a quiet, low-key, conversational tone:

'*She came with me one evening*
For air and friendly talk.
We crossed the quiet river
Took the embankment walk.'

But, reflecting the shift in the emotional relationship, the tone takes on a tense, excited note in verse two:

'*Traffic, holding its breath,*
Sky a tense diaphragm'

Try to trace the tonal development in the remaining verses of the poem. What do these various tonal shifts add to your understanding of the developing relationship between the two people?

ACTIVITY 5

Imagery

In this poem there is a tension set up between two main patterns of images, reflecting the emotional tension between the man and woman.

One pattern suggests a surface calmness and contrived casualness, which the couple try to maintain during their walk. This is communicated in images such as:

'*air and friendly talk*' (**line 4**)

'*the quiet river*' (**line 5**)

'*classic decorum*' (**line 17**)

'*deployed our talk with art*' (**line 18**)

See if you can pick out those images which form the second pattern, communicating the underlying emotions in the relationship. Try to indicate what specific emotions are being communicated in these selected images.

TEXT **B**   Clockwork

Broken clocks and watches were my father's hobby,
Killing time, he'd say, no irony intended, —
So grandfathers loitered dumbstruck in our lobby,
Hands salaaming as if begging to be mended.

5 Testimonial tokens of lifetimes on the job
Added to his pile their grateful mollusc gape.
Stammering snuff-stain, waistcoat fob —
Tick corrected by puff and scrape.

Eyeglass squinched, he'd read the auguries,
10 Pronounce and whistle, arrange his tiny tools,
Wind the watch until we'd hear it wheeze,
Teaching me to prod among the cogs and spools.

Though my cack-handedness loomed larger through the glass
He didn't mind the knack not passing on.
15 It's a stoic's pastime, letting time pass,
He knew with quartz and plastic his day had gone.

Now Dad's hands are slow and he's lost his spring
His face is scuffed by the emery-paper years
But he can value a clock by its pendulum swing
20 or a watch by the tact of the tick, that he hears

And on Sundays sometimes we will repair
To smile at every bang on mantel chime
So many hundred gloamings unwinding there
My father and I keeping perfect time.

Donny O'Rourke

■ **ACTIVITY 1**

Form and structure

> **BLOCK A**
>
> Understanding of main ideas,
> central concerns through: *form
> and structure; key words and
> phrases*

a) The poem is in the form of a character sketch of the narrator's father,
using his hobby of clock repairing as the vehicle for revealing something
of his personality.

 What characteristics of his father are revealed through the references to his
hobby?

b) Look carefully at the structure of *Clockwork,* including such aspects as:
   - title
   - number, length and shape of verses
   - line length
   - rhyme scheme
   - rhythm
   - time as a linking device.

What overall contribution do these aspects of structure make to:
- ◆ your impression of the father's character?
- ◆ your understanding of the relationship between father and son?

ACTIVITY 2
Key words and phrases

1	2	3	4
clockwork	eyeglass	broken	scrape
clocks	tiny tools	mended	whistle
watches	cogs and spools	corrected	wheeze
waistcoat fob		the knack	tick
			bang

The groups of words in this box highlight one of the central concerns of the poem, the skill and precision of the father's hobby of watch and clock repair.

What other main concerns are communicated through groups A and B, listed below?

GROUP A	GROUP B
lifetime	his day had gone
pastime	lost his spring
pendulum swing	scuffed
perfect time	hundred gloamings

ACTIVITY 3

Tone

BLOCK B

Understanding of significant detail through: *tone and imagery*

One of the keys to understanding the nature of the relationship between father and son featured in *Clockwork* is the recognition and interpretation of tone.

Can you recognize the tones of the following lines? What contribution does each quotation make to your understanding of this relationship?

'*Testimonial tokens of lifetimes on the job*' *(line 5)*

'*Eyeglass squinched, he'd read the auguries,
Pronounce and whistle, arrange his tiny tools,
Wind the watch until we'd hear it wheeze,
Teaching me to prod among the cogs and spools.*' *(lines 9–12)*

'*Though my cack-handedness loomed larger through the glass
He didn't mind the knack not passing on.*' *(lines 13–14)*

'*Now Dad's hands are slow and he's lost his spring.*' *(line 17)*

'*But he can value a clock by its pendulum swing.*' *(line 19)*

'*My father and I keeping perfect time.*' *(line 24)*

ACTIVITY 4

Imagery

Patterns of key images lead the reader to a clearer understanding of both the character of the father and of his son's relationship with him.

The picture of his father as a kind of high priest reading the 'auguries' or signs (line 9), to help him diagnose the problem with a broken watch or clock, reinforces our understanding that this man's hands can work miracles of repair.

a) Identify two or three other images which belong to this pattern, showing us the father is highly skilled at his hobby.

b) Pick out two or three examples from a second image pattern, which focuses on establishing the relationship between father and son.

CHAPTER 27 *Poetry*

BUILDING BLOCKS TO UNDERSTANDING

Demonstrating

Chapter 26 provided you with opportunities to develop the skills of recognizing and interpreting the **building blocks to understanding**. In this chapter the focus will be on demonstrating your new confidence in applying these techniques.

Accompanying the poem *My Rival's House*, you will find a commentary on those aspects which help us to build a fuller understanding of the main, as well as the detailed, concerns of the text. Use this model to help you in your own independent exploration of the final text in this chapter.

TEXT A

My Rival's House

My rival's house
is peopled with many surfaces
Ormolu and gilt, slipper satin,
lush velvet couches,
5 cushions so stiff you can't sink in.
Tables polished clear enough to see distortions in.

We take our shoes off at her door,
shuffle stocking-soled, tiptoe — the parquet floor
is beautiful and its surface must
10 be protected. Dust
cover, drawn shade,
won't let the surface colour fade.

Silver sugar-tongs and silver salver
my rival serves us tea.
15 She glosses over him and me.
I am all edges, a surface, a shell
and yet my rival thinks she means me well.
But what squirms beneath her surface I can tell.
Soon, my rival
20 capped tooth, polished nail
will fight, fight foul for her survival.
Deferential, daughterly, I sip
and thank her nicely for each bitter cup

And I have much to thank her for.
25 This son she bore —
first blood to her —
never, never can escape scot free
the sour potluck of family.
And oh how close
30 this family that furnishes my rival's place.

Lady of the house
Queen bee.
She is far more unconscious,
far more dangerous than me.
35 Listen, I was always my own worst enemy.
She has taken even this from me.

She dishes up her dreams for breakfast.
Dinner, and her salt tears pepper our soup.
She won't
40 give up.

Liz Lochhead

Sample commentary on *My Rival's House*

Form and structure

The poem adopts the form of a descriptive piece of writing, based apparently on a description of 'my rival's house'. But as the poem develops, the descriptive focus shifts subtly from the house to its owner, the 'rival'.

The structure appears, at first, to be rather edgy and disjointed, like the relationship which comes to be the focus of interest. But, in fact, there is a controlling structural pattern, based on a six-line stanza with a transitional section, where the focus shifts from house to woman, building to eleven lines to allow this subtle transition to take place. The poem closes with a shortened four-line stanza punching home its point.

The tension between this underlying, controlled framework and the uneven, edgy surface appearance sums up very well the nature of the balance in the relationship between the nervous girl and the controlling 'rival'.

Our understanding of the complex interplay between the characters in this scene is helped by the setting down of identification markers: '*we*' enters in line 7, followed by the anonymous '*rival*', who finally becomes '*she*' in line 15. '*She*', '*him*' and '*me*' come together in that same line. Thereafter '*daughterly*' (line 22), '*this son*' (line 25) and '*this family*' (line 30) help the reader to unravel the relationships.

Structure of sentences

The uneven line lengths reflect the uneasy relationship and the tug of the power struggle. Overall, the sentences tend to be short, clipped structures which reflect the tense atmosphere of the meeting:

'*She glosses over him and me.*'   **(line 15)**

'*But what squirms beneath her surface I can tell.*'   **(line 18)**

'*She has taken even this from me.*'   **(line 36)**

'*She won't
give up.*'   **(lines 39–40)**

The opening sequence of sentences in list form contribute to our awareness of the importance to the woman of showy, material possessions:

'Ormolu and gilt, slipper satin,
lush velvet couches,
cushions so stiff you can't sink in.'   *(lines 3–5)*

The contracted, verbless sentence:

'Lady of the house
Queen bee.'   *(lines 31–32)*

helps to communicate the idea of a tense power struggle between the two rivals.

Similarly, the use of repetition within some structures helps to reinforce this idea of a battle between two rival factions:

'Soon, my rival . . .
will fight, fight foul for her survival.'   *(lines 19–21)*

'She is far more unconscious,
far more dangerous than me.'   *(lines 33–34)*

Key words and phrases
The word 'surface' is repeated five times, giving a clear indication as to the poem's central theme. Other key words can be grouped under four main headings as set out below.

Luxury	Concealment	Conflict	Power
ormolu	distortions	rival	serves
gilt	dust cover	protected	deferential
satin	glosses	fight foul	thank her
lush velvet	shell	blood	lady of the house
silver sugar-tongs	capped tooth	escape	queen bee
silver salver	polished	dangerous	taken . . . from me
	dreams	worst enemy	
		won't give up	

Taken together, the words and phrases within each of these groups accumulate meanings so that the reader is given a build-up of verbal clues to the main ideas and central concerns running through the text.

Tone
Identifying and tracking the tonal shifts in the poem is an important key to understanding the situation and relationships.

The opening tone is mixed. There is a mocking note in the listings of the plush furnishings of the house:

'cushions so stiff you can't sink in'   *(line 5)*

but, at the same time, there is a note of awe in the description of the pair taking off their shoes and tiptoeing across the parquet floor as if they were entering a holy temple.

Then the tone becomes nervous as she feels *'all edges'* (line 16) but shifts again to a note of bitter realization when she acknowledges that this woman is going to *'fight foul'* to keep her son.

Finally, bitter resentment is heard in the closing lines:

*'She won't
give up.'*

Imagery

The image patterns in *My Rival's House* guide us to a clearer understanding of the various layers of meaning within the poem. By decoding the imagery, we begin to understand that this is a poem, not about an invitation to tea with the boyfriend's mother, but about a number of universally recognized themes:

- keeping up appearances
- power
- rivalry
- jealousy
- hypocrisy.

The woman keeps up appearances in the furnishings of her house and in her own grooming:

*'Ormolu and gilt, slipper satin,
lush velvet couches'*　*(lines 3–4)*

'capped tooth, polished nail'　*(line 20)*

Her power is conveyed through images such as:

'Queen bee'　*(line 32)*

and　*'Deferential, daughterly, I sip
and thank her nicely for each bitter cup.'*　*(lines 22–23)*

Rivalry is seen in the imagery of battle:

*'my rival ...
will fight, fight foul for her survival.'*　*(lines 19–21)*

and jealousy in images such as:

*'And oh how close
this family that furnishes my rival's place.'*　*(lines 29–30)*

Hypocrisy is likewise communicated through key images:

'But what squirms beneath the surface I can tell.'　*(line 18)*

The woman is all politeness on the surface, but the poet knows that this hides something much more sinister. Similarly, the girl hides her true feelings as she *'thanks her nicely for each bitter cup'.*　*(line 23)*

Demonstrating understanding

In summary, using the building blocks approach, several readings of this text have revealed in terms of meanings a clearer understanding of the following aspects:

- situation
- mood/atmosphere
- character
- relationships
- theme(s).

TEXT B

Girl

She is thin as a bird fallen from its nest,
Muscular contractions have violently
returned her to the foetal crouch
but if she is born she will breathe earth.
5   Tubes pour such nourishment into her
as she can bear.
Little grasshopper, are you alive?
She squeaks or gasps or tries
to speak, her eyes roll madly under light,
10   her brain tested says
not dead, tested
says not
dead, tested
says not
15   dead. Wait.
Her parents who are godfearing folk
have examined their consciences and announced on T.V.
they would like to '*see her die with dignity*',
i.e. to kill her. Her
20   priest has examined his rules and announced on T.V.
he sees no reason for not discontinuing
'*extraordinary measures*' of prolonging life,
i.e. killing her. One at least
of her doctors has said they will pull out
25   her life support systems over his dead body.
Wait. The court has tested, said,
not dead, not kill, not
dead, not
kill. And the parents appeal.
30   Wait. Hell smiles, prepares
their life support systems
though they are not ready for the earth.
Calmly they talk at the table, to the cameras.
Don't ever bury their dust
35   by their daughter's dust, that's all.

Edwin Morgan

ACTIVITY

Now, having worked your way through the model commentary on *My Rival's House*, it's your turn to demonstrate what you've learnt about decoding meaning by exploring the poem *Girl* by Edwin Morgan.

Use the following prompts to help direct your discussion of this text.

Form and structure

The poem is written as a single structure, rather than divided into verses.

- ◆ Can you identify the various stages within the structure? How are these stages linked so that meaning is made clear?
- ◆ The poem could be said to be written in a similar form to that of a newspaper article, reporting on the girl's condition and on the views of those involved in deciding her fate.

What similarities in structure can you see between the poem and a newspaper article? Does the visual appearance of the poem on the page contribute in any way to your understanding of the content?

Key words and phrases

Which words and/or phrases would you identify as key ones? Are any of these repeated or set up in opposition to each other?

Tone

- ◆ Can you hear a dominant tone running through the poem? Is so, how would you describe it?
- ◆ Is there more than one tone?
- ◆ How does tone help your understanding of specific aspects of meaning?

Imagery

- ◆ Has any one particular image helped you to unlock some important area of meaning? If so, discuss its significance with the rest of the group.
- ◆ Can you identify a number of similar images which group together to form a pattern? What does this pattern of images add to your understanding of situation and/or character and/or theme?

CHAPTER 28 *Poetry*

BUILDING BLOCKS TO ANALYSIS AND EVALUATION

 ## Learning

Armed with the building blocks to understanding dealt with in Chapters 25–27, you're now ready to extend your skills to enable you to respond more fully to poetry texts. Knowing how to **analyse** and **evaluate** a text will help you to do this.

Look at the SQA criteria for Textual Analysis at Higher.

ANALYSIS | 'Responses explain in some detail **ways in which** aspects of **structure/style/language** contribute to **meaning/effect/impact**.'

EVALUATION | 'Responses reveal **engagement** with the text or aspects of the text and stated or implied evaluation of **effectiveness**, using some **appropriate critical terminology** and substantiated with **some relevant evidence** from the text.'

The words in **bold** highlight key ingredients in the process of analysing and evaluating.

Some of these require further explanation.

Analysis

'**ways in which**' simply means *how* in a technical sense

'**style**' refers to the distinctive way in which an author uses the various tools of writing

'**effect**' relates to the particular response(s) produced in the reader as a result of the way in which an author has used a specific writing tool

NB Not to be confused with **effectiveness**. See below for note on 'effectiveness'.

Evaluation

'**clear engagement**' means obvious personal involvement with the text

'**effectiveness**' relates to the degree of success an author has had in using specific techniques to communicate effectively with the reader

'**appropriate critical terminology**' means the special vocabulary used when discussing specific literary features: for poetry, some of these terms would be *form, structure, rhythm, rhyme, figurative language …*

'**detailed and relevant evidence**' indicates that whatever statement is being made about a text or aspect of a text needs to be backed up by ample evidence which is directly related to that statement.

The SQA criteria indicate what skills a candidate needs to demonstrate in order to achieve a pass at Higher in Textual Analysis. Using these as our framework, let's see how they translate into useful **building blocks**.

Analysis in action

Using the following text, *Angus in his 80s* by Donny O'Rourke, let's explore further the **process** of analysis to see how it works in practice.

TEXT A

Angus in his 80s

In this peaty, puddled land
his spade's excalibur*;
3   at eighty-six, still claiming crop
from gale and sucking bog.
5   The Atlantic's a skiff away —
blue black as plums:
7   with hair like spume
and in gansey* and denims,
he's a fierce tide going out.

excalibur = the magic sword of King Arthur, in Arthurian legend
gansey = a dialectal word for jersey or pullover

Donny O'Rourke

The process of analysis could be said to involve three key stages: making a statement about an aspect of structure/style/language; providing relevant evidence to back up that statement; and then commenting on the effect of the selected aspect. For ease of memory, this process can be reduced to a neat acronym, **SEA**:

S   **statement**

E   **evidence**   **(SEA)**

A   **analysis**

Working with a few examples from *Angus in his 80s*, let's look at this process in action.

Example 1   **statement**

The poet manages to convey a vivid sense of landscape through **word choice** and **figurative language**.

evidence

The inhospitable land is described as '*peaty*' and '*puddled*' (line 1), a land against which Angus has to do battle to '*claim*' (line 3) his crop from '*gale and sucking bog*' (line 4). The seascape of the Atlantic dominates the description, with its waters '*blue black as plums*' (line 6) and its fierce tides.

analysis

The **alliterated** adjectives '*peaty*' and '*puddled*' suggest a dark, heavy soil, waterlogged and difficult to cultivate. The heavy vowel sound in '*puddled*' adds to this feeling of weightiness. This landscape is a challenge against which people like Angus have to do battle: the phrase '*claiming crop*' highlights this idea of an ongoing fight to rescue the crops from '*gale and sucking bog*'. In the **onomatopoeic** word '*sucking*' we can hear the water-soaked land taking down the crops and drowning them. The Atlantic acts as a backdrop to this landscape, with its waters '*blue black as plums*'. This striking **simile** captures the distinctive colour of the water but also suggests something of the changeable nature of the sea: sometimes dark and threatening but, at other times, smooth and velvety like ripe plums.

Example 2   **statement**

The personality of the old man, Angus, is conveyed, in part, through the poem's rhythm.

evidence and analysis

The rhythm is full of vital energy, like Angus. Alliteration in '*peaty*' and '*puddled*', in '*claiming crop*' and in '*blue black*' contributes to this sense of continuous movement. The regular use of the 's' sound in '*spade*', '*sucking*', '*skiff*' and '*spume*' helps to push the rhythm along, forcing its way through the lines like the old man's spade forcing its way through the peaty soil.

analysis

Angus is portrayed as a man of eighty-six, but someone who is a strong, determined and hardy character. The poem's muscular rhythm, helped by the short line lengths and small but strong words, helps us to see Angus as a physically active man, despite his age.

ACTIVITY 1

Using each of the following statements as your starting point, try to find evidence and analysis to support these statements, using the examples above to help you.

statement A

The poet uses carefully chosen examples of simile and metaphor to help paint a picture of the old man, Angus.

evidence

analysis

statement B

One of the poem's central themes could be said to be the enduring courage of man's spirit in the face of a hostile environment.

evidence

analysis

Evaluation in action

Although we've separated the two areas of analysis and evaluation for teaching purposes, they are, of course, very closely related. Often your evaluative comments will be based on specific aspects which you've already analysed. The emphasis, however, will be different. If you look at **building block D** again, you'll see that the focus is on assessing the **effectiveness** of a text or aspects of a text through the following elements:

personal response
relevant evidence
appropriate critical vocabulary

> **BLOCK D** *Evaluation*
> Assessing the **effectiveness** of a text through personal response, supported by relevant evidence and appropriate critical vocabulary.

Let's go back to *Angus in his 80s* to see some examples of the **evaluative process** in action.

Example 1   I find the poem very effective in managing to do a number of things within a very short structure (**PR**). It conveys a strong sense of the nature of both land and sea while, at the same time, Angus comes alive through word choice and metaphor (**CV**). Like the legendary King Arthur, he can work magic on the difficult soil by using his '*excalibur*', his spade (**E**). The contrast between Angus's advancing years and his physical strength and determination is particularly appealing (**PR**): metaphorically (**CV**), he is a '*fierce tide*' but he is also '*going out*' (**E**). In one sense, this suggests the end of his life but, as a tide must turn and come back in, perhaps it also hints at Angus's renewed energy, despite his age. He's a youthful-looking character in his '*gansey and denims*', but with white wispy hair, like the spume from breaking waves (**E**). In a space of nine short lines, Donny O'Rourke successfully communicates a deep sense of affection and admiration for Angus (**PR**).

(PR = personal response; E = evidence; CV = critical vocabulary)

Example 2   I think the poet's word choice (**CV**) is striking and very appropriate (**PR**). The rainy landscape is described as '*puddled*' and, in places, it is a '*sucking bog*'. (**E**) The Atlantic is so near it is only a stone's throw away, '*a skiff away*' as the poet expresses it (**E**). The old man is described in the language of the sea: his hair is '*like spume*' and his force and energy is '*a fierce tide going out*' (**E**). It is as though Angus and his environment are one.

ACTIVITY 2

I found this a very inspiring picture of an old man. The poet succeeds in convincing the reader that this is a man to be admired and respected (**PR**).

Try to expand on this response, using 'relevant evidence' (**E**) and 'appropriate critical vocabulary' (**CV**) to back up what you say. Use the examples above to help you.

CHAPTER 29 *Poetry*

BUILDING BLOCKS TO ANALYSIS AND EVALUATION

 Developing

The next two poetry texts aim to provide you with opportunities to develop specific analytical and evaluative skills by focusing on key aspects of each text and exploring *how* individual poets have achieved particular effects as well as assessing their effectiveness.

TEXT Ⓐ

A Silver Air Force

> They used to spin in the light, monoplanes,
> Biplanes, a frivolous deterrent to
> What had to happen. Silver-winged campaigns,
> Dogfights against death, she blew, and I blew,
> 5 The mobile spun: Faith, Hope and Charity,
> Wing and a Prayer, shot down, shot down in flames.
> I watched, and thought, 'What will become of me
> When she is dead?' I scramble in my dreams
> Again, and see these secret Spitfires fly
> 10 As the inevitable aces of the sky,
> Hanging from threads, a gentle violence.
> But day by day they fell, and each plane crashed
> On far, hereafter wheatfields in God's distance –
> White strings of hope a summer blueness washed.

Douglas Dunn

 ACTIVITY

a) Focus of interest for analysis: creating a unified structure.

How?

Areas for consideration:
- extended metaphor of flying
- connotations (positive and negative)
- contrast
- colour.

Using the four listed areas for consideration as the basis for your discussion, explore *how* each of these areas helps the writer to hold together the central concerns running through the poem.

Remember to support your statements with evidence and analysis. Use the examples in Chapter 28 to remind you of the process of analysis.

b) Focus of interest for evaluation: the communication of feeling.

How successful do you feel the writer has been in communicating his feelings both before and after the death of the person he speaks of in the poem?

Remember to show a personal response to the text, using relevant evidence and appropriate critical vocabulary. Use the examples in Chapter 28 to remind you of the process of evaluation.

TEXTS B

This house has been far out at sea all night,
The woods crashing through darkness, the booming hills,
Winds stampeding the fields under the window
Floundering black astride and blinding wet.

5 Till day rose; then under an orange sky
The hills had new places, and wind-wielded
Black-light, luminous black and emerald,
Flexing like the lens of a mad eye.

From Wind *by Ted Hughes*

Rain. Floods. Frost. And after frost, rain.
Dull roof-drumming. Wraith-rain pulsing across purple-bare woods
Like light across heaved water. Sleet in it.
And the poor fields, miserable tents of their hedges.
5 Mist-rain off-world. Hills wallowing
In and out of a grey or silvery dissolution. A farm gleaming.
Then all dull in the near drumming. At field-corners
Brown water backing and brimming in grass.

From Rain *by Ted Hughes*

The tractor stands frozen — an agony
To think of. All night
Snow packed its open entrails. Now a head-piercing gale,
A spill of molten ice, smoking snow,
5 Pours into the steel.
At white heat of numbness it stands
In the aimed hosing of ground-level fieriness.

It defies flesh and won't start.
Hands are like wounds already
10 Inside armour gloves, and feet are unbelievable
As if the toe-nails were all just torn off.

I stare at it in hatred. Beyond it
The copse hisses – capitulates miserably
In the fleeing, failing light. Starlings,
15   A dirtier sleetier snow, blow smokily, unendingly, over
Towards plantations eastward.
All the time the tractor is sinking
Through the degrees, deepening
Into its hell of ice.

From Tractor *by Ted Hughes*

ACTIVITY

a) Focus of interest for analysis: recreating weather.

How?

Areas for consideration:

- ◆ imagery
- ◆ originality of language
- ◆ sound (including alliteration and onomatopoeia)
- ◆ rhythm.

Using the four listed areas for consideration as the basis for your discussion, explore how each of these areas helps the writer to convey the particular weather conditions in each of the three extracts from *Wind*, *Rain* and *Tractor*.

Remember to support your statements with evidence and analysis. Use the examples in Chapter 28 to remind you of the process of analysis.

b) Focus of interest for evaluation: creating mood.

How successful is Ted Hughes in conveying an appropriate mood to match the weather conditions as described in each of the three extracts?

Remember to show a personal response to the extract, using relevant evidence and appropriate critical vocabulary. Use the examples in Chapter 28 to remind you of the process of evaluation.

CHAPTER 30 *Poetry*

BUILDING BLOCKS TO ANALYSIS AND EVALUATION

 Demonstrating

Demonstrating analysis and evaluation

In Chapter 27 we explored Liz Lochhead's poem *My Rival's House*, using the building blocks to understanding in order to provide a working model as preparation for your independent study of a text.

Now we're going to apply the **building blocks of analysis and evaluation** to this same text in preparation for your own independent study of another unseen poem.

BLOCK C *Analysis*	**BLOCK D** *Evaluation*
Examining aspects of structure, style, language to show HOW they contribute to meaning and effect.	Assessing the effectiveness of a text through personal response, supported by relevant evidence and appropriate critical vocabulary.

But first, as part of that preparation, remind yourself about the difference between **denotation** and **connotation**. See page 139 in Chapter 24.

Sample commentary on *My Rival's House*

Use the following sample commentary to help you in your own independent exploration of the second, unseen poem in this chapter.

TEXT **A**

My Rival's House

My rival's house
is peopled with many surfaces
Ormolu and gilt, slipper satin,
lush velvet couches,
5 cushions so stiff you can't sink in.
Tables polished clear enough to see distortions in.

We take our shoes off at her door,
shuffle stocking-soled, tiptoe — the parquet floor
is beautiful and its surface must
10 be protected. Dust
cover, drawn shade,
won't let the surface colour fade.

Silver sugar-tongs and silver salver
my rival serves us tea.
15 She glosses over him and me.
I am all edges, a surface, a shell

and yet my rival thinks she means me well.
But what squirms beneath her surface I can tell.
Soon, my rival
20   capped tooth, polished nail
will fight, fight foul for her survival.
Deferential, daughterly, I sip
and thank her nicely for each bitter cup

And I have much to thank her for.
25   This son she bore —
first blood to her —
never, never can escape scot free
the sour potluck of family.
And oh how close
30   this family that furnishes my rival's place.

Lady of the house
Queen bee.
She is far more unconscious,
far more dangerous than me.
35   Listen, I was always my own worst enemy.
She has taken even this from me

She dishes up her dreams for breakfast.
Dinner, and her salt tears pepper our soup.
She won't
40   give up.

Liz Lochhead

Analysis of form and structure

The poem is written in the form of a narrative with a very detailed description of setting, a carefully constructed atmosphere, in-depth characterization, together with a strong first-person narrative voice.

The structure of the first section is orderly and controlled — six-line verses with regular use of rhyme, often in the form of rhyming couplets as in 'door'/ 'floor' or 'shell'/'well' (lines 7–8 and 16–17). It has a neat, organized appearance, in keeping with the tidy, orderly house — everything fixed and in its place. This controlled opening, with its tight use of rhyme, reflects the tense, restrained atmosphere of the characters in the narrative: they are all putting on an appearance of politeness which imposes a strain on all of them.

As the poem develops, this initial control becomes looser and more uneven as the narrator sees underneath the surface of the woman's personality and realizes that '*she is ... far more dangerous*' than herself. The woman's brutal determination to fight to control her son's life, as well as the girl's final realization of the absolute strength of that determination, is expressed through a more irregular structure. The final four-line verse punches home the conclusion that:

'*She won't
give up.*'

The structure is held together by the use of key words such as '*surface(s)*' and '*rival*' and by the characters themselves, the '*she*' and '*him*' who form the '*family*', set against the '*I*' and '*me*'. The use of a first-person narrator likewise acts as a unifying device, as all the aspects of the scene are viewed from her sole perspective and related through her voice.

Analysis of sound effects

The predominance of particular consonants, often used in alliterated phrases, helps to establish mood. For example, the sharp 's' sound appears very regularly, suggesting the tense, strained atmosphere of the meeting between the mother and her son's girlfriend, or possible future daughter-in-law. The false, surface smoothness of the atmosphere which accompanies their arrival at the house is conveyed in alliterated phrases such as '*slipper satin*', '*so stiff*', and '*shuffle stocking-soled*'. There is a showy artificiality about the meeting, reflected in the '*silver sugar-tongs*' and '*silver salver*': this atmosphere of deception is reinforced in the hard 'd' sounds of the phrase '*deferential, daughterly*'. The woman '*glosses over*' her son and his girlfriend: the combination of the hard 'g' sound and the double 's' captures her brittle hypocrisy, while the 's' and soft 'c' in '*surfaces*' reinforce this notion of an outward smoothness hiding harsh truths.

We can hear the atmosphere become more biting in the aggressive 'd' and 't' sounds of '*capped tooth*', '*fight*', '*bitter*', '*dishes up her dreams*'. Some other individual words which heighten this atmosphere through sound are: '*distortions*', '*edges*', '*squirms*', '*blood*', '*never*' and '*won't*'.

Analysis of imagery

A number of patterns of images run through the poem, carrying the main themes. The most obvious of these is the group which conveys the central idea of superficiality and hypocrisy. The opening metaphor introduces the theme:

> '*My rival's house*
> *is peopled with many surfaces.*'

The rival, like her house, has many sides to her personality: she is not all that she appears to be, hiding behind her many surfaces, which the narrator later realizes when she observes:

> '*But what squirms beneath her surface I can tell.*' (**line 18**)

Here the word '*squirms*' conveys unpleasant connotations of worms or some other wriggling creatures, writhing about beneath the surface – like the woman's unseen thoughts.

Once the girl realizes this hidden side to her rival's nature, she recognizes that:

> '*She is far more unconscious,*
> *far more dangerous than me.*' (**lines 33–34**)

'*Unconscious*' suggests that there is much more going on deep within the woman than is obvious from her outward behaviour, hence making her a much more serious threat. Inside, she '*dreams*' her son's future, which does not include the girl.

The second image pattern carries the idea of showiness or ostentation: her house is like a museum, full of rich exhibits which remain under dust covers to protect them. They do not contribute to making a 'home', just a kind of show house. The house shows off its furniture:

> *'Ormolu and gilt, slipper satin,*
> *lush velvet couches,*
> *cushions so stiff you can't sink in.*
> *Tables polished clear enough to see distortions in.' (lines 3–6)*

Ironically the cushions, which would normally be luxurious and soft, in this case are uncomfortably stiff. The highly polished tables reflect *'distortions'*, false, twisted images of reality. The *'silver sugar-tongs'* and *'silver salver'* are used as status symbols to show off to her visitors.

Another group of images carries connotations of conflict and power, highlighting the struggle between the two women over 'possession' of the son. Right from the start, despite the fact that she is 'serving' them tea, the woman seems to have the upper hand as she makes the girl feel ' … *all edges, a surface, a shell'* (line 16). And the girl responds to the situation by feigning politeness:

> *'Deferential, daughterly, I sip*
> *and thank her nicely for each bitter cup.' (lines 22–23)*

The word *'deferential'* suggests the idea of bowing before someone you respect or regard as superior. *'Nicely'* carries overtones of a child who has been trained by parents to thank people politely for their hospitality. In this case she is thanking her for *'each bitter cup'*: she knows this conflict will be bitter, bringing pain and suffering.

Some of the images highlight the conflict more directly. For example, the girl begins to recognize that it is going to be open warfare when she says:

> *'Soon, my rival,*
> *capped tooth, polished nail*
> *will fight, fight foul for her survival.' (lines 19–21)*

The second line here echoes the expression 'to fight tooth and nail'. The mother, armed with the 'weapons' of her *'capped tooth'* and *'polished nail'* will do battle with the girl: it will be a dirty fight to the last to ensure the mother's survival. It is literally a matter of life and death for the mother, who sees her role and purpose in life being threatened by a rival for her son's heart.

The girl knows she is going to lose against a rival who is *'far more dangerous'* than herself. She also knows she is her *'own worst enemy'*: she will be too busy fighting against her own nature to engage in battle with this woman who is so determined to win that:

> *'She won't*
> *give up.' (lines 39–40)*

Evaluating effectiveness

How convincing is the character of the 'rival'?

The mother figure seems very credible, someone most people will come across at some point in their lives (**PR**). The poet's effective choice of imagery (**CV**) places her in a setting (**CV**) which reflects her character: like the rather Victorian-style furniture with its '*ormolu and gilt*' (**E**), reminders of a past age, she too lives in the past, unwilling to accept change represented by the girl. She wants things to remain as they are, like the furniture which is protected from change by '*dust cover*' and '*drawn shade*' (**E**).

Her '*silver sugar-tongs and silver salver*' (**E**) not only link her to a past era but also act as status symbols, showing her up as someone who likes to impress by being seen to be doing things '*properly*'. She likes to be the '*lady of the house*', the '*queen bee*'. We can all recognize the type, whether the status symbol is the family silver, the designer clothes or the expensive car (**PR**). We can also recognize the fiercely protective mother whose '*first blood*' is often particularly precious. She is possessive and will do anything to retain that possession. We are told she '*will ... fight foul*' (**E**) to ensure her own survival as the '*queen bee*' (**E**). People like her are dangerous, as the girl recognizes: their determination to keep a hold on the past and to control their children's future, whatever the cost, make them powerful rivals to any contenders (**PR**). The fact that she '*won't give up*' (**E**) the fight makes her particularly ruthless.

The use of first person narrator (**CV**) further ensures that the mother emerges as a believable character: we identify with the narrator's position when she says she feels '*all edges*' (**E**) or when she puts on a veneer of politeness and thanks her '*nicely*' (**E**) for the tea. We also sympathize with the fact that she feels that the mother is a rival: having built a relationship with the son, she is now faced with hostility from his mother.

Liz Lochhead uses a variety of effective techniques (**CV**) to create a believable character. She provides an appropriate and detailed setting (**CV**) for the character, she builds striking images (**CV**) to reinforce aspects of her personality and uses a first-person narrative voice (**CV**) to heighten the tone (**CV**) and create a tense relationship between the narrator and the woman. I found she reminded me of people I have met who live similar lives and whose attitudes to their children's boyfriends or girlfriends, I could imagine, could be very similar to the 'rival's' (**PR**).

Demonstrating analysis and evaluation

In summary, using the building blocks approach to analysis and evaluation, our study of this text has revealed a clearer awareness of the **effect** and **effectiveness** of the following aspects:

- form and structure
- narrative voice
- rhythm
- rhyme
- sound effects
- word choice and imagery
- mood/atmosphere

◆ tone
◆ personal response to all of the above.

TEXT **B**

All Leave Cancelled
(for PC Stephen O'Rourke)

In the temporary mortuary
at the ice rink, you spent Christmas Day
body bagging those the pathologist's knife
had gourded*. You'd asked us round and Life

5   Goes On ... I carved the turkey in your absence
shirking comparisons. Dorothy was tense
the children muted – the crackers they pulled
imploding like a Boeing's pressurised hull

in the dead air space over Lockerbie.
10 While we scoured the floor for debris
of a shattered toy, your colleagues searched
the Galloway Hills for fragments. Perched

on the edge of your empty seat we passed the day
resisting the emblems of Tragedy –
15 in cinnamon-scented candles and kitchen smells;
the reek of putrefaction – parallels.

*gourded = from 'gourd', the fruit of certain types of plants whose dried shells are used for
ornaments or drinking cups

Donny O'Rourke

ACTIVITY
Now it's your turn to demonstrate what you've learnt about analysis and
evaluation by exploring the poem *All Leave Cancelled* by Donny O'Rourke.

Directing discussion on analysis and evaluation
Use the following prompts to help direct your discussion.
◆ How do word choice and imagery help to point up the parallels
between the Christmas lunch and the Lockerbie air disaster? (Analysis)
◆ Comment on the contribution made by punctuation and word
placement to the atmosphere of the Christmas Day scene. (Analysis)
◆ To what extent does the poet succeed in sharing with the reader the
terrible irony of the circumstances surrounding the Christmas Day
'celebrations'? (Evaluation)

CHAPTER 31 *Drama*

BUILDING BLOCKS TO UNDERSTANDING

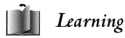 *Learning*

Introduction

Understanding, analysing and evaluating a drama text involves the same core skills as those employed in the textual analysis of prose and poetry. But the genre does have its own distinctive features. Firstly, a play is a visual, as well as a verbal medium: this means it is meant to be watched as a performance, not just read. Secondly, a drama text has its own individual structure: it is usually divided into acts and scenes, and set down as dialogue with stage directions adding important information about such aspects as action, reaction (including facial expression and tone of voice), gesture and so on.

When we read the text of a play, rather than watch it being performed, therefore, we have to take these distinctive features into account.

In the following chapters, you will explore a variety of extracts from drama texts, learning how to build on your skills of understanding, analysis and evaluation. Successive chapters will focus on developing and demonstrating these skills, using a similar building blocks approach to the one which you've already seen in action in the Prose and Poetry chapters.

Building blocks to understanding drama

BLOCK A	BLOCK B
Understanding of main ideas, central concerns through: *structure; dialogue; key words and phrases*	Understanding of significant detail through: *stage directions; punctuation; dramatic conflict*

Let's begin with a specific extract from the drama text *Death of a Salesman* by Arthur Miller, to see how these building blocks work in action to help reveal meaning.

EXTRACT A (Willy Loman is an ageing, failed salesman who cannot understand why his son, Biff, has not experienced the kind of success that his boyhood friend, Bernard, has achieved. In this scene, Willy meets up with Bernard, who is now a respected lawyer.)

Willy *(sitting down)*: What're you going to do in Washington?
Bernard: Oh, just a case I've got there, Willy.
Willy: That so? *(indicating the rackets)* You going to play tennis there?
Bernard: I'm staying with a friend who's got a court.
Willy: Don't say. His own tennis court. Must be fine people I bet.
Bernard: They are, very nice. Dad tells me Biff's in town.

impressed by status symbols: concludes this must make the owners 'fine people'

5

Willy: *(with a big smile)* Yeah, Biff's in. Working on a very big deal, Bernard.

Bernard: What's Biff doing?

Willy: Well, he's been doing very big things in the West. But he decided to establish himself here. Very big. We're having dinner. Did I hear your wife had a boy?

Bernard: That's right. Our second.

Willy: Two boys! What do you know!

Bernard: What kind of a deal has Biff got?

Willy: Well, Bill Oliver — very big sporting-goods man — he wants Biff very badly. Called him in from the West. Long distance, *carte blanche*, special deliveries. Your friends have their own private tennis court?

Bernard: You still with the old firm, Willy?'

Willy *(after a pause)*: I'm — I'm overjoyed to see how you made the grade, Bernard, overjoyed. It's an encouraging thing to see a young man really — really — Looks very good for Biff — very — *(He breaks off, then)* Bernard — *(He is so full of emotion, he breaks off again)*

Bernard: What is it, Willy?

Willy *(small and alone)*: What — what's the secret?

Bernard: What secret?

Willy: How — how did you? Why didn't he ever catch on?

Bernard: I wouldn't know that, Willy.

Willy *(confidentially, desperately)*: You were his friend, his boyhood friend. There's something I don't understand about it. His life ended after that Ebbets Field game. From the age of seventeen nothing good ever happened to him.

Bernard: He never trained for anything.

Willy: But he did, he did. After high school he took so many correspondence courses. Radio mechanics; television; God knows what, and never made the slightest mark.

Bernard *(taking off his glasses)*: Willy, do you want to talk candidly?

Willy *(rising, facing Bernard)*: I regard you as a very brilliant man, Bernard. I value your advice.

Bernard: Oh, the hell with the advice, Willy. I couldn't advise you. There's just one thing I've always wanted to ask you. When he was supposed to graduate, and the math teacher flunked him —

Willy: Oh, that son-of-a-bitch ruined his life.

Bernard: Yeah, but Willy, all he had to do was to go to summer school and make up that subject.

Willy: That's right, that's right.

Bernard: Did you tell him not to go to summer school?

Willy: Me? I begged him to go. I ordered him to go!

Bernard: Then why wouldn't he go?

Willy: Why? Why? Bernard, that question has been trailing me like a ghost for the last fifteen years. He flunked the subject, and laid down and died like a hammer hit him!

Bernard: Take it easy, kid.

Willy: Let me talk to you — I got nobody to talk to. Bernard, Bernard, was it my fault? Y'see? It keeps going around in my mind, maybe I did something to him. I got nothing to give him.

Bernard: Don't take it so hard.

Willy: Why did he lay down? What is the story there? You were his friend!

10

15

20

25

30

35

40

45

50

55

Margin annotations:

repetition of 'very big' suggests a boastful character who wishes to impress: suspect exaggeration

his second reference to the 'private tennis court' underlines how impressed he is by this feature

stage directions, as well as the dashes, give clear indication of Willy's emotional state

captures the intensity of Willy's anguish

indicates Bernard's values

contradicts what he says above about Biff doing 'very big things'

forceful language indicates level of blame

simile conveys the idea of being haunted by the unanswered question; 'trailing' suggests being shadowed by something sinister

dramatic expression hints at the crisis which Bernard describes

theme of guilt & blame

Willy's dialogue is punctuated by the question mark

Bernard: Willy, I remember, it was June, and our grades came out. And he'd   60
flunked math.

Willy: That son-of-a-bitch!

Bernard: No, it wasn't right then. Biff just got very angry, I remember, and
was ready to enrol in summer school.

Willy   *(surprised)*: He was?   65

Bernard: He wasn't beaten by it at all. But then, Willy, he disappeared from
the block for almost a month. And I got the idea that he'd gone up
to New England to see you. Did he have a talk with you then?

(Willy stares in silence)

Bernard: Willy?

Willy   *(with a strong edge of resentment to his voice)*: Yeah, he came to Boston.   70
What about it?

Bernard: Well, just that when he came back — I'll never forget this, it always
mystifies me. Because I'd thought so well of Biff, even though he'd
always taken advantage of me. I loved him, Willy, y'know? And he
came back after that month and took his sneakers — remember those   75
sneakers with 'University of Virginia' painted on them? He was so
proud of those, wore them every day. And he took them down in the
cellar, and burned them up in the furnace. We had a fist fight. It
lasted for at least half an hour. Just the two of us, punching each
other down the cellar, and crying right through it. I've often   80
thought of how strange it was that I knew he'd given up his life.
What happened in Boston, Willy?

(Willy looks at him as an intruder.)

Bernard: I just bring it up because you asked me.

Willy   *(angrily)*: Nothing. What do you mean, 'What happened?'   85
What's that got to do with anything?

Bernard: Well, don't get sore.

Willy: What are you trying to do, blame it on me? If a boy lays down is
that my fault?

From Death of a Salesman *by Arthur Miller*

Annotations (left margin):

short, dramatic stage direction arrests our attention

words suggest defensiveness, hinting that Willy is feeling guilty about the meeting in Boston

compelling narrative holds our attention

echoes Willy's earlier words 'laid down and died'.

the question arouses our interest by hinting at some secret from the past

'intruder' suggests Willy feels threatened by Bernard who is forcing his way into Willy's hidden past like a burglar breaking into one's house

structure of dialogue reflects Willy's defensiveness

key words highlighting central theme

BLOCK A

Understanding of main ideas, central concerns through: *structure; dialogue; key words and phrases*

ACTIVITY 1

Recognizing and interpreting structure of extract

The extract opens as a conventional, polite conversation between two people who haven't seen each other for some time. They catch up with the news:

'What's Biff doing?'
'You still with old firm, Willy?'

a) At what stage in the extract do you detect a turning point in the conversation as it shifts from the general to the specific? What topic now forms the focus for the dialogue between Willy and Bernard?

b) Bernard's detailed account of the fight in the cellar has a key function in the overall structure. How would you describe the part it plays?

   What contribution does it make to your understanding of what might have happened between Willy and Biff on that visit to Boston?

c) The extract ends with Willy's two rhetorical questions:

'What are you trying to do, blame it on me? If a boy lays down is that my fault?'

How is your understanding of one of the main themes of this extract helped by these final questions?

ACTIVITY 2
Recognizing and interpreting structure of dialogue

a) Much of the extract's dialogue is structured as a series of short questions and answers.

What do you gather from this about:
   - Willy's mood?
   - Bernard's mood?

b) The nature of the dialogue changes from this series of short questions and answers during Bernard's extended speech (lines 72–82).
   - What changes do you notice?
   - What impact does this different type of structure have on the atmosphere?

c) 'What happened in Boston, Willy?' (line 82)

What impact does this closing question have on the mood of the remainder of the extract?

ACTIVITY 3
Recognizing and interpreting key words and phrases

The repetition of specific words or phrases within an extract can help the reader to grasp main ideas.

For example, Willy repeats the word 'very' in 'very big' and 'very badly' on four separate occasions. This helps us to see Willy as someone who is prone to exaggeration, perhaps even to lying.

Look at the groups of repeated or similar key words and phrases that Willy uses. They are set out on the next page.

Try to suggest what contribution is made by individual words or phrases to your understanding of character, situation or theme.

The letter **R** indicates a repeated word or phrase.

	1		2		3	
R	secret		own tennis court	R	my fault	
R	that son-of-a-bitch		private tennis court		did something to him	
R	why?				blame	
R	what happened?					

	4
	ruined his life
R	lay/laid down
	died
	beaten
	given up his life

BLOCK B

Understanding of significant detail through: *stage directions; punctuation; dramatic conflict*

ACTIVITY 4

Recognizing and interpreting features of stage directions

Stage directions are the playwright's instructions to the director about a character's actions and reactions, sometimes indicating facial expression and tone of voice. They are recognizable as 'directions' by their distinctive font and by their separation, usually by brackets, from the scripted dialogue.

The information contained in stage directions can add significantly to our understanding of any or all of the following: situation; atmosphere; character; relationships and themes.

For example, in the *Death of a Salesman* extract, one of the stage directions, referring to Willy, reads:

> *He is so full of emotion he breaks off again.* **(line 22)**

This information helps us to understand Willy's fragile emotional state and his reaction to that state.

Look closely at the following stage directions as they are used in context.

(after a pause)	*(line 19)*
(small and alone)	*(line 24)*
(confidentially, desperately)	*(line 28)*
(Willy stares in silence)	*(line 68)*
(with a strong edge of resentment to his voice)	*(line 70)*
(Willy looks at him as an intruder)	*(line 83)*

What does each of these directions contribute to your understanding of any of the following:
- ◆ situation
- ◆ atmosphere
- ◆ character
- ◆ relationships
- ◆ theme(s)?

ACTIVITY 5

Recognizing and interpreting punctuation

a) This extract is dominated by the question mark: this is a scene about two people looking for answers to important questions about the past. If we look more closely, however, we find that the questions are not all of the same kind: some are superficial, others are more searching.

For example, in the early part of the scene, Willy and Bernard ask innocent, general questions:

Willy: What're you going to do in Washington?

Bernard: What's Biff doing?

Later on, however, more significant and quite specific questions are asked by both characters.

Find examples of this type of question. Explain what part they play in giving us clues about Biff's past behaviour.

b) Other significant punctuation marks used in this extract include the exclamation mark and the dash.

Find examples of both and comment on what each tells us about:

◆ atmosphere
◆ character.

ACTIVITY 6

Recognizing and interpreting features of dramatic conflict

At the heart of all drama is conflict: between people; between ideas; within relationships; within individuals. Being able to identify and understand how these conflicts affect action and character is an important skill in textual analysis.

a) One of the most significant types of conflict evident in this extract is the conflict within Willy himself. Find some examples where you recognise this inner conflict at work. In each case, try to describe what is happening to Willy.

b) Identify another type of conflict which the playwright explores in this extract. Give some examples to support your findings. In each case, explain what you learn of the conflict from your given example.

CHAPTER 32 *Drama*

BUILDING BLOCKS TO UNDERSTANDING

 *Developing*

BLOCK A

Understanding of main ideas, central concerns through: *structure; dialogue; key words and phrases*

BLOCK B

Understanding of significant detail through: *stage directions; punctuation; dramatic conflict*

Practice in developing understanding

In Chapter 31 you learned to recognize and interpret aspects of meaning within an extract from a drama text by applying the building blocks to understanding.

With more practice, you will become more skilled, boosting your confidence in being able to apply these techniques to an unseen text.

Below you will find two further drama extracts with discussion questions to help you develop confidence in recognition and interpretation of the keys to understanding.

EXTRACT A

(Living in war-torn Belfast, Marie and Cassie are victims of the 'troubles': Cassie's husband, Joe, is in prison and Marie's husband, Michael, has been killed.)

Marie: Have you been seeing someone Cassie?
(*Cassie doesn't answer for a minute, hesitating, then she drops her eyes*)
Cassie: No.
Marie: Well I'm just saying I wouldn't blame you if you had Cassie, I
wouldn't blame you at all.   5
Cassie: What about the sacred bonds of marriage? What about my martyred
            wee Joe, pining for me in his prison cell?
Marie: I'm not saying you wouldn't be doing wrong, but it's wrong that's been
            done to you often enough. Sure, there's worse things you could be doing.
Cassie: Marie Donnelly, I'm surprised at you.   10
Marie: Oh I'm just the wee prude amn't I? Cleaner than a prayer book me.
Cassie: You're drunk.
Marie: I am not. Just — well if you are Cassie, you need to be more careful.
Cassie: If I was, Marie, you'd all know for sure. You can't keep a secret in this
            place. It's like trying to keep a snake in a matchbox. Oh they'll have me   15
            tarred and feathered before the week's out.
Marie: Don't joke about it, Cassie.
Cassie: Who's joking?
Marie: I don't know how you coped with all Joe's carry on. I don't. You were
            the martyr there, Cassie.   20
Cassie: It gave me peace.
Marie: No but I couldn't have stood that, just the lying to you, the *lying* to you.
            I used to say to Michael, 'If you go with someone else it'll tear the
            heart out of me but tell me, just tell the truth 'cause I'd want to know,
            I couldn't bear not to know.' He never did though. So I never worried.   25
Cassie: No.

Marie: Do you know he was like my best friend. Well, sure you're my best friend but if a man can be that kind of friend to you he was to me, could tell each other anything. That's what I miss most. The crack. The *sharing.*

Cassie: Marie ...   30

Marie: What?

Cassie: Aw Jesus I hate this place! *(She gets up, kicking the ground)*

Marie: We'll get a weekend in Donegal again soon, the three of us and the kids. Sure we could all do with a break.

Cassie: I'm leaving.   35

Marie: What? *(Cassie says nothing)* What do you mean, you're leaving?

Cassie: Do you know she gives me a tenner before every visit to go up to town and buy fruit for them, 'poor Martin' and 'poor Joe'. That's all she's allowed to give them, all she can spoil them with, fruit, so she wants them to have grapes and melons and things you've never heard of   40 and shapes you wouldn't know how to bite into. I'll bring her home something that looks and smells like the Botanic gardens and she'll sniff it and stroke it like it was her favourite son himself, 'stead of his dinner ... And I'll have three or four hundred pounds safe in my pocket, saved, sure she doesn't have a clue of the price of kiwi fruit.   45 *(Pause)* I've two hundred pounds saved. I'm going, Marie.

Marie: Going where?

Cassie: It's desperate, isn't it? Thirty-five years old and she's stealing from her mummy's purse. Well I thought about asking the broo for a relocation grant or something you know, but it seems to me all they can offer you   50 is the straight swap of one hell hole for another.

Marie: You talking about a holiday?

Cassie: I'm talking about getting out of here.

Marie: Cassie, where would you go with two kids for two hundred pounds? *(Cassie says nothing for a moment)*   55

Cassie: Sure, you'd need thousands wouldn't you? Enough to buy yourself into a different country and a different kind of house and a different kind of life altogether. Thousands. *(Shaking her head)* But I'm going.

From Bold Girls *by Rona Munro*

BLOCK A

Understanding of main ideas, central concerns through:

structure; dialogue; key words and phrases

ACTIVITY 1

Structure of extract

The basic structure of the extract is held together by two main themes. One is dishonesty or betrayal, introduced by Marie's question:

'Have you been seeing someone, Cassie?'

a) Trace the line of this idea through the rest of the extract, using relevant quotations to mark out the stages of its development.

b) What would you say is the other main theme? Look, in particular, at the section of dialogue from Cassie's words:

'Aw Jesus I hate this place!'   *(line 32)*

to the end of the extract:

'But I'm going'.   *(line 58)*

c) These two themes interweave at times, helping to unify the different stages of the structure. Can you identify those places in the script where there is an overlapping of the two themes?

ACTIVITY 2

Structure of dialogue

The structure of the dialogue reflects the development of the two main themes.

a) Look carefully at the first half of the extract down to where Marie asks, 'What?' *(line 31)*

What do you notice about the length and type of much of Cassie's dialogue in this section?

Which of the two characters seems to be shaping and directing the conversation here?

b) Look carefully at the second half of the extract from:

'Aw Jesus I hate this place!' *(line 32)*

What do you notice about the length and type of much of Cassie's dialogue in this section?

Which of the two characters seems to be shaping and directing the conversation here?

ACTIVITY 3

Key words and phrases

The repetition of specific words or phrases within an extract can help the reader to grasp main ideas.

For example, Marie repeats the two key, oppositional words 'truth' and 'lying' while Cassie repeats the word 'different' in three separate phrases.

Marie's words point to one of the central ideas in the extract, the theme of dishonesty or betrayal: Cassie's repetition of 'different' sums up the second main concern, the theme of imprisonment and escape.

Look at these groups of repeated or similar key words and phrases that the two characters use. Try to suggest what contribution is made by individual words or phrases to your understanding of situation and theme.

The letter **R** indicates a repeated word or phrase.

	1		2		3	4		5
R	blame		secret		bonds	sacred		prison cell
R	wrong		snake	R	best friend	martyr		matchbox
			carry on		sharing	peace		a break
		R	lying		spoil them	truth	R	leaving
			hate		favourite son			going
			stealing					hell hole
								holiday
								getting out

BLOCK B

Understanding of significant detail
through: *stage directions;
punctuation; dramatic conflict*

ACTIVITY 4

Stage directions

All the stage directions in this extract relate to the character Cassie.

Discuss what each of the following contributes to your understanding of character and/or situation:

(Cassie doesn't answer for a minute, hesitating, then she drops her eyes)   **(line 2)**
(She gets up, kicking the ground)   **(line 32)**
(Cassie says nothing)   **(line 36)**
(Pause)   **(line 46)**
(Cassie says nothing for a moment)   **(line 55)**

ACTIVITY 5

Punctuation

The question mark, dash, series of dots, quotation mark and exclamation mark are all significant aids to understanding this extract.

For example:

'What?'   *(line 31)*
'Going where?'   *(line 47)*
'You talking about a holiday?'   *(line 52)*
'Cassie, where would you go with two kids for two hundred pounds?'*(line 54)*

Marie's series of questions tells us that she is confused and disbelieving that Cassie should even be considering escaping from her environment.

Look at the remaining key forms of punctuation used here and show how each example furthers your understanding of some aspect of meaning.
- the question mark after a rhetorical question
- the dash (ellipsis)
- series of dots
- quotation marks
- exclamation mark.

ACTIVITY 6

Dramatic conflict

There are a number of different types of dramatic conflict that emerge from this extract. The majority of them are centred on Cassie. They include:
- Cassie's inner conflict
- Cassie's conflict with her husband
- Cassie's conflict with community values
- Cassie's conflict with her physical environment.

Identify those areas in the extract where you recognize each of these conflicts operating. For each one, find a quotation which seems to illustrate the nature of the conflict.

EXTRACT (B) (The setting is Glasgow in 1915. Aidan Quinn, a deserter, is in hiding at home.)

(Aidan wakes up, gets up. He realises he's alone in the house and finds this strange, eerie but beautiful — the space. Then he becomes frightened. When he folds up his blankets they aren't even approximately folded. Mrs Black comes in.)

Mrs Black:	Aidan! Aidan Quinn! But you're with the 6th Royal Munsters.
Aidan:	How did you get in?
Mrs Black:	The door was open. The door's always open.
Aidan	*(aggressively)*: I've just folded up my blankets — I've just got up! Where's my mother? I woke up and there was no one here.
Mrs Black:	I don't know, it's not like your mother to be out. Especially in a fog like that.
Aidan:	So she *wants* to frighten me. She either wants me to think she has gone to the authorities or she *has* gone to the authorities.
Mrs Black:	Why should she want to do that?
Aidan:	Because I'm a deserter!
Mrs Black:	I don't believe it, Aidan Quinn. That's an unholy lie.
Aidan:	I see. You're one of these people who for the duration of the war will refuse to see what's in front of their eyes. Deserters, for example. Or the unusual number of soldiers who return from the front missing an index-finger. Have you noticed that? Our 'lads' are chopping off their own fingers.
Mrs Black:	Oh Aidan — now I *know* you're making things up.
Aidan:	So that they can't fire their rifles! Of course I never went to the front but I have an imagination. That is the whole problem with us Quinns. We have an imagination which we can ill afford.

(Elizabeth comes in)
(Pause)
(Mrs Black decides to carry on as if she has not seen Aidan)

Mrs Black:	Oh Mrs Quinn. I got a letter! The War office has found my son! What a thing it is for a mother to have her son restored to her after so long. I'm so happy I don't know myself.
Elizabeth:	I'm very pleased for you, Mrs Black. So where is he?
Mrs Black:	Oh I forget the name of the place. The letter said the hospital was nicely situated.
Elizabeth:	So — you'll soon have your wounded hero back in your arms. Like me.
Aidan:	I've already told Mrs Black I'm a deserter. What else was she to think — she walked in and saw me like this! *(Slight pause)* Oh? You don't care? You don't care I made it public because you have just gone and betrayed me to the authorities! See! She doesn't deny it.
Elizabeth:	Yes I've been to the authorities. I informed them that since my son is a deserter I am no longer entitled to my nine shillings Separation Allowance. I handed in my book.
Aidan:	You went to the authorities today?
Elizabeth:	Yes. I opened a drawer this morning and the first thing I saw was my Allowance book. I don't want it in my house any more.
Aidan:	My own mother. What else did you say? Nothing probably — you wouldn't want any fuss, you'd rather I quietly disappeared. You've always wanted rid of me. That's why I joined the army in the first place.

5

10

15

20

25

30

35

40

45

Elizabeth: No one listening to your tone of voice, Aidan, would imagine you joined the 6th Royal Munsters of your own free will and volition.

Aidan: Yes — I volunteered. Ha! On the other hand I was aware you would rather have me dead than a post-office clerk.

Elizabeth: I agree you had limited ability. I thought you might make an officer. 50

(Elizabeth sits on her stool)

Aidan: I was a perfectly good post-office clerk! That was too ridiculous for words of course. It carries connotations of petty cash, as well as the ignominy of being a minor public servant. Your enthusiasm for the war on the other hand was fanatic. You talked of nothing 55 else. You knew exactly how many of those awarded VC were Catholics. You knew the official number of casualties in every major engagement. We were up to our waists in offal. Finally I volunteered. This was how I could stop being ridiculous.

Elizabeth: You always were too sensitive. We loved you, Aidan. 60

Aidan: Who's 'we'? Don't say 'we' like that! It makes me feel like I'm being dressed. Also — I would have preferred it if you had simply hated me. If you had simply hated me all the time that would at least have been consistent.

Mrs Black: That's not your son, Mrs Quinn. Your son wouldn't have come 65 home and — announced — he was a deserter. And the language he's used — 'love'! In front of his own mother. That woman's not well. She's stopped eating. She can do without abuse from you.

Aidan *(forceful, pleading, desperate)*: Have you noticed how often things disappear from round about you? I don't mean only material things 70 though I notice there is less and less here all the time. But now people are disappearing too. Why? What is it you do? Why for example did your husband simply vanish?

(Aidan finishes up on his knees in front of her, appealing to her as a son. We see her wanting to respond — a mother.) 75

Elizabeth: You could ask him.

Aidan: I can't ask him. He's vanished!

Elizabeth: We had an argument.

Aidan: About what? Something petty?

Elizabeth *(points to the piano)*: That thing. 80

Aidan: You argued about that all my life.

Elizabeth: We argued all your life because I was too good for him! *(Pause)* Or rather, he was too good for me. I was a liar. *(She clasps Aidan's head and takes it in her lap)* The piano was his wedding present to me. He couldn't afford it and I couldn't play it. Though we led each other 85 to believe the opposite. When I married I imagined I would never be poor again.

From Elizabeth Gordon Quinn *by Chris Hannan*

BLOCK A

Understanding of main ideas,
central concerns through:
*structure; dialogue; key words
and phrases*

ACTIVITY 1

Structure of extract

The structure of this extract follows the pattern of a mini narrative:

- a clear beginning (Mrs Black's entrance);
- a middle section in which background narrative details are filled in and relationships develop;
- a definite climax with mother and son both breaking down, reaching what appears to be a possible turning point in their relationship.

a) Can you identify where each of these narrative stages begins and ends?

b) Apart from the climax, where else do you recognize specific turning points in the structure?

ACTIVITY 2

Structure of dialogue

Look carefully at the dialogue given to each of the three characters, making notes on the following:

- quantity
- length
- content.

Supporting your views with evidence, try to justify the following statement:

The character Aidan moves the dialogue on, controlling its structure: the other characters simply react to what he says.

ACTIVITY 3

Key words and phrases

Both individual words and groups of words and phrases with some shared meaning are important keys to understanding situation, as well as the central relationship between Aidan and Elizabeth revealed in this extract. For example, the following single words are repeated several times, adding significance to their meaning:

A	**B**
deserter	frightened
authorities	ridiculous
volunteer	argued
help us to understand background to situation	*highlights tensions in the relationship*

a) Find other examples of key individual words which are repeated. Try to show what aspect of the situation or relationship they highlight.

b) Each of the following key words or phrases shares some elements of meaning with one or two other words or phrases in the extract. See if you can find words/phrases to match each of them.

(line 12) don't believe   *(line 34)* don't care   *(line 47)* free will

(line 54) enthusiasm   *(line 83)* liar   *(line 87)* poor

What do you learn about situation and character from these key groups?

ACTIVITY 4

Stage directions

The stage direction at the start of this extract illustrates very effectively how the playwright's contextualized comments can help our understanding.

(Aidan wakes up, gets up. He realises he's <u>alone</u> in the house and finds this <u>strange, eerie</u> but <u>beautiful</u> — the <u>space.</u> Then he becomes <u>frightened</u>. When he folds up his blankets they <u>aren't even</u> <u>approximately folded</u> . . .)

From what we are told here of his actions and his reactions, we begin to realize that Aidan is in an emotionally fragile state. In the context of what follows, we understand why: he is a deserter from the 6th Royal Munsters and is on the run; we can guess he has been living in cramped army conditions in a disciplined environment, surrounded by other men. When he finds himself '*alone*' with '*space*' to himself, therefore, he feels a mix of emotions: initially the experience is simply '*strange*' but '*beautiful*' but once he realizes he really is on his own, or remembers that he is on the run, he becomes '*frightened*'. The discipline of his army training is lost as he tries in vain to fold his blanket neatly, fear perhaps affecting his ability to carry out this task.

Study the following stage directions carefully. How is your understanding of the relationship between Aidan and his mother helped by these directions?

(forceful, pleading, desperate)   **(line 69)**

(Aidan finishes up on his knees in front of her, appealing to her as a son. We see her wanting to respond — a mother)   **(lines 74–75)**

(She clasps Aidan's head and takes it into her lap)   **(lines 83–84)**

ACTIVITY 5

Punctuation

Aidan's speech is characterized by the use of question and exclamation marks, giving his speech a nervous tension.

For example:

'I've just got up! Where's my mother?'   *(lines 4–5)*

Pick out some other examples, suggesting in each case how it develops your understanding of Aidan's emotional state.

ACTIVITY 6

Dramatic conflict

Understanding the nature of dramatic conflict is a key to a fuller appreciation of this extract. Here the central conflict between mother and son is introduced early on when Aidan says:

'So she *wants* to frighten me. She either wants me to think she has gone to the authorities or she has gone to the authorities.'

Using the following list of quotations to anchor your discussion, trace the development of this conflict, highlighting any aspects of the conflict which you think are of particular significance.

'So she *wants* to frighten me.'   *(line 8)*

'That is the whole problem with us Quinns. We have an imagination which we can ill afford.'   *(lines 20–21)*

'Oh? You don't care? You don't care I made it public because you have just gone and betrayed me to the authorities!'   *(lines 33–35)*

'You went to the authorities today?'   *(line 39)*

'My own mother ... You've always wanted rid of me.'   *(lines 42–44)*

'I agree you had limited ability. I thought you might make an officer.'   *(line 50)*

'I was a perfectly good post-office clerk! That was too ridiculous for words of course.'   *(lines 52–53)*

'Also – I would have preferred it if you had simply hated me.'   *(lines 62–63)*

'Why? What is it you do?'   *(line 72)*

'You argued about that all my life.'   *(line 81)*

CHAPTER 33 *Drama*

BUILDING BLOCKS TO UNDERSTANDING

Demonstrating

So far you've been concentrating on learning to identify and interpret the building blocks of meaning. In this chapter, you will be given an opportunity to demonstrate that you are now able to explore an unseen drama extract, using the tools of textual analysis to uncover what may be several layers of meaning.

Below is an extract from *Valley Song* by the South African dramatist, Athol Fugard. Following this, you will find a full commentary, showing how the key elements of building blocks A and B have helped the reader to an understanding of this extract. Use this sample commentary to help you in your own independent exploration of the final extract in this chapter.

EXTRACT Ⓐ (Living in a remote village in the Karoo region of South Africa, a Coloured man, Buks, and his granddaughter, Veronica, find themselves under threat from the White man who is interested in buying a house and land on which Buks and his father before him have grown vital crops.)

Buks:	No! Leave the Government out of it. Every time they stick their nose in your business you get to pay something. I know what I'm talking about, my child. Government is trouble. I'll be very happy if they don't know where we are.
Veronica:	Well, God certainly knows where the village is so I'm going to pray to Him to do something.
Buks:	That's better ... but God also helps those who help themselves. I think maybe I must go try to speak to the Whiteman myself ... I see his car is still standing there in front of the Guest House.
Veronica:	What are you going to say to him, Oupa*?
Buks:	Tell him about myself and those akkers* – if he'll listen ... Ask him, nicely, if I can carry on there.
Veronica:	I hate to see Oupa like this.
Buks:	Like what?
Veronica:	Like you are now. All worried and down and ... I don't know ... upset.
Buks:	I also don't like it, but what can I do? Anyway he doesn't look so bad. He greeted me nicely last time when they came to look at the house. And, as Stella said, maybe there is also a good side to this business. If he does buy the house and fixes it up and comes to live here in the village, who knows, maybe there's a chance for you in there.
Veronica *(alarmed)*:	What do you mean, Oupa?
Buks:	Work, my girl. For you, Ja! Stella is right. They're going to need somebody to clean the house and do the washing.
Veronica:	No, Oupa!
Buks:	No? I think you are old enough for it now, Veronica.

5

10

15

20

25

Veronica	*(panic)*: Yes, I know I am but ... No, no, no! *(A few seconds of surprised silence at her outburst. She is desperate and flustered.)* I know Oupa means good for me ... and I'm very grateful ... but No! ... Oupa mustn't just ... decide like that ... what I mean is you promised, Oupa, that when the time came we could talk about these things first ... yes you did! ...
Buks:	Veronica?
Veronica:	What I'm trying to say, Oupa, is that I also got ideas ... other ideas about what I want to do ... about my future and everything ... so Oupa mustn't decide just like that ...
Buks:	You're talking too fast for me. I don't understand what you are saying. Speak so that I can understand you.
Veronica:	I don't want to do housework.
Buks:	But you do it here every day, Veronica.
Veronica:	This is different, Oupa. This is our house. I'm doing it for us. I don't want to do it for other people. I don't want to do it for a living. Specially that house.
Buks:	What is wrong with getting work there? Your Ouma* cleaned that house.
Veronica:	Exactly, Oupa! That's what I have been trying to say. Isn't it supposed to be different now?
Buks:	What must be different?
Veronica:	Our lives and ... and everything. Isn't that why there was an election? Oupa voted in it ... and all that talk that was going on about how things was going to change and be different from now on. Well, this doesn't look like it. Here we are carrying on and talking just like the 'klomp arme ou kleurling'* we've always been, frightened of the Whiteman, ready to crawl and beg him and be happy and grateful if we can scrub his floors ...
Buks:	Veronica? Where does all this nonsense come from? Who's been giving you these ideas?
Veronica:	Nobody, I don't need other people to give me ideas. They're my own. And it's not nonsense, Oupa ...
Buks:	Veronica! *(It takes him a few seconds to control his anger before he can speak coherently)* Okay – now you listen to me very carefully, my child. I've never talked to you like this before and I don't ever want to talk to you like this again. You wouldn't be alive today, standing there insulting the memory of your Ouma ...
Veronica:	No! I didn't!
Buks	*(ignoring her)*: ... insulting the memory of your Ouma, if that 'arme ou kleurling' hadn't gone to the city and rescued you. Ja. You would most probably be lying in the same grave as your mother if Betty Bruintjies hadn't climbed into that railway bus and found you and brought you back here. Broken hearted as she was she nursed you and gave you a start in life. Ja, it's true she scrubbed floors in that Landman house, went down on her hands and knees and scrubbed and polished, but if you can walk through your life with even half of the pride that that woman had in herself and her life, then you will be a very lucky girl. As for this 'arme ou kleurling' ... you're right – I've done a lot of crawling and begging in my life and I am ready to do it again for those few akkers. You want to know why, Veronica? So that I can grow food there for you to eat, just as I

grew food there for your mother and your Ouma to eat, and as my
father grew food for me to eat.   80
Veronica *(struggling to hold back tears)*: I'm sorry, Oupa.

These are all Afrikaans expressions.
Oupa = grandfather
akkers = a small plot or piece of ground
Ouma = grandmother
'klomp arme ou kleurling' = a derogatory phrase which means a bunch of poor old Coloureds

From Valley Song *by Athol Fugard*

Sample commentary on extract from *Valley Song*

Structure of extract

The extract opens suddenly, mid-conversation, arousing our curiosity about the subject of the conversation between Buks and Veronica. 'Maybe there's a chance for you in there' (line 21) marks a turning point where the focus shifts from the wider topic of the threat posed by the Whiteman to Buk's future, to the very specific theme of the conflicting aspirations of grandfather and granddaughter. The extract builds to a powerful climax during Buk's speech beginning, 'Veronica! ... Okay – now you listen to me very carefully, my child' (lines 60–61) and culminates in the answer to his own question. 'You want to know why, Veronica?' (lines 77–78). Finally, Veronica's apology draws a definite closure to the structure.

Structure of dialogue

Buks's dialogue dominates the extract: for the majority of the scene, he controls and directs the conversation. Veronica attempts to challenge this dominance, at first hesitantly:

   'Yes, I know I am but ... No, no, no!'   *(line 27)*

and then more confidently in the speech:

   'Isn't that why there was an election? ... if we can scrub his floors.'   *(lines 49–55)*

But the grandfather regains absolute dominance of the dialogue in the extended speech:

   'Veronica! ... Okay – now you listen to me very carefully.'   *(lines 60–61)*

ignoring Veronica's interruption, 'No! I didn't!' (line 65) and carrying straight on to a powerful finish.

Key words and phrases

If we look closely at the following groups of words and phrases, many of which are repeated (**R**), some of which share elements of meaning (**S**), we can see that they give us significant clues about the main concerns running through the extract.

	1		**2**		**3**
R	akkers	R	talk(ing)	R	nicely
R	work	S	tell	S	means good
R	grow food	R	listen	S	happy
		S	ask	S	grateful
		S	decide	S	lucky

	4		**5**		**6**		**7**		**8**
S	all worried	R	crawl	S	change	R	no	S	a chance
S	down	R	beg	S	other ideas	S	don't understand	S	future
S	upset	R	scrub floors	R	different	S	don't want	S	a start in life
S	frightened								

The extract's main concerns are:

- Buk's anxiety about holding on to his cherished 'akkers'
- Buk's belief that, in order to survive, his people have to be prepared to 'ask nicely', to 'crawl' and to 'beg' in the Whiteman's world
- Veronica's opposing belief that there should be a different kind of future for them in a post-apartheid South Africa.

Stage directions

As we've already noted, stage directions can give us vital information about such key aspects as situation, atmosphere, character and relationships. In this extract there are a few key directions which add to our understanding of both characters, as well as contributing to our awareness of atmosphere.

Veronica

'(alarmed)' (line 22)
'(panic)' (line 27)
'(A few seconds of surprised silence at her outburst. She is desperate and flustered)' (lines 27–28)

Buks

'(It takes him a few seconds to control his anger before he can speak coherently)' (lines 60–61)
'(ignoring her)' (line 66)

The atmosphere becomes tense as Veronica registers alarm and panic: this tension heightens as Buks struggles to *'control his anger'*. Veronica's *'surprised silence'* tells us that she is not accustomed to speaking to her grandfather in this challenging way. We understand Veronica's desperation as she does not wish to upset her grandfather but, at the same time, feels she must protest about his suggested plans for her. Her conflicting loyalties to Buks and to her own principles confuse her, making her *'flustered'*.

From the stage directions, we realize the depth of Buk's emotion as he struggles to *'control his anger'*, which is so extreme that it takes him a few seconds before he can *'speak coherently'*. The power of this emotion is further conveyed by the direction telling us that he ignores Veronica's protest.

Punctuation

This extract is dominated by question marks, exclamation marks and series of dots indicating unfinished or interrupted statements.

In many cases the question mark indicates uncertainty or confusion about the situation:

'What are you going to say to him, Oupa?' *(line 10)*
'I also don't like it, but what can I do?' *(line 17)*

In other cases, it communicates a tension between the two characters as one struggles to understand the other's viewpoint:

'What do you mean, Oupa?' *(line 22)*
'What must be different?' *(line 48)*

Occasionally, it marks a rhetorical question:

'Isn't that why there was an election?' *(lines 49–50)*

The exclamation mark is used very effectively to communicate strength of emotion, helping us to understand better both characters' perspectives on the situation. Buk's opening 'No!' shows quite clearly that he is strongly opposed to any Government interference in the situation. Later on, we are helped to understand why Buks feels so passionately about the need to fight for his small parcel of land when he abruptly interrupts his granddaughter, shouting 'Veronica!'

Similarly, we learn something of Veronica's state of mind through her use of the exclamation. For example, we first hear her oppose her grandfather when she repeatedly shouts 'No!' (line 27) and then again two lines later. She continues to challenge him:

' ... yes you did! ... '

'No! I didn't!'

showing both a desperate and a courageous side to her character.

In the frequent use of the ellipsis (series of dots), particularly in Veronica's dialogue, we can detect a mixture of hesitation, uncertainty, even fear:

'All worried and down and ... I don't know ... upset.' *(lines 15–16)*

'Yes, I know I am but ... No, no no!' *(line 27)*

'What I'm trying to say, Oupa, is that I also got ideas ... other ideas about what I want to do ... about my future and everything ... so Oupa mustn't decide just like that ... ' *(lines 34–36)*

Dramatic conflict

We've already observed that conflict lies at the heart of all drama and this extract is no exception. Here the dramatist explores a number of different types of conflict – personal and universal – each one of which contributes to our understanding of situation, character and theme. These are:
- The conflict between people and the Government
- The conflict between races (Buks and the Whiteman)

- The conflict between generations (Buks and his granddaughter)
- The conflict between past and present values
- Inner conflict (within both characters)

Demonstrating understanding

In summary, using the building blocks approach, several readings of this extract have revealed in terms of meanings a clearer understanding of the following aspects:

- situation
- mood/atmosphere
- character
- relationships
- theme(s).

EXTRACT Ⓑ (Rita, a hairdresser from Liverpool, has embarked on an Open University course with Frank as her tutor. He has invited Rita to a dinner party he is hosting but she fails to turn up.)

Frank: Now I don't mind: two empty seats at the dinner table means more of the vino for me. But Julia — Julia is the stage-manager type. If we're having eight people to dinner, she expects to see eight. She likes order — probably why she took me on — it gives her a lot of practice —

(Rita starts sharpening her pencils)   5

Frank: — and having to cope with six instead of eight was extremely hard on Julia. I'm not saying that I needed any sort of apology; you don't turn up that's up to you, but ...

Rita: I did apologise.

Frank: 'Sorry can't come', scribbled on the back of your essay and thrust   10
through the letter box? Rita, that's hardly an apology.

Rita: What does the word 'sorry' mean if it's not an apology? When I told Denny we were goin' to yours he went mad. We had a big fight about it.

Frank: I'm sorry. I didn't realise. But look, couldn't you have explained? Couldn't you have said that was the reason?   15

Rita: No. Cos that wasn't the reason. I told Denny if he wasn't gonna go, I'd go on me own. An' I tried to. All day Saturday, all day in the shop I was thinkin' what to wear. I got back, an' I tried on five different dresses. They all looked bleedin' awful. An' all the time I'm trying to think of things I can say, what I can talk about. An' I can't remember anythin'.   20
It's all jumbled up in me head. I can't remember if it's Wilde who's witty an' Shaw who was Shavian or who the hell wrote *Howards End.*

Frank: Oh God!

Rita: Then I got the wrong bus to your house. It took me ages to find it. Then I walked up your drive, an' I saw y' all through the window, y'   25
were sippin' drinks an' talkin' an' laughin'. An' I couldn't come in.

Frank: Of course you could.

Rita: I couldn't. I'd bought the wrong sort of wine. When I was in the off licence I knew I was buyin' the wrong stuff. But I didn't know which was the right wine.   30

Frank: Rita, for Christ's sake; I wanted *you* to come along. You weren't expected to dress up or buy wine.

Rita *(holding all the pencils and pens in her hands and playing with them)*: If you go out to dinner don't you dress up? Don't you take wine?

Frank: Yes, but ...

Rita: Well?

Frank: Well what?

Rita: Well you wouldn't take sweet sparkling wine, would y'?

Frank: Does it matter what I do? It wouldn't have mattered if you'd walked in
with a bottle of Spanish plonk.   40

Rita: It was Spanish.

Frank: Why couldn't you relax? (*He gets up and goes behind Rita's chair, then leans on
the back of it*) It wasn't a fancy dress party. You could have come as
yourself. Don't you realise how people would have seen you if you'd
just — just breezed in? Mm? They would have seen someone who's   45
funny, delightful, charming ...

Rita (*angrily*): But I don't wanna be charming and delightful: funny. What's
funny? I don't wanna be funny. I wanna talk seriously with the rest of
you, I don't wanna spend the night takin' the piss, comin' on with the
funnies because that's the only way I can get into the conversation. I   50
didn't want to come to your house just to play the court jester.

Frank: You weren't being asked to play that role. I just wanted you to be
yourself.

Rita: But I don't want to be myself. Me? What's me? Some stupid woman
who gives us all a laugh because she thinks she can learn, because she   55
thinks that one day she'll be like the rest of them, talking seriously,
confidently, with knowledge, livin' a civilised life. Well, she can't be like
that really but bring her in because she's good for a laugh!

Frank: If you believe that's why you were invited, to be laughed at, then you
can get out now. (*He goes to his desk and grabs a pile of essays, taking them to the* 60
window desk. He stands with his back to **Rita** *and starts pushing the essays into his
briefcase*) You were invited because I wished to have your company and
if you can't believe that then I suggest you stop visiting me and start
visiting an analyst who can cope with paranoia.

Rita: I'm all right with you, here in this room; but when I saw those people   65
you were with I couldn't come in. I would have seized up. Because I'm
a freak. I can't talk to the people I live with any more. An' I can't talk
to the likes of them on Saturday, or them out there, because I can't
learn the language. I'm a half-caste. I went back to the pub where
Denny was, an' me mother, an' our Sandra, an' her mates. I'd decided I   70
wasn't comin' here again.

(*Frank turns to face her*)

Rita: I went into the pub an' they were singin', all of them singin' some song
they'd learnt from the juke-box. An' I stood in that pub an' thought,
just what the frig am I trying to do? Why don't I just pack it in an'   75
stay with them, an' join in the singin'?

Frank: And why don't you?

Rita (*angrily*): You think I can, don't you? Just because you pass a pub
doorway an' hear the singin' you think we're all O.K., that we're all
survivin', with the spirit intact. Well I did join in with the singin', I   80
didn't ask any questions. I just went along with it. But when I looked
round me mother had stopped singin', an' she was cryin', but no one
could get it out of her why she was cryin'. Everyone just said that she
was pissed an' we should get her home. So we did, an' on the way I
asked her why. I said, 'Why are y' cryin', Mother?' She said, 'Because —   85
because we could sing better songs than those.' Ten minutes later,

Denny had her laughing and singing again, pretending that she hadn't said it. But she had. And that's why I came back. And that's why I'm staying.

From Educating Rita *by Willy Russell*

ACTIVITY

Now it's your turn to demonstrate what you've learnt about decoding meaning by exploring the extract from the play *Educating Rita* by Willy Russell.

Use the following prompts to help direct your discussion of the extract.

Structure of extract
How does the overall structure of the extract help to shape the reader's understanding of the situation?

Structure of dialogue
Can you identify any key turning points that help shape the direction of the dialogue? What seems to be the main function of Frank's dialogue in this scene? To what extent could Rita's dialogue be said to shape the scene?

Key words and phrases
Identify any key words and phrases. What contribution do they make to your awareness of atmosphere and/or character and/or theme?

Stage directions
What contribution is made by stage directions to your understanding of any of the following:
- atmosphere
- character
- theme?

Punctuation
Are there any features of punctuation which you recognize as contributing to your understanding? If so, identify them and show what contribution is made.

Dramatic conflict
Can you recognise several different types of conflict running through the extract? What part do they play in developing your understanding of both Frank and Rita?

CHAPTER 34 *Drama*

BUILDING BLOCKS TO ANALYSIS AND EVALUATION

 ## *Learning*

Armed with the building blocks to understanding dealt with in Chapters 31 to 33, you're now ready to extend your skills to enable you to respond more fully to extracts from drama texts. Knowing how to **analyse** and **evaluate** such extracts will help you to do this.

Look at the SQA criteria for Textual Analysis at Higher.

ANALYSIS	'Responses explain accurately and in some detail **ways in which** aspects of **structure/ style/language** contribute to **meaning/effect/impact**.'
EVALUATION	'Responses reveal **clear engagement** with the text or aspects of the text and stated or implied evaluation of **effectiveness**, using **appropriate critical terminology** and substantiated with **detailed and relevant evidence** from the text.'

The words in **bold** highlight key ingredients in the process of analysing and evaluating. Some of these require further explanation.

Analysis

'**ways in which**' simply means *how* in a technical sense

'**style**' refers to the distinctive way in which an author uses the various tools of writing

'**effect**' relates to the particular response(s) produced in the reader as a result of the way in which an author has used a specific writing tool

NB Not to be confused with **effectiveness**. See below for note on *effectiveness*.

Evaluation

'**clear engagement**' means obvious personal involvement with the text

'**effectiveness**' relates to the degree of success an author has had in using specific techniques to communicate effectively with the reader

'**appropriate critical terminology**' means the special vocabulary used when discussing specific features relating to that genre: for drama, some of these terms would be *character, dialogue, stage directions, dramatic conflict, climax, set design, sound and lighting effects*

'**detailed and relevant evidence**' indicates that whatever statement is being made about a text or aspect of a text, this needs to be backed up by ample evidence directly related to that statement.

The SQA criteria indicate the skills a candidate needs to demonstrate in order to achieve a pass at Higher in Textual Analysis. Using these as our framework, let's see how they translate into useful **building blocks**.

> **BLOCK C** *Analysis*
> Examining aspects of structure, style, language to show HOW they contribute to meaning and effect.

> **BLOCK D** *Evaluation*
> Assessing the effectiveness of a text through personal response, supported by relevant evidence and appropriate critical vocabulary.

Analysis in action

Using the following extract from *The Devil's Disciple* by George Bernard Shaw, let's explore further the **process** of analysis to see how it works in practice.

EXTRACT Ⓐ   (Richard Dudgeon, having impersonated Judith Anderson's husband, allowing the latter to escape during the American War of Independence, awaits execution.)

Sergeant:	Your good lady, sir.	
Richard	*(going to her)*: What! My wife. My adored one. *(He takes her hand and kisses it with a perverse, raffish gallantry)* How long do you allow a brokenhearted husband for leave-taking, Sergeant?	
Sergeant:	As long as we can, sir. We shall not disturb you till the court sits. You may count on twenty minutes, sir, and by your leave I won't waste any more of them. *(He goes out, locking the door. Richard immediately drops his raffish manner and turns to Judith with considerate sincerity)*	5
Richard:	Mrs Anderson, this visit is very kind of you. And how are you after last night? I had to leave you before you recovered; but I sent word to Essie to go and look after you. Did she understand the message?	10
Judith	*(breathless and urgent)*: Oh, don't think of me: I haven't come here to talk about myself. Are they going to – to – *(meaning 'to hang you')*?	
Richard	*(whimsically)*: At noon, punctually. At least that was when they disposed of Uncle Peter. *(She shudders)* Is your husband safe? Is he on the wing?	15
Judith:	He is no longer my husband.	
Richard	*(opening his eyes wide)*: Eh?	
Judith:	I disobeyed you. I told him everything. I expected him to come here and save you. I wanted him to come here and save you. He ran away instead.	20
Richard:	Well, that's what I meant him to do. What good would his staying have done? They'd only have hanged us both.	
Judith	*(with reproachful earnestness)*: Richard Dudgeon, on your honour, what would you have done in his place?	
Richard:	Exactly what he has done, of course.	25
Judith:	Oh, why will you not be simple with me – honest and straightforward? If you are so selfish as that, why did you let them take you last night?	
Richard	*(gaily)*: Upon my life, Mrs Anderson, I don't know. I've been asking myself that question ever since; and I can find no manner of reason for acting as I did.	30
Judith:	You know you did it for his sake, believing he was a more worthy man than yourself.	
Richard	*(laughing)*: Oho! No: that's a very pretty reason, I must say; but I'm not so modest as that. No: it wasn't for his sake.	35

Judith	*(after a pause, during which she looks shamefacedly at him, blushing painfully)*: Was it for my sake?
Richard	*(gallantly)*: Well, you had a hand in it. It must have been a little for your sake. You let them take me, at all events.
Judith:	Oh, you think I have not been telling myself that all night? Your death will be at my door. *(Impulsively, she gives him her hand, and adds, with intense earnestness)* If I could save you as you saved him, I would do it, no matter how cruel the death was.
Richard	*(holding her hand and smiling, but keeping her almost at arms length)*: I am very sure I shouldn't let you.
Judith:	Don't you see that I can save you?
Richard:	How? By changing clothes with me, eh?
Judith	*(disengaging her hand to touch his lips with it)*: Don't *(meaning 'don't jest')*. No, by telling the court who you really are.
Richard	*(frowning)*: No use: they wouldn't spare me; and it would spoil half his chance of escaping. They are determined to cow us by making an example of somebody on that gallows today. Well, let us cow them by showing that we can stand by one another to the death. That is the only force that can send Burgoyne back across the Atlantic and make America a nation.
Judith	*(impatiently)*: Oh, what does all that matter?
Richard	*(laughing)*: True: what does it matter? What does anything matter? You see, men have these strange notions, Mrs Anderson; and women see the folly of them.
Judith:	Women have to lose those they love through them.
Richard:	They can easily get fresh lovers.
Judith	*(revolted)*: Oh! *(Vehemently)* Do you realise that you are going to kill yourself?
Richard:	The only man I have any right to kill, Mrs Anderson. Don't be concerned: no woman will lose her lover through my death. *(Smiling)* Bless you, nobody cares for me. Have you heard that my mother is dead?
Judith:	Dead?
Richard:	Of heart disease — in the night. Her last word to me was her curse: I don't think I could have borne her blessing. My other relatives will not grieve much on my account. Essie will cry for a day or two; but I have provided for her: I made my own will last night.
Judith	*(stonily, after a moment's silence)*: And I?
Richard	*(surprised)*: You?
Judith:	Yes, I. Am I not to care at all?
Richard	*(gaily and bluntly)*: Not a scrap. Oh, you expressed your feelings towards me very frankly yesterday. What happened may have softened you for the moment; but believe me, Mrs Anderson, you don't like a bone in my skin or a hair on my head. I shall be as good a riddance at 12 today as I should have been at 12 yesterday.
Judith	*(her voice trembling)*: What can I do to shew you that you are mistaken?
Richard:	Don't trouble. I'll give you credit for liking me a little better than you did. All I say is that my death will not break your heart.
Judith	*(almost in a whisper)*: How do you know? *(She puts her hands on his shoulders and looks intently at him)*

40

45

50

55

60

65

70

75

80

85

> **Richard** (*amazed – divining the truth*): Mrs Anderson! (*The bell of the town clock strikes the quarter. He collects himself, and removes her hands, saying rather coldly*) Excuse me: they will be here for me presently. It is too late.

From The Devil's Disciple *by George Bernard Shaw*

As we saw when looking at prose on page 132 and poetry on page 162, the process of analysis could be said to involve three key stages: making a statement about an aspect of structure/style/language; providing relevant evidence to back up that statement; and then commenting on the effect of the selected aspect. For ease of memory, this process can be reduced to a neat acronym, **SEA**:

S	**statement**	
E	**evidence**	**(SEA)**
A	**analysis**	

Working with a few examples from *The Devil's Disciple* extract, let's look at this process in action.

Example 1   **statement**
Dramatic tension is created through situation and setting.

evidence
The setting is a prison cell and it is literally a life and death situation with Richard about to be hanged in place of Judith's husband.

analysis
The cell door is locked, heightening the tension: there is no escape from this situation. The awkward and tense meeting between the two characters takes place in a confined space, further straining the atmosphere. Time is very limited: the Sergeant gives them twenty minutes and we are made aware of time passing when we hear the clock strike the quarter hour. Time is literally running out for Richard and we feel the tension mounting as we realize the sacrifice he is about to make.

Example 2   **statement**
The dramatic nature of the dialogue contributes to the tense atmosphere.

evidence
The general pace of the dialogue is urgent with much of the exchange in the form of question and answer. For example:

> **Richard:** Is your husband safe? Is he on the wing?
> **Judith:**   He is no longer my husband.
> **Richard:** Eh? (*lines 15–17*)

The emotional nature of Judith's dialogue adds to the tension. For example:

> 'Oh, why will you not be simple with me – honest and straightforward?' (*lines 26–27*)

'Oh, you think I have not been telling myself that all night? Your death will be at my door.'   *(lines **40–41**)*

'Yes, I. Am I not to care at all?'   *(line **75**)*

Richard's direct, sometimes even cold, dialogue acts as a foil to Judith's, further heightening the dramatic tension. For example:

Judith: Do you realise that you are going to kill yourself?

Richard: The only man I have any right to kill, Mrs Anderson. Don't be concerned: no woman will lose her lover through my death. *(lines **62–65**)*

Judith: Yes, I. Am I not to care at all?

Richard *(gaily and bluntly)*: Not a scrap. Oh, you expressed your feelings towards me very frankly yesterday ... I shall be as good a riddance at 12 today as I should have been at 12 yesterday. *(lines **75–80**)*

analysis

The pattern of question and answer sets up expectations in the reader, who is curious to hear the response, particularly when the question has been of a challenging nature – as when Judith asks Richard: 'Was it for my sake?' The pattern seems particularly appropriate as much of the scene is about two people questioning the nature of their relationship, which ebbs and flows throughout the extract, setting up tensions.

The contrasting tone of the two characters' dialogue helps to sustain the tension. While Judith is direct in her emotional appeals, Richard moves from a false playfulness to a detached bluntness which can seem cruel, as in his response to Judith:

'Don't trouble. I'll give you credit for liking me a little better than you did. All I say is that my death will not break your heart.'   *(lines **82–83**)*

Example 3   ### statement
The theme of loyalty contributes to the dramatic tension.

evidence
Judith indicates that she has abandoned her loyalty to her husband when she says:

'He is no longer my husband.'   *(line **16**)*

Her actions have been prompted by her own disappointment in her husband's apparent lack of loyalty: when she 'told him everything' she had expected him to come and save Richard; instead he runs away. Richard questions her apparent switch of loyalties, unconvinced until the end that she has really changed her opinion of him. He demonstrates his own commitment to the idea of loyalty when he says that he feels that the only way their side can stand up to the opposing forces is:

' ... by showing that we can stand by one another to the death.' *(line **53**)*

analysis

The theme sets up tensions: the loyalties explored in the extract affect people dramatically. Judith has thrown convention to the wind and abandoned her husband, openly declaring her feelings for Richard. At the time, her actions would have been regarded as scandalous. She declares her love just at the point where Richard is about to save her husband from the gallows.

ACTIVITY 1

Now try to provide **evidence** and **analysis** to support the following statements, using the examples above to help you.

statements

1   The playwright uses stage directions to heighten tension.

2   The extract employs dramatic irony to help sustain tension.

3   The interaction between the two characters makes a vital contribution to the tense mood.

Evaluation in action

Although we've separated the two areas of analysis and evaluation for teaching purposes, they are, of course, very closely related. Often your evaluative comments will be based on specific aspects which you've already analysed. The emphasis, however, will be different. If you look at building block D again, you'll see that the focus is on assessing the **effectiveness** of a text or aspects of a text through the following elements:

personal response relevant evidence appropriate critical vocabulary	**BLOCK D** *Evaluation* Assessing the **effectiveness** of a text through personal response, supported by relevant evidence and appropriate critical vocabulary.

Let's go back to *The Devil's Disciple* extract to see some examples of the **evaluative process** in action.

Example 1   I was impressed by the way in which the playwright kept a firm grip on the structure (CV) of the scene, despite the emotional nature of the meeting (PR). His control of dialogue (CV), in particular, showed his craftsmanship. For example, when the character Judith threatens to lose emotional control in the line:

'Are they going to – to – (*meaning "to hang you"*)?',

Richard controls the situation by responding '*whimsically*':

'At noon punctually.' (E)

Thereafter he redirects the dialogue by asking Judith if her husband has made a safe getaway. A little later, his short, direct response to another emotive question: 'Exactly what he has done, of course' (E) has a similar effect in controlling the mood and pace (CV) of the dialogue.

(PR = personal response; E = evidence; CV = critical vocabulary)

Example 2   Both characters develop as fascinating individuals (PR), partly because of the way in which they act as foils (CV) to each other and partly because of the different ways in which they react to the situation. Judith comes across as courageous, even reckless, prepared to sacrifice her own life, if it would save Richard's:

> 'If I could save you as you saved him, I would do it, no matter how cruel the death was.' (E)

She also risks being rejected by Richard when she shows her feelings openly, as conveyed in the stage directions (CV), as well as in her dialogue. When Richard says:

> 'All I say is that my death will not break your heart', (E)

she asks '*(almost in a whisper)*: How do you know?', then '*she puts her hands on his shoulders and looks intently at him*'.

Richard, on the other hand, is portrayed as a cool individual who will be ruled by his head, rather than his heart. I found him absorbing because of this apparent indifference to Judith's emotional appeals (PR). According to the stage directions, sometimes he is teasing in his manner to her, taking her hand and kissing it '*with a perverse, raffish gallantry*' or speaking '*whimsically*' and '*gaily*' or openly '*laughing*' (E).

ACTIVITY 2

I feel that the playwright successfully builds a scene full of dramatic tension (PR).

Try to expand on this response, using 'relevant evidence' (E) and 'appropriate critical vocabulary' (CV) to back up what you say. Use the examples above to help you.

CHAPTER 35 *Drama*

BUILDING BLOCKS TO ANALYSIS AND EVALUATION

 *Developing*

Practice in developing the skills of analysis and evaluation

The next two extracts aim to provide you with opportunities to develop specific analytical and evaluative skills by focusing on key aspects of each text, exploring *how* individual playwrights have achieved particular effects and assessing their effectiveness.

EXTRACT A

(The church of Hellya, with dark pews and plain windows. Four elders — John Rosey the factor, William Kolson the merchant, Thomas Manson of Blinkbonny, and Obadiah Corrigall of Skaill — are speaking together. It is an afternoon in January 1664. Already the darkness is coming down.)

Rosey:	There's too much clinging to the past in this island. We must think in the way of progress, men. Look at the wooden cart I shipped over from Scotland in the spring. It brought all Mr Faa's corn in one morning to the mill. We'll be hearing more about wheels and machines. In a few generations ...
Manson:	But it mightn't be the Lord's will, Mr Rosey. *(He stamps his feet)* I wish the minister would hurry. It's very cold in the kirk.
Kolson:	He'll be lingering over his drop of toddy. He's a man for his toddy, Mr MacFarland.
Manson:	If he doesn't turn up soon, we'll have to light the lamps. More expense.
Corrigall:	Ah, God knows, this is a poor business that brings us together, a lass in trouble.
Rosey:	Worse, maybe, than any of you think. *(He turns to Kolson)* A mare of thine was it died, William?
Kolson:	Suddenly, on Yule night, a fine healthy garron. It was just back from being shod in the Smithy.
Rosey:	Just back from the Smithy, was it? Just so. There's a power of ill-luck in the parish nowadays.

(Enter the Minister)

Minister:	Sorry to have kept you waiting, men. A lot to do these short winter days. Where is the young woman?
Kolson:	We kept her in the vestry until such time as you arrived. We had things to talk about that weren't for her ears.
Corrigall	*(opening the vestry door)*: Come in, Sigrid lass.

(Sigrid comes in shyly)

Kolson	*(in a low voice)*: A shameless slut.
Minister:	Come here, girl, and look at us. Do you know why you are here?
Sigrid:	Yes, sir.
Minister:	Is it true you're going to bear a child?
Sigrid:	So the old women say.
Rosey:	Who's the father? Speak up.

Sigrid:	I never went with any man but one.	
Manson:	Give his name.	
Sigrid:	Storm Kolson that's vanished.	35
Minister:	Where had you your liaison with that young man?	
Sigrid:	In the laird's cornfield. *(The four elders look at one another)*	
Minister:	When?	
Sigrid:	The night of the wedding in Blinkbonny. It was midsummer. Storm was my partner.	40
Minister:	Then, Sigrid Thomson, you admit all this?	
Sigrid:	Yes.	
Minister:	Do you realise that you have committed a most serious crime against God and his kirk?	
Sigrid:	No doubt, sir, but I have.	45
Minister:	Are you sorry for it? *(A pause)*	
Sigrid:	No, Storm and I, we did what we had to do.	
Rosey:	Ah ha!	
Corigall:	An honest lass, God help her.	
Minister:	You realise what you must do? Three Sabbaths running, you must sit in sackcloth on the stool of penitence before the whole congregation. If the father had been available, he would have had to do likewise.	50
Sigrid:	I'll do it.	
Minister:	Well, then, I think you can go now, under the cloud of our displeasure.	55
Rosey	*(slowly and ponderously)*: Not yet, I think. I have a more serious charge still to bring against this woman. *(He pauses and says quietly)* I accuse her of witchcraft.	

(A long silence. Their eyes shift from one to another, avoiding the girl. Only John Rosey's eye is steady, fixed on a white doomed face. The other eyes shift and speculate round it. A web is beginning to be spun.) 60

Adapted from A Spell for Green Corn *by George Mackay Brown*

ACTIVITY
a) Focus of interest for analysis: creation of appropriate mood/atmosphere.

How?
Areas for consideration:
- setting
- language of dialogue
- stage directions

How would you describe the mood or atmosphere of this extract?

Using the three listed areas for consideration as the basis for your discussion, explore *how* each of these areas helps the writer to build atmosphere.

Remember to support your statements with evidence and analysis (SEA). Use the examples in Chapter 34 to remind you of the process of analysis.

b) Focus of interest for evaluation: effectiveness of structure.

How successful do you feel the dramatist is in the way in which he builds this scene?

Remember to show a personal involvement with the extract, using appropriate critical vocabulary when making your evaluation. Use the examples in Chapter 34 to remind you of the process of evaluation.

EXTRACT **B** (Queen Elizabeth I of England was the daughter of Henry VIII and Anne Boleyn. Anne was executed on the orders of the king. Robert Dudley, The Earl of Leicester, was a favourite of Queen Elizabeth, but she never married.)

(She is lying down asleep. She rolls over moaning and murmuring.)

Elizabeth: Leicester? Dad ... Dad ... Mother? Robert?
(In dream lighting and strange music, very stylised, Fiddler comes on with a doll whose head is chopped off and she holds it separate by the hair. She is like a child and she is crying her eyes out. But slowly, silently. In real time and like a child, Elizabeth, still asleep, is crying for her dead mama (and her dead dreams of marrying Leicester too, probably, and tossing and turning.) 5
No! No! Don't ... don't kill her. Dad? Want my Mam. Want Robert!
(Shadowy figure (Dad) puts something — not a crown but an improvised and very clear representation of one — on Fiddler's head. Everyone cheers weirdly. 10
Dad-figure chucks doll away.)
Don't want — I want — Don't want to be Daddy's little princess. Yes!
(All the men throw Fiddler from one to the other, kissing her. Her crown keeps nearly falling off but she holds it on. They blindfold her, spin her round, a game of blindman's bluff. She goes to one man very slowly, deliberately, head held high. 15
They are 'married' by the others. She turns round to kiss him, eyes shut, trusting. He steals her crown. All the 'dream-people' laugh in a surreal, nightmarish, horrible way. Elizabeth wakes up with a cry. Dream snaps out. She is sobbing and crying.)
Robert!

(Enter Marian) 20
Marian: Madam ... What on earth's the matter? Bad dream again, only a dream. Ssh.
(Comforts her like a child. Elizabeth is sobbing all through next)
Elizabeth: I couldn't have married him, Marian ...
Marian: Well ... no madam ... Perhaps not. 25
Elizabeth: I told him! Leicester, if I married you and we lay down together as King and Queen, then we should wake as plain Mister and Mistress Dudley. The Nation would not have it.
Marian: Surely the scandal would have died down? Can't you marry him secretly and — 30
Elizabeth: She trumped us. His bloody wife. Why couldn't she let him decently divorce her? Oh no, she has to commit suicide. Now everyone is sure he murdered her. If he'd bloody murdered her, he'd have done it a lot better than that. Made quite sure it looked as though she had taken her own life. 35
Marian: Marry him secretly! In six months ... a year ... everyone will have forgotten she ever lived.
Elizabeth: Too late! I've told him I want him to marry Madam o'Scots.
Marian: Who?

Elizabeth:	Queen Mary and take him off to Edinburgh.
Marian:	Madam!
Elizabeth:	Why not? I hear she is very attractive, though I've yet to set eyes on her.
Marian:	But madam —
Elizabeth:	Oh yes! Bit on the tall side, of course, and hair that reddish colour that makes the complexion sickly looking — oh, and a virgin too, although she has been married. Altogether doing it exactly the wrong way round for my taste, but still, she is a Queen after all, so —
Marian:	He loves you!
Elizabeth:	I'm sure she'll make him happy, that'll shut all their mouths and we'll have a loyal Englishman — I think we may depend on him to remain a loyal Englishman — in her bed. Well, we really cannot have her married in France again, else the French King can straddle England with one foot in Calais, the other in Edinburgh, and piss down on us all fire, brimstone and poison. Besides, I have already broached it with the Scotch Ambassador.

(Marian looks on her with amazement. Elizabeth holds her defiance, then suddenly it crumbles, breaks, and she is sobbing in real abandonment and agony. Marian holds her, hushes her. Soon she calms again.)

No more. What shall it profit a woman if she can rule a whole kingdom but cannot quell her own rebellious heart? Robert, you are more dangerous to me than a thousand, thousand Northern Catholics poised and armed. I am not proud I love him — but I am proud that loving him, still I will not let him master me.

From Mary Queen of Scots Got Her Head Chopped Off *by Liz Lochhead*

ACTIVITY

a) Focus of interest for analysis: the character of Elizabeth.

How?

Areas for consideration:
- stage directions
- dialogue
- tone.

Using the three listed areas for consideration as the basis for your discussion, explore *how* each of these areas helps the dramatist to show the conflicting sides of Elizabeth's personality: the strong, decisive regal side and the troubled, vulnerable human side.

Remember to support your statements with evidence and analysis (SEA). Use the examples in Chapter 34 to remind you of the process of analysis.

b) Focus of interest for evaluation: recreating an historical figure.

Queen Elizabeth I is a figure from history. How successful is the dramatist in portraying her as someone who could also be seen as a 'modern' woman?

Remember to show a personal response to the extract, using appropriate critical vocabulary when making your evaluation. Use the examples in Chapter 34 to remind you of the process of evaluation.

CHAPTER 36 *Drama*

BUILDING BLOCKS TO ANALYSIS AND EVALUATION

 ## *Demonstrating*

Demonstrating analysis and evaluation

In Chapter 31 we explored an extract from *Death of a Salesman*, using the building blocks to understanding in order to provide a working model as preparation for your independent study of a text.

Now we're going to apply the **building blocks of analysis and evaluation** to this same extract in preparation for your own independent study of another, unseen extract.

BLOCK C *Analysis*	**BLOCK D** *Evaluation*
Examining aspects of structure, style, language to show HOW they contribute to meaning and effect.	Assessing the effectiveness of a text through personal response, supported by relevant evidence and appropriate critical vocabulary.

But first, as part of that preparation, a reminder about **denotation** and **connotation**.

Analysis of language

Look back at what was said on this important aspect in Chapter 24 of the Prose section for Higher (page 139).

Dramatists, like novelists and poets, rely heavily on their ability to tap into the connotative layers of language.

For example:

> **Lucy:** If that's all you can say, I think I'll go.
> **David:** Go then, and take your dreams with you. I've no wish to spend the rest of my life $\boxed{\text{tiptoeing round the edges}}$ of your $\boxed{\text{leftover}}$ dreams.
> **Lucy:** No, you'd rather $\boxed{\text{trample}}$ across them, $\boxed{\text{crushing}}$ each one in turn with your favourite $\boxed{\text{weapon}}$ — $\boxed{\text{cold, factual reality}}$.

In this example, when we look more closely at the boxed words and phrases, we find a rage of interesting associations: 'tiptoeing round the edges' suggests elaborate care being taken not to disturb something or someone — travelling round the edges, rather than straight across or through the middle for fear of the centre collapsing; 'leftover' carries a derogatory tone as if the speaker thinks Lucy's dreams are worthless, only fit for the scrap heap; 'trample' and 'crushing' suggest violent, destructive actions — they set up an effective contrast to 'tiptoeing'; 'weapon' is associated with combat and that, in turn, presents a picture of David metaphorically going to war, armed with 'cold, factual reality' with which he will destroy Lucy's dreams.

Your analysis of language features should always explore any relevant **connotations**.

Sample commentary on *Death of a Salesman* extract

Use the sample commentary which follows this extract to help you in your own independent exploration of the second, unseen extract in this chapter.

EXTRACT A (Willy Loman is an ageing, failed salesman who cannot understand why his son, Biff, has not experienced the kind of success that his boyhood friend, Bernard, has achieved. In this scene, Willy meets up with Bernard, who is now a respected lawyer.)

Willy	*(sitting down)*: What're you going to do in Washington?	
Bernard:	Oh, just a case I've got there, Willy.	
Willy:	That so? *(indicating the rackets)* You going to play tennis there?	
Bernard:	I'm staying with a friend who's got a court.	
Willy:	Don't say. His own tennis court. Must be fine people I bet.	5
Bernard:	They are, very nice. Dad tells me Biff's in town.	
Willy	*(with a big smile)*: Yeah, Biff's in. Working on a very big deal, Bernard.	
Bernard:	What's Biff doing?	
Willy:	Well, he's been doing very big things in the West. But he decided to establish himself here. Very big. We're having dinner. Did I hear your wife had a boy?	10
Bernard:	That's right. Our second.	
Willy:	Two boys! What do you know!	
Bernard:	What kind of a deal has Biff got?	
Willy:	Well, Bill Oliver – very big sporting-goods man – he wants Biff very badly. Called him in from the West. Long distance, *carte blanche*, special deliveries. Your friends have their own private tennis court?	15
Bernard:	You still with the old firm, Willy?	
Willy	*(after a pause)*: I'm – I'm overjoyed to see how you made the grade, Bernard, overjoyed. It's an encouraging thing to see a young man really – really – Looks very good for Biff – very – *(He breaks off, then)* Bernard – *(He is so full of emotion, he breaks off again)*	20
Bernard:	What is it, Willy?	
Willy	*(small and alone)*: What – what's the secret?	
Bernard:	What secret?	25
Willy:	How – how did you? Why didn't he ever catch on?	
Bernard:	I wouldn't know that, Willy.	
Willy	*(confidentially, desperately)*: You were his friend, his boyhood friend. There's something I don't understand about it. His life ended after that Ebbets Field game. From the age of seventeen nothing good ever happened to him.	30
Bernard:	He never trained for anything.	
Willy:	But he did, he did. After high school he took so many correspondence courses. Radio mechanics; television; God knows what, and never made the slightest mark.	35

Bernard *(taking off his glasses)*: Willy, do you want to talk candidly?

Willy *(rising, facing Bernard)*: I regard you as a very brilliant man, Bernard. I value your advice.

Bernard: Oh, the hell with the advice, Willy. I couldn't advise you. There's just one thing I've always wanted to ask you. When he was supposed to graduate, and the math teacher flunked him —   40

Willy: Oh, that son-of-a-bitch ruined his life.

Bernard: Yeah, but Willy, all he had to do was to go to summer school and make up that subject.

Willy: That's right, that's right.   45

Bernard: Did you tell him not to go to summer school?

Willy: Me? I begged him to go. I ordered him to go!

Bernard: Then why wouldn't he go?

Willy: Why? Why? Bernard, that question has been trailing me like a ghost for the last fifteen years. He flunked the subject, and laid down and died like a hammer hit him!   50

Bernard: Take it easy, kid.

Willy: Let me talk to you — I got nobody to talk to. Bernard, Bernard, was it my fault? Y'see? It keeps going around in my mind, maybe I did something to him. I got nothing to give him.   55

Bernard: Don't take it so hard.

Willy: Why did he lay down? What is the story there? You were his friend!

Bernard: Willy, I remember, it was June, and our grades came out. And he'd flunked math.

Willy: That son-of-a-bitch!   60

Bernard: No, it wasn't right then. Biff just got very angry, I remember, and was ready to enrol in summer school.

Willy *(surprised)*: He was?

Bernard: He wasn't beaten by it at all. But then, Willy, he disappeared from the block for almost a month. And I got the idea that he'd gone up to New England to see you. Did he have a talk with you then?   65

(Willy stares in silence)

Bernard: Willy?

Willy *(with a strong edge of resentment to his voice)*: Yeah, he came to Boston. What about it?   70

Bernard: Well, just that when he came back — I'll never forget this, it always mystifies me. Because I'd thought so well of Biff, even though he'd always taken advantage of me. I loved him, Willy, y'know? And he came back after that month and took his sneakers — remember those sneakers with 'University of Virginia' painted on them? He was so proud of those, wore them every day. And he took them down in the cellar, and burned them up in the furnace. We had a fist fight. It lasted for at least half an hour. Just the two of us, punching each other down the cellar, and crying right through it. I've often thought of how strange it was that I knew he'd given up his life. What happened in Boston, Willy?   75   80

(Willy looks at him as an intruder)

Bernard: I just bring it up because you asked me.

Willy *(angrily)*: Nothing. What do you mean, 'What happened?' What's that got to do with anything?   85

Bernard: Well, don't get sore.

> **Willy:**   What are you trying to do, blame it on me? If a boy lays down is
> that my fault?

From Death of a Salesman *by Arthur Miller*

BLOCK C *Analysis*

Examining aspects of structure, style, language to show HOW they contribute to meaning and effect.

Analysis of character through language

The language Willy uses is a useful marker, signposting aspects of his personality. For example, in the early part of the extract, he tends to repeat exaggerated phrases: 'a very big deal'; 'very big things'; 'very big sporting-goods man'; 'wants Biff very badly'; 'looks very good for Biff'. This repeated use of **hyberbole** suggests a man prone to boasting, perhaps without due cause: on the one hand, at this point in the conversation, he talks in these terms about Biff, but, on the other hand, at a later point, he tells Bernard that 'from the age of seventeen nothing good ever happened to' Biff. This would seem to imply that Willy's story about 'the very big deal' is exaggerated, even false.

This contradiction is further apparent when Willy says Biff: 'laid down and died like a hammer hit him'. He boasts that things are 'looking very good' for Biff, but here the **simile** suggests that at a certain point in his life, Biff has given up completely as if he had been felled by a huge blow. There is a clear **tension** here between a man in touch with reality and someone who lives in the world of make-believe.

Other language features combine to create a picture of Willy as a broken man who senses that he may have contributed to his son's failure, but cannot accept the blame for it. For example, he asks Bernard a series of questions: 'What's the secret?', 'Why didn't he ever catch on?' and 'Why did he lay down?'

We feel sorry for someone who thinks that it is all a matter of learning the 'secret' of success, rather than putting in the hard work. 'Catching on' implies that life is a merry go round and to be successful you have to reach out and grab hold of it before it passes you by. A sense of despair, perhaps even humiliation, is evident in the phrase 'lay down': Biff has gone down without a fight, simply succumbing to failure.

Analysis of mood

The extract opens on a light, conversational note, creating a mood of polite warmth. After Willy breaks down and asks 'What – what's the secret?' in a voice described as *'small and alone'*, the mood changes to one charged with emotional tension. Willy's repeated, angry outburst in the phrase 'that son-of-a-bitch' sustains this tension, making us very aware that Willy is at breaking point.

This tension is reflected in the urgent pace of Willy's dialogue at times. For example:

'Me? I begged him to go. I ordered him to go.'

'Why? Why?'

'Why did he lay down? What is the story there? You were his friend!'

Towards the end of the extract, the mood becomes angry and hostile as Willy becomes defensive about Bernard's questions. He *'stares in silence'*, then answers Bernard *'with a strong edge of resentment to his voice'*. When he *'looks at him as an intruder'* — as if Bernard were probing Willy's inner secrets, breaking into his conscience — we sense the mood has changed dramatically from the amiable opening.

BLOCK D *Evaluation*

Assessing the effectiveness of a text through personal response, supported by relevant evidence and appropriate critical vocabulary.

Evaluating effectiveness in communicating theme

One of the main themes (CV) which emerges from this extract is the idea of success versus failure. I think Arthur Miller's skill as a playwright is very evident in the subtle way in which he weaves both sides of this theme into the dialogue (PR). Willy is clearly impressed by symbols of success as is seen in his references to 'own tennis court' and to 'their own private tennis court' (E). He says they 'must be fine people' (E) simply because they have their own tennis court. His use of language betrays this emphasis on success: things are not just big, they are 'very big' and Bernard is not just clever, he is 'very brilliant' (E).

There is dramatic irony (CV), however, in the way in which success sits alongside frequent references to failure. Referring to Biff, Willy says:

'From the age of seventeen nothing good ever happened to him.'

(he) 'never made the slightest mark'

'He flunked the subject, and laid down and died … ' (E)

Bernard's success is used as a dramatic foil (CV) to Biff's failure, effectively reinforcing the theme. We feel a deep sense of personal tragedy that Willy has had to face the evident success of Bernard, while, at the same time, speaking of his own son in terms of absolute failure (PR).

Demonstrating analysis and evaluation

In summary, using the building blocks approach to analysis and evaluation, several readings of this extract have revealed a clearer awareness of the following aspects:

- style
- language
- situation
- mood/atmosphere
- dialogue
- character
- theme
- personal response to all of the above.

EXTRACT B (Ernest Worthing, also known as Jack, has proposed to Gwendolen, daughter of Lady Bracknell. He discusses the outcome with his friend, Algernon.)

Algernon:	Didn't it go off all right, old boy? You don't mean to say Gwendolen refused you? I know it is a way she has. She is always refusing people. I think it is most ill-natured of her.
Jack:	Oh, Gwendolen is as right as a trivet. As far as she is concerned, we are practically engaged. Her mother is perfectly unbearable. Never

5

met such a gorgon ... I don't really know what a gorgon is like, but I am sure that Lady Bracknell is one. In any case, she is a monster, without being a myth, which is rather unfair ... I beg your pardon, Algy, I suppose I shouldn't talk about your own aunt in that way before you. 10

Algernon: My dear boy, I love hearing my relations abused. It is the only thing that makes me put up with them at all. Relations are simply a tedious pack of people who haven't got the remotest knowledge of how to live, nor the smallest instinct about when to die.

Jack: Oh, that is nonsense! 15

Algernon: It isn't!

Jack: Well, I won't argue about the matter. You always want to argue about things.

Algernon: That is exactly what things were originally made for.

Jack: Upon my word, if I thought that, I'd shoot myself ... You don't 20
think there is any chance of Gwendolen becoming like her mother in about a hundred and fifty years, do you, Algy?

Algernon: All women become like their mothers. That is their tragedy. No man does. That's his.

Jack: Is that clever? 25

Algernon: It is perfectly phrased! And quite as true as any observation in civilised life should be.

Jack: I am sick to death of cleverness. Everybody is clever nowadays. You can't go anywhere without meeting clever people. The thing has become an absolute public nuisance. I wish to goodness we had a 30
few fools left.

Algernon: We have.

Jack: I should extremely like to meet them. What do they talk about?

Algernon: The fools? Oh! about the clever people, of course.

Jack: What fools! 35

Algernon: By the way, did you tell Gwendolen the truth about your being Ernest in town and Jack in the country?

Jack: My dear fellow, the truth isn't quite the sort of thing one tells to a nice sweet refined girl. What extraordinary ideas you have about the way to behave to a woman! 40

Algernon: The only way to behave to a woman is to make love to her, if she is pretty and to someone else if she is plain.

Jack: Oh, that is nonsense.

Algernon: What about your brother? What about the profligate Ernest?

Jack: Oh, before the end of the week I shall have got rid of him. I'll say 45
he died in Paris of apoplexy. Lots of people die of apoplexy, quite suddenly, don't they?

Algernon: Yes, but it's hereditary, my dear fellow. It's the sort of thing that runs in families. You had much better say a severe chill.

Jack: You are sure a severe chill isn't hereditary, or anything of that kind? 50

Algernon: Of course it isn't.

Jack: Very well, then. My poor brother Ernest is carried off suddenly in Paris, by a severe chill. That gets rid of him.

Algernon: But I thought you said that ... Miss Cardew was a little too much interested in your poor brother Ernest? Won't she feel his loss a 55
good deal?

Jack: Oh, that is all right. Cecily is not a silly romantic girl, I am glad to say. She has got a capital appetite, goes long walks, and pays no attention at all to her lessons.

Algernon: I would rather like to see Cecily.   60

Jack: I will take very good care you never do. She is excessively pretty, and is only just eighteen.

Algernon: Have you told Gwendolen yet you have an excessively pretty ward who is only just eighteen?

Jack: Oh! One doesn't blurt these things out to people. Cecily and   65 Gwendolen are perfectly certain to be extremely good friends. I'll bet you anything you like that half an hour after they have met, they will be calling each other sister.

Algernon: Women only do that when they have called each other a lot of other things first.   70

From The Importance of Being Earnest *by Oscar Wilde*

ACTIVITY

Now it's your turn to demonstrate what you've learnt about analysis and evaluation by exploring the drama extract from *The Importance of Being Ernest* by Oscar Wilde.

Directing discussion on analysis and evaluation

Use the following prompts to help direct your discussion of the extract.

a) What techniques does Wilde use to produce witty, fast-paced dialogue? You may wish to consider some or all of the following aspects:
- rhythm
- expression
- tone

(Analysis)

Give examples and comment on effects.

b) How does the playwright communicate attitudes to women? You may wish to consider some or all of the following aspects:
- characterization
- expression
- tone

(Analysis)

Give examples and comment on effects.

c) The play is set in a past era: how successful is the dramatist in entertaining today's reader/audience? You may wish to consider some or all of the following aspects:
- situation
- character
- relevance of themes
- style of expression

(Evaluation)

APPENDIX

Decoding the question

A very important part of preparing for any assessment is learning to recognize the language of the questions, so that you feel confident that you know *exactly* what you are being asked to do. Hopefully, you will have prepared yourself as well as possible to meet the demands of the examination, but if you misunderstand what the question is asking of you, all that preparation will have been in vain.

Remember that those who set the examination papers are trying to help you by asking questions which have a straightforward structure and a clearly recognizable vocabulary.

The **Textual Analysis** paper forms the first part of the **Analysis and Appreciation** examination. Here, you are being tested on three main areas:

- ◆ your ability to **understand** the main points, as well as details, of an extract (or text)
- ◆ your ability to **analyse** how the writer has used particular techniques to communicate his ideas
- ◆ your ability **to evaluate** how successful the writer has been in communicating his or her ideas in an interesting and effective way.

Analysing and **evaluating** will also require you to show you can support points by using **evidence** from the text, and that you can use the **appropriate critical vocabulary** in your comments.

Let's look at some examples of questions from past **Analysis and Appreciation** examination papers (2000 and 2001).

Intermediate 2
(from SQA Analysis and Appreciation 2000 paper)

5   Look at lines 24–27
     Give two reasons why the staff of Petty's Hotel might think that she had got the wrong address.

6   In the last line we are told: 'She had decided to study glass.'
     What decision did she make in line 14?

4(b) Refer to **two** of Sol's actions in lines 22–24 and *suggest what* each reveals about his personality. You should refer to the text in support of your answer.

(from SQA Analysis and Appreciation 2001 paper)

4   *Explain the significance* of the vase in the story.

> **Higher**
> (from SQA Analysis and Appreciation 2000 paper)
>
> 3   *What* attitude about the writer's time in school seems to emerge in lines 6–8?
>
> 6(a)   *Why* might each of these be hoped for?
>
> (from SQA Analysis and Appreciation 2001 paper)
>
> 6   *What do you think* is an important theme in this poem?

These questions are all testing **understanding**. You can tell these are 'understanding' questions by the language: the key words **what; why; give reasons** and **explain** signal this type of question.

Similarly, questions that are designed to test your ability to **analyse** can be recognized by the use of key words. Look at these examples.

> **Intermediate 2**
> (from SQA Analysis and Appreciation 2000 paper)
>
> 1(a)   *How* is this impression created? You should refer closely to the text in your answer.
>
> 2   *How* does the *sentences structure* of this paragraph help to reinforce the idea of time passing on Lucinda's journey through the harbour?
>
> 3(b)   *Explain how* it does so.
>
> 3(c)   By selecting two other single words from lines 8–14, *show how* this impression is reinforced.

> **Higher**
> (from SQA Analysis and Appreciation 2001 paper)
>
> 1(b)   *Explain* in detail *how* a contrast is created between the poet and her brothers in the rest of verse one (lines 4–8).
>
> 2(b)   'Some are slow,' (line 9) 'Others are sudden' (line 11)
> *Show how* the poet highlights features of each emigration in lines 9–14. You should refer to word choice, sentence structure and sound in your answer.
>
> 4   *Explain how* the language of lines 17–21 helps you to appreciate the change introduced by the word 'but'.
>
> (from SQA Analysis and Appreciation 2000 paper)
>
> 4   *In what way* do lines 9–10 link the ideas of verses one and two?

As you can see, **how**, either on its own or in phrases such as **show how** or **explain how**, is a very important word which signals the question is asking you to **analyse. In what way** is simply another way of asking **how**.

Finally, questions which are testing your ability to **evaluate** a text are also recognizable by their own code words. Look at these examples.

Intermediate 2
(from SQA Analysis and Appreciation 2000 paper)

7(a) One of the main functions of this extract is to expand the reader's knowledge of Lucinda's personality and characteristics.

How successful do you think the writer has been in conveying Lucinda's inexperience and self-consciousness in lines 17–28? You should support your answer by close reference to the text.

(from SQA Analysis and Appreciation 2001 paper)

9 In this short story there are three main characters.

By selecting one significant detail for each character, explain *how successful* you think the writer has been in establishing their feelings.

Higher
(from SQA Analysis and Appreciation 2001)

3(b) *How effective* do you find the image in this context (lines 15–16)?

6 What do you think is an important theme in this poem? *How effectively* do you feel the poem has explored this theme?

How successful, **how effectively** – these phrases signal that the questions are asking you to evaluate particular aspects of the text.

To sum up: if you are going to be successful in any assessment, you need to learn to recognize what the question is asking you to do. In the case of Textual Analysis, you should recognize the following groups of key words being used to signal those questions which are testing **understanding** or **analysis** or **evaluation**:

Understanding	what; why; where; who; explain; give reasons; identify
Analysis	how; show how; explain how; comment on the effect of; indicate how; in what way
Evaluation	how successful; how effective; how well

Decoding exercise

Read the following questions and see if you can recognize which of the three key aspects is being tested: **understanding**, **analysis** or **evaluation**.

1 Based on the information given in the first paragraph, why do you think the child was reluctant to join in the game?

2 Show how the imagery of the second sentence (lines 2–4), contributes to the mood of the opening paragraph.

3   How effective is the dialogue in paragraph two in establishing the character of Lucy?

4   What **two** details do you see as significant in determining Amy's actions?

5   Explain how sentence structure and punctuation contribute to the tone of paragraph 3 (lines 15–21).

6   The extract focuses on the development of the relationship between Lucy and Brian. How successful do you think the writer is in making the reader sympathetic to the difficulties both characters face in this relationship?